Checking Out Quick Planning Tips

For the best planning, follow these tips:

- **Know all you can about reverse mortgages before you walk into your counselor's or originator's office.** It pays to be well-informed, and you'll be more relaxed when you know what to expect.

- **Make sure you qualify for the loan (you're at least 62 and own your home).** When in doubt, just go for it. It never hurts to go talk to the counselor, and if you don't qualify the counselor may know of another program that can solve your financial situation.

- **Get to know the loan options.** Read about each one, and consider which works best for you based on your home value, county, and age. Get your family's input as well, but always do what feels right to you. After all, it's your loan!

- **Plan your repayment carefully.** Don't leave this important step to the last minute or unresolved for your heirs. Lay out a plan and be sure to record it in your will. Talk to your family about their future responsibilities.

- **When you go to your counselor meeting, take along a friend or family member who can help you take notes, ask additional questions, and weigh in afterward.** Sometimes it helps to have someone there to bounce options off of, or just hold you hand while your counselor explains your choices.

- **Get your money's worth out of your originator.** Ask as many questions as you can think of, call if anything comes up before or after the loan closes, and feel free to ask for help along the way. You're paying for their services — make it count.

- **Before your appraiser arrives, spruce up your house (within reason).** Give everything a good scrubbing and fix the little things that are broken. Try to look at your home from an appraiser's point of view and be realistic in your expectations of your home's value.

- **If you're an adult child of someone who's thinking of getting a reverse mortgage, find out all you can about the loan, and be a part of the process if your parent allows it.**

- **If you're a baby boomer, start planning now!** Pay off as much of your current mortgage as you can afford, and get your home ready to be a retirement paradise.

- **Most importantly, if you ever have questions or don't feel comfortable with some part of the loan, stop!** Ask questions and get them resolved before you move on.

Reverse Mortgages For Dummies®

Cheat Sheet

Getting Instant Gratification

If you want to get started on your reverse mortgage right away, here's where to start:

- ✔ **Request a meeting with a reverse mortgage counselor.** For information about finding an approved counselor, see Chapter 8. You can get a personalized list of options and examples of what you might be able to expect from your loan.

- ✔ **Start searching for a reverse mortgage originator.** Look online, in senior-oriented publications, pay attention to radio ads, and peruse the list of National Reverse Mortgage Lenders Association members listed on www.reversemortgage.com. Ask your friends for a good recommendation. There's no charge to talk to the originator, so feel free to check out a few of them and pick the one you like best.

- ✔ **Gather your current mortgage information (particularly how much you still owe, if anything), your outstanding debts, and other pertinent financial information.** This way you can be ready to bring it all to your counselor meeting, giving him or her a better idea of what you need from a reverse mortgage.

Making Big Decisions

Getting some of these big decisions out of the way can tie up loose ends quickly and make the process go smoothly:

- ✔ **Make sure you have enough money handy to pay for your closing costs upfront.** They can range from a couple thousand dollars to tens of thousands of dollars — not many people can shell out that kind of cash. You have the option to finance your closing costs, but remember: You're paying interest on that, too.

- ✔ **Decide whether you want to continue taking care of your property taxes and homeowners insurance or whether you want to let the lender start paying those for you using your reverse mortgage funds.** You have to pay them regardless, and if you fall too far behind you may get a notice from the lender saying that they'll end the loan unless you start paying again. If you don't want to have to worry about it, let the lender bear responsibility for you. You're paying them enough for your loan, put them to work!

- ✔ **Figure out how badly do you need a reverse mortgage today.** Keep in mind that the longer you wait, the more money you can get (based on age). Plus, lending limits go up every year or so, which means your available loan amount may go up as well. Can you wait three or more years?

For Dummies: Bestselling Book Series for Beginners

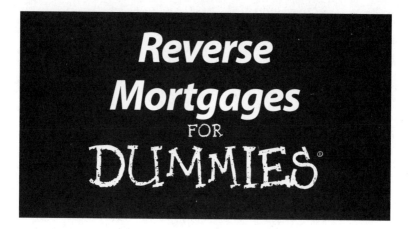

Reverse Mortgages FOR DUMMIES®

by Sarah Glendon Lyons and John E. Lucas

WILEY

Wiley Publishing, Inc.

Reverse Mortgages For Dummies®

Published by
Wiley Publishing, Inc.
111 River St.
Hoboken, NJ 07030-5774
www.wiley.com

Copyright © 2005 by Wiley Publishing, Inc., Indianapolis, Indiana

Published simultaneously in Canada

For general information on our other products and services, please contact our Customer Care Department within the U.S. at 800-762-2974, outside the U.S. at 317-572-3993, or fax 317-572-4002.

For technical support, please visit www.wiley.com/techsupport.

Wiley also publishes its books in a variety of electronic formats. Some content that appears in print may not be available in electronic books.

Library of Congress Control Number: 2005923784

ISBN-13: 978-07645-8446-6

ISBN-10: 0-7645-8446-4

Manufactured in the United States of America

10 9 8 7 6 5 4 3 2

1B/QW/RQ/QV/IN

WILEY

About the Author

Sarah Glendon Lyons is a San Diego-based writer with a diverse portfolio of housing-industry experience. She holds a B.A. in English Language and Literature from the University of Arizona, and studied at Australia's University of Wollongong before joining Hanley Wood LLC, publishers of over 75 consumer home magazines. As an editor for Pfingsten Publishing's *Mortgage Originator* magazine, she has written hundreds of articles for mortgage professionals. Although she has developed a wide scope of lending insight, her particular expertise is in the reverse mortgage field. Sarah has been interviewed on the topic of reverse mortgages by leading mortgage executives and sales trainers, and offers reverse mortgage information to originators and consumers around the country. Her perspective as an unbiased researcher and consultant allows her to provide readers with both the benefits and challenges of reverse mortgages.

John E. Lucas has been in the mortgage banking industry for over 39 years, actively originating mortgage loans in the Van Nuys, Ca. area. When the Department of Housing and Urban Development (HUD) introduced the HECM reverse mortgage in 1989, he worked with one of the companies HUD chose to participate in the test program. His involvement in this process led him to concentrate his career on reverse mortgages, rather than the typical "forward" mortgage. John has lectured on the subject of reverse mortgages to a wide variety of organizations and groups such as senior centers, realtors, CPAs, financial planners, elder law attorneys, service clubs and university groups, and is a member of the National Reverse Mortgage Lenders Association.

John will tell anyone he comes in contact with about reverse mortgages, and admits he has a "passion" for the program. He feels strongly about expanding the public's awareness of reverse mortgages, because he has seen how a reverse mortgage can change a senior's quality of life. As a senior himself, he understands the needs of seniors and is committed to continue originating reverse mortgages for the foreseeable future.

Dedication

We would like to dedicate this book to all those who have taken an active role in their future finances, whether through a reverse mortgage or by other means. To all those baby boomers who are planning early, to all those adult children who have set aside the time to help their parents with this essential decision, and of course, to all of our senior readers who chose to be in control of their own financial destiny. We wish you the best of luck!

Author's Acknowledgments

We would like to thank everyone who made this book possible, all those who supported our efforts, and our friends and family who sat patiently by as we toiled away through weekends and holidays. Thank you to our acquisitions editor Mikal Belicove for your personal, kind attention to this project. Thank you Jennifer Connolly for all of your hard work editing this manuscript and for being such a great source of ideas. Thank you Peter Bell for acting as Technical Editor and offering your and the National Reverse Mortgage Lenders Association's support. Thank you Carole Sparrow, reverse mortgage counselor, and Mary Beth Johnson, appraiser, for your time and efforts providing information and proofing the chapters you inspired.

Sarah Glendon Lyons: I would especially like to thank Pfingsten Publishing and *Mortgage Originator* magazine for the constant encouragement and interest in this project. Thank you David Branfman for your legal council and generosity. John Obradovich, thank you for recommending me as the reverse mortgage expert. Thank you to my co-author, John Lucas, for your dedication and commitment to this book. I'm particularly grateful to my parents, family, and friends who consistently asked about "the book" and learned more than they ever wanted to know about reverse mortgages, all with a smile. To Adam, thank you for waiting patiently while I worked, and always offering to read over these pages. To everyone who helped make this book a possibility, my sincere thanks.

John E. Lucas: I want to thank Sarah Lyons for the opportunity to participate in the writing of this book. I believe the reverse mortgage is a very important program that helps alleviate difficult financial problems for seniors. In most cases, the reverse mortgage will change the quality of a senior's life, sometimes rather dramatically. Working with seniors and helping them to obtain reverse mortgages has been the most satisfying portion of my professional career. Playing a role in the writing of this book has been a privilege.

Publisher's Acknowledgments

We're proud of this book; please send us your comments through our Dummies online registration form located at www.dummies.com/register/.

Some of the people who helped bring this book to market include the following:

Acquisitions, Editorial, and Media Development

Project Editor: Jennifer Connolly

Acquisitions Editor: Mikal Belicove

Copy Editor: Jennifer Connolly

Technical Editor: Peter Bell

Editorial Manager: Michelle Hacker

Editorial Supervisor: Carmen Krikorian

Editorial Assistants: Hanna Scott, Melissa Bennett

Cartoons: Rich Tennant (www.the5thwave.com)

Composition Services

Project Coordinator: Adrienne Martinez

Layout and Graphics: Carl Byers, Andrea Dahl

Proofreaders: David Faust, Joe Niesen, Carl William Pierce, TECHBOOKS Production Services

Indexer: TECHBOOKS Productions Services

Publishing and Editorial for Consumer Dummies

Diane Graves Steele, Vice President and Publisher, Consumer Dummies

Joyce Pepple, Acquisitions Director, Consumer Dummies

Kristin A. Cocks, Product Development Director, Consumer Dummies

Michael Spring, Vice President and Publisher, Travel

Kelly Regan, Editorial Director, Travel

Publishing for Technology Dummies

Andy Cummings, Vice President and Publisher, Dummies Technology/General User

Composition Services

Gerry Fahey, Vice President of Production Services

Debbie Stailey, Director of Composition Services

Contents at a Glance

Table of Contents

Introduction

*W*elcome to *Reverse Mortgages For Dummies*! You've just done yourself a huge favor. By picking up this book, you're that much closer to finding out if a reverse mortgage is right for you and to discovering how to go about securing this rapidly growing loan option for yourself. You may have heard about reverse mortgages before, and you probably have some reservations about them — it's okay, it's good to be skeptical about any financial matter that you're not entirely comfortable with. Don't worry, you won't hurt our feelings if you're reading this with one hesitant eyebrow raised. Our job is to put your mind at ease and give you the tools you need to make a fully informed decision about reverse mortgages.

Reverse mortgages aren't for everyone, and this book is in no way an advertisement for the loan. We're not here to sell you on reverse mortgages; in fact, we've included an entire chapter on determining whether or not this loan is right for you (see Chapter 2). What we do want to accomplish by writing this book is to open your mind to the idea of reverse mortgages and squelch some of the old-fashioned myths that some people have about the loan. It's like you probably said to your kids — we just want what's best for you. If the answer to your financial situation is a reverse mortgage, great! If not, pass this on to a friend or family member who may benefit from a reverse mortgage.

About This Book

We wrote *Reverse Mortgages For Dummies* to make this loan accessible to all seniors and anyone who may benefit from the loan sometime in the future. We wanted to give you all the methods and resources you need to get a reverse mortgage, feel confident in your decision, and fully enjoy the benefits of the loan. Because we want you to be well-prepared and have the best reverse mortgage resources at your fingertips, this book covers a wide range of topics. Inside, you can find information on the pre-loan process (what you need to do before you even apply), how to select a reverse mortgage originator, what to expect during the loan process, what happens afterward, and ways you and your family can find additional help. We've also included sections just for adult children, who may be helping their senior parents make this important financial decision.

Conventions Used in This Book

In the mortgage community, the term *lender* may apply to the person whose office you sit in, filling out forms; it may mean the company that actually shells out the money; or it may mean the even bigger company that funds a smaller company's loans. Within these pages, we use *lender* to mean the companies who fund your loan. The person you come in contact with, who takes your application and walks you through the loan process, is the *originator*.

Any lending limits mentioned in this book are as of the time of publication and are subject to change. Reverse mortgage providers like HUD and Fannie Mae usually raise their limits every year or so — if you're reading this book after 2005, check with your originator or counselor to find out what the current limits are.

All examples of calculations, loan scenarios, and estimated loan values are for illustrative purposes only and are not to be used as concrete proof of what you personally will experience. All loans are based on individuals and, like snowflakes and fingerprints, no two loans are exactly alike.

Foolish Assumptions

You don't need to be a financial wizard to get the most out of this book. In fact, you don't need to know much about mortgages at all! As we wrote this book, we did make a few assumptions about you:

- We assume you currently own a home and are somewhat familiar with the basics of mortgages. We do not, however, expect you to be an expert. You may not even remember what was involved your last mortgage process, and that's okay.

- We assume you are currently thinking about getting a reverse mortgage, or are a loved one of someone who could benefit from this loan. You may know a little about reverse mortgages, but probably aren't aware of all your options.

- We assume you want to get the facts about reverse mortgages before you seek out an originator.

- We assume you have already thought about what you want to do with your reverse mortgage money, whether it's to remodel your kitchen, pay for medical expenses, or take a trip to Spain.

✔ We assume you're no dummy. You may not be the expert on reverse mortgages (yet), but you're a smart, capable person who's ready to see how you can help yourself live more comfortably in your retirement.

How This Book Is Organized

Reverse Mortgages For Dummies is organized in five parts, all of which are designed to be read in any order. You can start at Chapter 1 and read this book cover to cover (if nothing else you'll get your money's worth!), or pick and choose the chapters that interest you most. Perhaps you already know everything you need about reverse mortgages but don't know how to go about setting your financial gears in motion: just turn to Part III! Want to give this book to an adult child who needs some help? Flip to Part IV. There's no right or wrong way to read this book. Below we give you a rundown of the five parts and what each one encompasses — go ahead and skip around when you see a part that has the information you need.

Part I: Understanding the Basics of a Reverse Mortgage

You may have misconceptions about reverse mortgages based on what you've heard in the past. Or, you may be so new to the idea that you don't have any preconceived notions at all. This part clears up the myths and explains the ins and outs of reverse mortgages.

In Chapter 1 you can find general information about how the loan works. After reading this chapter, you'll have a pretty good grasp of the loan itself and what's involved in the loan process.

Chapter 2 gives you some answers to the question, "is it right for me?" and includes tips on budgeting for your new loan, additional options that may be a better choice for you than a reverse mortgage, and a checklist that can guide you through determining whether you're ready to proceed.

Chapter 3 explains who can qualify, the best age at which to get a reverse mortgage, and what you can do to prepare for the loan process. You can find comparisons of hypothetical borrowers at different ages and home values, and which housing types are eligible.

Chapter 4 covers how you pay the loan back, with tons of ideas to make repayment easier on you and your family.

Part II: Going Shopping: Product Options

We highlight three main types of reverse mortgage products in this book. Part II goes into detail on all three, in three individual chapters — the Home Equity Conversion Mortgage, Home Keeper, and Jumbo Cash Account — with tips on which may be right for you, qualifying, costs, interest rates, and how to choose a payment plan.

Part III: Taking the Plunge

Once you've decided on a loan that may work for you (see the Chapters in Part II), Part III ushers you into the next steps. We include lots of great tips (if we do say so ourselves) to equip you so there are no surprises as you take each step of the reverse mortgage process on your own.

Chapter 8, the first step, gives you the scoop on arranging a meeting with a reverse mortgage counselor, what to expect during the visit, and what you can do to make the meeting go smoothly.

Chapter 9 covers the procedure of choosing an originator, applying for a loan, and the loan approval process.

Getting your home appraised may be a familiar experience, but Chapter 10 gives you some tips from reverse mortgage originators on how to make a good impression and how to boost your home's value.

Last but not least, Chapter 11 gives an overview of the closing process. This is the part where you sign those last documents and get your first check, so we give you all the info you need to make it hassle-free.

Part IV: Giving Advice for Adult Children

We dedicate this part to all of the caring, loving children out there who are helping their senior parents get a reverse mortgage. This part covers helping your parents both hands-on and hands-off, setting your mind at ease, resources for outside help, and what role you play in all of this.

Chapter 12 gives adult children and other loved ones ideas for helping your parents during the loan process and afterward. We list a lot of great Web sites and support groups that deal specifically with assisting your parents at every level.

Chapter 13 deals with the question on every adult child's mind: the inheritance. How does a reverse mortgage affect your future bounty? Find out here.

For those who need to take an even more proactive stance in their parents' finances, Chapter 14 explains how to assist your parent through a durable power of attorney. We've included symptoms that indicate you need to step in, the best ways to secure your parents' financial future, and additional options.

Part V: The Part of Tens

The Part of Tens is a standard device in every *Dummies* book, and ours is no exception. You may even want to read this part first, to get some instant-gratification answers!

Chapter 15 answers some of seniors' most common questions with the Top 10 What Ifs (such as, what if my spouse doesn't qualify or what if I need more money).

Chapter 16 lists our favorite resources for seniors and their families and why you need to check them out.

The biggest mistakes that borrowers all too commonly make are pointed out in Chapter 17. Take this opportunity to learn from other borrowers' mistakes — they didn't have access to this useful chapter, but you do!

Icons Used in This Book

If you've ever read a *For Dummies* book before, you know this book is littered with little icons next to some paragraphs. Each one has its own connotation, but they're all intended to point out something important so you can get the most out of this book.

A tip icon like this means you're about to read a time-saver, money-saver, or a headache-saver. Tips ensure that you get the most out of your reverse mortgage experience and keep you sane while you do it. Pretty soon you should be a calm, cool reverse mortgage guru.

If you see a warning icon, pay close attention! Since reverse mortgages have been around for over 20 years, there have been plenty of trail-blazing borrowers before you. You can learn from others' common mistakes, as well as get a heads up on things that may cause problems for you down the road.

Are you a savvy senior? You should be after you read the paragraphs with a remember icon next to them. We want you to have an edge when you're ready to go after your loan; when you see this icon, you know it's a chance to boost your reverse mortgage confidence quotient.

Like sidebars, you can save these paragraphs for a rainy day or just skip them altogether. Sometimes, we explain a technical fact or define a situation that, quite frankly, isn't vital to your understanding of the reverse mortgage process, although they may enhance your knowledge of reverse mortgages and its finer points. We love the topic of reverse mortgages and deal with them every day, so some of these tidbits we just couldn't bear to leave out!

Where to Go from Here

This is the easy part: You bought the book, you're wearing your I heart Reverse Mortgages T-shirt, and you poured yourself a nice hot cup of reverse mortgage coffee. Now what? You can open this book to Chapter 1 and settle in for a quiet afternoon of absorbing everything you can about reverse mortgages if that's your style. For those on the go, you can pick up this book for ten minutes a day and flip through looking for topics that interest you. If you're a gambler, just let the book fall open and start reading wherever fate decides. That's the beauty of a book like this one — all of our chapters are meant to be read either as part of a whole book, or just on their own. You should never feel lost if you skip around or your dog eats Chapter 2. So go ahead and dive right in. Ready? Set? Reverse Mortgage!

Part I

Understanding the Basics of a Reverse Mortgage

The 5th Wave   By Rich Tennant

"So, a reverse mortgage is like a mortgage, but it doesn't act like one. I had a wife like that once."

In this part . . .

You may have misconceptions about reverse mortgages based on what you've heard in the past. Or, you may be so new to the idea that you don't have any preconceived notions at all. This part clears up the myths and explains the ins and outs of reverse mortgages.

In Chapter 1 you can find general information about how the loan works. After reading this chapter, you'll have a pretty good grasp of the loan itself, and what's involved in the loan process.

Chapter 2 gives you some answers to the question, "is it right for me?" and includes tips on budgeting for your new loan, additional options that may be a better choice for you than a reverse mortgage, and a checklist that can guide you through determining whether you're ready to proceed.

Chapter 3 explains who can qualify, the best age to get a reverse mortgage, and what you can do to prepare for the loan process. You can find comparisons of hypothetical borrowers at different ages and home values, and which housing types are eligible.

Chapter 4 covers how you pay the loan back, with tons of ideas to make repayment easier on you and your family.

Chapter 1

Figuring Out the Reverse Mortgage Basics

*W*elcome to the beginning of your new, financially independent life. Simply by picking up this book, you've taken a proactive step to ensure a safe, stress-free retirement by using the equity in your home today. Congratulations! You've probably heard a lot about reverse mortgages lately, as they're quickly becoming a popular, safe, simple way to supplement seniors' retirement income. In this chapter, you can see the basics of modern reverse mortgages and get a feel for whether these loans are right for you or someone you love. By the end of this chapter, you should be able to explain the rudiments of reverse mortgages to anyone like a pro.

Understanding Reverse Mortgages

People tend to shy away from the very idea of reverse mortgages, in part because of their former bad rap, and in part because of all the scary terminology. If you're one of millions of people who are unfamiliar with real estate terms, when someone starts spouting off about how you can "utilize the equity in your home on deferred payments with a conversion mortgage," chances are pretty good you're going to tune it out. In fact, that's why we wrote this book: to give seniors and their families facts and tips about reverse mortgages in language that's as approachable as a big-eyed puppy (unless you're a cat person, then just think of it as a little fluffy kitten). We want you to fully understand the benefits and disadvantages of getting a reverse mortgage. We want you to walk into that loan originator's office knowing exactly what you want. And most importantly, we want you to feel good about whatever decision you make for your financial future.

Checking out how it works

Reverse mortgages pay you to continue living in your home. You can think of your home as the Bank of You: You're borrowing money that you would have earned had you sold your house. You can then use the money for whatever you want. Anything your heart desires (and your wallet can handle) is yours for the taking, whether it's a vacation in Switzerland, moving your master bedroom to the first floor, or sending yourself to college!

The concept is kind of abstract if you've been paying a lender for the past 30 years or so, and it may be difficult to grasp at first. Take a look at the quick reference points below. Once you get the gist of it, you can educate your friends and family about reverse mortgages. Next time you're at a cocktail party, holiday dinner, social lunch, or any time reverse mortgages come up in conversation, you can dazzle everyone with your knowledge.

Here's a quick rundown:

- You're a homeowner who owes little or nothing on your home. You decide you need more money to live the lifestyle you want, but your biggest asset is your home and you certainly don't want to sell it to get the money you need.

- A reverse mortgage lender figures out how much it can lend you based on your home value, your age, and interest rates, and loans you some percentage of the money you would have gotten if you'd decided to sell your home.

- You still own your home and continue to live in it, but now you're getting payments from the lender, so your cash flow problem is solved.

- You pay the loan back (with interest) only when you don't live in the house full time anymore, usually due to moving out or death.

- You never owe more than your home is worth, no matter how much you've accumulated in debt.

- You keep any leftover equity after the sale of the house; if you owe the lender $67,000 and your home sells for $200,000, you put the difference in your pocket and walk away smiling.

A reverse mortgage is sometimes called a *deferred payment* loan, and for a very good reason. Instead of paying off the home loan as you borrow money, the payments are put off (deferred). This is why reverse mortgages can be such a good choice for seniors; when you're on a fixed income or living off of your savings, it can help to have some extra cash in hand to supplement. Because payment is deferred, you are spending the equity in your home, rather than earning it (as you would with a traditional forward mortgage). Since equity is an intangible value, you never feel the effects of the equity going down, but you sure feel the money flowing steadily into your checking account!

Being over the hill pays off

There is a lot of ageism in society today, especially from employers and retailers. Even Hollywood starlets have a hard time finding work at a certain age. After a while you may start to think that the only advantage to old age is the 10-percent-off discount on Tuesdays at the local Bar & Grille. But reverse mortgages operate for seniors and seniors only — whippersnappers need not apply. If you are a homeowner age 62 or older, you will probably qualify for a reverse mortgage. There are no credit checks, and no income requirements.

Even better, the older you are, the more money you can usually get from your reverse mortgage. That's because the reverse mortgage lenders (big companies like the department of Housing and Urban Development, Fannie Mae, and Financial Freedom) are playing the odds. If you're 86, chances are good that they won't have to service your loan for very long — you may need to move to assisted living or pass away within only a few years, thus ending the loan. A 62-year-old, by contrast, probably has about 20 good years before the lender even needs to think about ending the loan. When has your age ever worked to your advantage like this?

Getting rid of common misconceptions

Seniors often tell us that they were considering a reverse mortgage until a friend or relative said something like, "Reverse mortgage?! Don't you dare! They'll take your house! Stay away!" We'd like to say that these fears are completely unfounded; unfortunately, they stem from a very old version of reverse mortgages (which are no longer done) that, in hindsight, weren't such a hot idea. Today's reverse mortgages are safe, effective, and definitely in the best interest of the borrower. It's a whole new generation of loans.

Although they were revamped and vastly improved in the past 20 or so years, people still tend to think of them as a poor choice for seniors. We're here to fix that. Take a look at the misconceptions below, and the truths that follow:

- ✔ **The lender gets your house.** This is by far the most widely misunderstood fallacies about reverse mortgages. In fact, you keep ownership of your home. The lender has no rights to your home and can't foreclose on you as long as you keep up with your taxes and insurance. Part of the confusion about this area stems from the fact that many reverse mortgage borrowers choose to sell their homes to pay off the loan when they move. And it makes perfect sense — what do you need with that house if you're not living there? But remember, you're selling to another regular buyer, not the lender.

- ✔ **You'll have no estate left.** This one is sort of up to you. If you own anything when you die, you'll have an estate left. If you spent all your money on pinball machines and then donated everything else to charity, you won't. Many seniors are concerned that a reverse mortgage keeps them from leaving anything to their children. The fact is, the way you pay off your loan is up to you and your heirs. Chapters 7 and 13 go into detail about this and show you several options for fulfilling your repayment obligations. It's also up to you to decide who you want to leave your estate to. Unless you form an emotional bond with your lender and leave your estate to them, your family or whomever you name in your will is the inheritor of your estate. Of course, they need to pay back the loan, but it's up to them how they carry out that responsibility.

- ✔ **You won't qualify because of poor credit.** If you have bad credit, or even moderate credit, you may have been turned down for a loan in the past. It's embarrassing, frustrating, and inconvenient. Reverse mortgages work differently: You can never be denied a loan because of bad credit — it's not even a consideration in your approval. The originator or lender runs a credit report, but it's only to make sure you don't owe the government any money (usually in back taxes). If you do, you have to use a portion of your reverse mortgage money to pay back those debts before you can start spending on yourself.

- ✔ **You have to be debt free.** While you are required to own a home in order to get a reverse mortgage, you do not have to own it "free and clear." One of the benefits of a reverse mortgage is that it can help pay off your remaining forward mortgage, leaving you without house payments for what may be the first time in your adult life. Here's how it works: The lender determines how much it can let you borrow and then deducts the amount you still owe from your available funds.

That money pays off the first loan, and then you're free to do what you wish with the rest of the money.

✔ **Only desperate people get reverse mortgages.** At one time, this may have been true. However, today's reverse mortgage borrower is more likely to get a loan out of want, rather than need. In fact, a growing number of people who have no immediate need are taking out these loans because they like the security of having a financial cushion, or are planning for future expenses. Take a look around and ask yourself if you could use several thousand dollars. Who doesn't? Don't let an antiquated stigma keep you from getting the money you want or need.

Knowing what it isn't

A reverse mortgage can be a lot of things: a way to make ends meet, a nice chunk of change for a rainy day, a fabulous dream vacation, or a remodeled kitchen. But there's one thing it's definitely not — free money. There's no free lunch here. While reverse mortgages offer many wonderful benefits, your loan will need to be paid back, just like any other loan (whether it's due when you move or upon your death).

There are fees involved that are explained in more detail in Part II, but they can include payments to the originator, the appraiser, postage fees, flood certificate fees, recording fees . . . the list goes on and on. Of course, these are the same sort of fees you paid for the mortgage that bought you the home you live in now. You also have to pay interest on your loan, which is generally right around the interest rates on traditional mortgages. You only pay interest on what you borrow, so any money that you don't use from your pool of reverse mortgage funds isn't charged. People still get the idea, however, that lenders simply hand you checks every month out of the goodness of their hearts. Now, they're not bad people, but they certainly aren't looking to give away billions of dollars per year in reverse mortgages.

Because it's not a cheap loan, a reverse mortgage is also not the best way to pay off a small debt. Would you really want to spend several thousand dollars in fees and closing costs just to pay back a $900 credit card debt? You know that wouldn't make sense. But what if you owed the IRS $12,000 in back taxes? In most cases, a reverse mortgage is still too costly for this kind of debt. Okay, that's easy for us to say, and if it looks like the best option then by all means take the first step and call a reverse mortgage counselor (see Chapter 8 for more). If you're in a similar situation, you may also contact a financial planner who specializes in seniors' money.

In fact, you can probably ask a reverse mortgage originator to refer you to someone good. They love to hand out referrals.

A reverse mortgage is also not a direct value-to-dollar loan. In other words, they aren't going to lend you the actual value of your home; what they lend is a percentage of that value, based on age, interest rates, and area. For example, a 66-year-old in a high-end county with a $500,000 home may expect to receive around $163,000 with a Home Equity Conversion Mortgage (depending on interest rates). Don't expect the full value of your home, or you'll be very disappointed. Before you make plans to spend money you don't yet have, go online to www.reversemortgage.org and click on the reverse mortgage calculator. This very cool tool gives you an estimate of what you may be able to borrow. Remember, you're not selling your home for the amount you're lent — you are simply borrowing equity that you already own.

Lastly, a reverse mortgage is not a panacea, or some kind of all-encompassing loan that's right for everyone. Just because you qualify by being a 62-year-old homeowner doesn't mean you're an ideal candidate. The next chapter lays out some questions you can ask yourself to find out whether or not a reverse mortgage is right for you, but here are a few of the basics:

- ✔ Are you at least 62 and own your own home?

- ✔ Do you plan to be in your home for at least 5 years?

- ✔ If you're getting the loan to purchase or pay off something specific, have you looked into other options for financing those expenses?

- ✔ Are you comfortable with the terms of the loan?

The more of these questions you can answer "yes" to, the more ready you are for a reverse mortgage. When you feel you meet all of these suggested criteria, you're ready to seek out a reverse mortgage counselor (see Chapter 8).

Choosing a Loan Product

There are two ways to pick a reverse mortgage loan product:

- ✔ Throw darts at a list of mortgage products and see which one fate chooses for you.

- ✔ Talk to your counselor and originator and let them lay out your options for you in an easy-to-understand, straightforward manner.

We suggest the last one. Besides, you could put an eye out with those darts.

Part of the reverse mortgage process involves using your best judgment and the tools at your disposal (the plethora of information your counselor and originator give you) to make an informed and wise decision. No pressure, right? Actually, it can be a pretty easy choice to make once you see what each loan product has to offer and how each fits into with your goals and financial plans. Keep in mind that all loans have the same basic requirements, but they each have their little idiosyncrasies that may make one a clear choice for you.

Home Equity Conversion Mortgage

By far the most prevalent of the three main options, the Home Equity Conversion Mortgage (HECM, sometimes pronounced heck-um; look in Chapter 5 for more details) provides the most payment choices, low interest rates, and the added mental security of being insured by the Department of Housing and Urban Development (HUD), a government organization. Take a look at some of the main points of an HECM loan:

- ✔ The loan is calculated based on the age of the youngest qualified borrower.

- ✔ Eligible homes include most single-family, condos, townhouses, and manufactured homes built after 1976 (ask your originator about HUD guidelines and requirements for manufactured homes).

- ✔ Lending limits (the amount you can borrow, also called the principal) are lower than other options, yet you can often get a higher principal than you would with others because of lower interest rates.

- ✔ Loans top out at $312,896 in high-home-value areas, $172,632 in lower-home-value areas (based on 2005 county lending limits).

- ✔ Interest rates can be based on monthly interest adjustments or annual adjustments (you won't pay anything until the loan is due, it just accumulates).

- ✔ Your money is easily accessible and payment options are very flexible.

Do these benefits sound like a good fit for you? If so, what the heck-um are you waiting for? Flip to Chapter 8 and make an appointment with a reverse mortgage counselor today.

Home Keeper

There are two loans created by Fannie Mae, America's largest loan funder, but they both have the same basic foundation. Since the Home Keeper and the Home Keeper for Purchase were modeled after the HECM, you may see lots of similarities when you look closer in Chapter 6. There are, however, some quirks that separate these loans from the pack:

- Home Keeper for Purchase lets you use a reverse mortgage to help buy a new home.

- Loan calculations are based on the combined ages of the qualifying borrowers, so married couples get less than singles.

- Eligible homes are single-family homes, condos, homes in planned unit development projects, townhouses, or manufactured homes that meet Fannie Mae requirements.

- Lending limits are based on an adjusted property value, which is a national lending limit rather than a county limit.

- The national lending limit is $359,650 (based on 2005 lending limits).

- Home Keeper often costs less than HECM but you'll probably receive less money in the long run.

Although Fannie Mae's Home Keeper loans may not bring you as much income as an HECM, their benefits (such as the ability to buy a new house with the reverse mortgage money) may make these the loans for you.

Jumbo Cash Accounts

For the house-rich among you, the Financial Freedom Cash Account is probably your best bet. Although it doesn't offer the flexibility of the other two major loans, Financial Freedom's reverse mortgage provides bundles of cash that HECM and Home Keeper only dream of. Chapter 7 goes into detail about the loan, but here are some of its general characteristics:

- There's no maximum lending limit; in theory, you could get a cash account reverse mortgage on a $20 million mansion and expect to receive a pretty hefty amount.

- Designed for homes valued at $359,651 or above (but is best when your home is worth at least $700,000).

- Almost all homes will qualify, including some co-ops.

> ✔ Interest rates and fees are usually higher than other loans.
>
> ✔ There are three types of Cash Accounts — each with different costs involved — that may generate different available funds for you.

If reverse mortgages aren't for everyone, then the Cash Account is for even fewer — rates and fees are higher, and there are some restrictions to the ways you can withdraw your money. However, if you own a high-priced home the tradeoff is probably worth it. Consult your counselor and financial planner about your Cash Account choices.

Figuring Out the People in Your Mortgage

Unlike most loans in today's Internet-crazy world, you can't simply go online and get a reverse mortgage from a pool of competing lenders. Reverse mortgages are a highly personal, interactive loan, and there are several people who make them happen and help you out along the way. Work closely with these people and let yourself be helped. You know what's best for you, but they know reverse mortgages. Together, you're an unstoppable equity-borrowing machine.

Counselor

Your first stop on the road to reverse mortgages is the counselor. They're not here to analyze your childhood or interpret your dreams; instead, these counselors offer up sound advice and the information necessary for you to make an informed decision about your own loan. They are required to remain completely unbiased and can only give you the facts — they never tell you what to choose or take away your power to make the best choice for you. It sounds great now, but come choosing time, you may probably wish someone would just tell you what to do!

Even the most independent homeowners are required to seek the advice and educational offerings of an approved counselor. Typically, an "approved" counselor refers to HUD-approved, but Fannie Mae and Financial Freedom each have their own set of preferred counselors. Unless you know for a fact that you need the Home Keeper or Cash Account loan, it's usually best to see a HUD counselor. These professionals are acceptable for any of the major loans discussed in this book, and if you decide to get an HECM (even after you've been to a Fannie Mae or Financial Freedom counselor) you still need to make an appointment with a HUD counselor as well. You can save time and energy by going to a HUD-approved counselor from the get-go.

Many counselors (especially HUD) operate free of charge, although some have a nominal fee for their services (usually around $75). Unless you live in an area where the only counselor for 50 miles charges a fee, try to use one who's free. The ones who charge offer the same exact information, so if you have a choice, go with the free ride.

During your counseling session, the counselor asks you all sorts of personal questions about your finances, your health, your family, your home, and your lifestyle. Don't keep anything from them or stretch the truth even a little bit. Counselors only have about an hour with you and need all the information they can get in that time to show you the options that may work best for you. It can be a bit off-putting to spill the beans to a stranger, but it's necessary to make a smart decision regarding your loan. You can rest assured that counselor sessions are completely confidential — only you and your counselor have access to the information you provide, unless, of course, you bring someone with you to the meeting.

It's a good idea to bring along any trusted family members or friends who may be able to help you get a better perspective, supply information, ask questions you hadn't even thought of, or just lend you some moral support. Counselors encourage families to come together, and you may probably find that you're glad to have someone else there. This isn't a requirement by any means, but consider it when you make your appointment. For more on counselors, how to find them, and what to expect at an appointment, flip ahead to Chapter 8.

Originator

Your originator is the person who sets your loan in motion. The originator meets with you to determine whether the loan you've decided on is really the best for your unique circumstances, helps you fill out the application, and submits it to the underwriters (who verify your information) and the lender (who actually signs your checks). You'll probably have at least two meetings with the originator: one to fill out the application and another to finalize details at closing. However, most people end up at their originator's office three, four, or more times over the course of their loan process. You may not choose a loan to apply to right away, have questions regarding your loan in progress, need to bring in additional information, or a whole host of other reasons to visit. That's why you and your originator become such close friends before your loan is completed.

Time is money, and although originators don't charge by the hour, there are fees involved for originators' services. Many of the fees you see on the Good Faith Estimate originators are required to provide are additional closing costs unrelated to the originator's efforts. A Good Faith Estimate lists all of the approximate costs involved in getting your loan, from appraisal services to stamps. All told, these fees can add up to several thousand dollars. That's a whole lotta cash to plunk down all at once, and the originators and lenders realize that it may present a burden. After all, if you had a few thousand dollars to spend, you may not need this loan. Because of this, you can roll the amount of most, if not all of your fees and closing costs into your loan. That way, the costs are absorbed into the reverse mortgage and become spread out over several years.

Finding a reverse mortgage originator is easy once you know where to look. Chapter 9 gives you all the tools you need to find a great originator, but keep these points in mind when you're narrowing down the search:

- **Originators should be experienced in reverse mortgages.** Do not pick a traditional loan originator, because they probably don't have the expertise that a reverse mortgage originator has.

- **While it's not a requirement, you may feel better if your originator is a member of the National Reverse Mortgage Lenders Association (NRMLA).** They have access to all kinds of resources and materials that others may not.

- **Your originator should be patient, never pressure you, and encourage your family to attend your meetings (if you feel comfortable having them there).**

- **Most of all, you have to feel comfortable with your originator.** If he or she doesn't feel like someone you'd trust with your future financial well being, trust your instincts. You won't hurt his or her feelings.

Appraiser

Unlike the counselor and originator (who hold meetings at their office), the appraiser comes to you. No matter which reverse mortgage product you decide on, an appraiser is required to come out to your home and give it the once over to determine its value.

Straightening out the facts

Lending limits, loan value, and home value can be misleading terms. When your home is appraised, the value is not necessarily equal to the amount of money you can borrow. In fact, you'd have to be very, very old to get a loan for 100 percent of your home's value — we're talking born around the turn of the century. Lenders factor in your age, current interest rates (they change constantly, more on that shortly), and earned equity to come up with a percentage of the home value that they can lend. The younger you are (early 60's to early 70's), the less they are going to approve because they know that you will probably stay in the home longer than someone in their 80's or 90's. So, while your home may be worth $250,000, they may only lend you $125,000.

Depending on home values in your area and the last time you had your home appraised, you may be pleasantly surprised to find out what your home is worth in today's market. Keep in mind that appraisals are largely subjective, and although they follow a certain protocol, appraisers have to simply use their best judgment to set your home's fair market value. Chapter 10 gives a full description of what goes on in the appraisal, including what the appraiser looks for.

The appraisal visit is nothing to worry about, as long as you've kept up your home maintenance over the years. Either way, it couldn't hurt to do a bit of sprucing up; clear your yard of any debris, clean your home the way your would if very special company was coming over, and fix any little things that you've been putting off if you can reasonably afford to do it. Also, gather up your home records — if you've ever had work done on the home (and who hasn't?) try to find those statements. The appraiser will be impressed by a home that's well-kept, but they won't be impressed by receipts for granite countertops. Don't start waving your credit card statement under the appraiser's nose to prove how much you spent refurbishing the master suite. The money you put into a home never fetches an equal value when it's appraised.

Since you can't sway the appraiser's evaluation with cookies or compliments, the best thing you can do during the process is sit back and let him or her work. Be ready to answer questions, but don't hover or even follow the appraiser from room to room. If you need something to do, make a list of all the fabulous things you can do with your reverse mortgage income.

Getting Paid

Of course, what you're really interested in is the money. This is one time in your life when it's perfectly okay to be focused on material things. After all, that's what a reverse mortgage is all about — lending you the money you need to buy the things you want. This is also the easiest part of getting a reverse mortgage: The lender determines how much you can borrow and you simply pick your payment option and start receiving money. No sweat. Still, there are some things you need to know about payments, your current financial issues, and the country's financial issues before you make a decision.

Figuring out how much you can get

Without sitting down with an originator, there's no way to tell you for sure what you can borrow from a reverse mortgage. We wish we could give you a simple formula, but there just isn't one. As we mention in this chapter (and elsewhere), the amount you can borrow is calculated using:

- ✔ **Your age:** Generally, the older you are, the better off your loan situations because the lender figures it won't have to work on your loan as long as if you were a spring chicken.

- ✔ **Your home value:** More equity equals more money available to borrow.

- ✔ **Your area:** Higher home values in the area means higher loan values for you if you choose an HECM or Home Keeper (which both use county medians to determine your loan principal).

- ✔ **Interest rates:** This is the one factor where less is more — the lower the interest rates, the higher the principal.

If you can wait a few years to get your loan, it will be worth it in the increased principal. Most people who wait at least five years are pleasantly surprised to find their loan amount has gone up . . . to the tune of a few thousand dollars. Don't wait so long that you can't enjoy the cash flow — that trip down the canals of Venice will probably be a lot more fun at 68 than at 98 — but don't rush out and get a loan on your 62nd birthday if you don't really need it yet.

Also, each loan has its own system of determining loan value. For example, no matter what your home is worth, Fannie Mae's Home Keeper bases the amount available to you on a scale as compared to the national lending limit ($359,650). On the other hand, the

Cash Account has no set limit. It bases its principal solely on your age, home value, and interest rates.

You can get an estimate of what each loan may be able to offer you using online reverse mortgage calculators. The NRMLA calculator (find it at www.reversemortgage.org) is a good indicator because it breaks down the entire loan, from what your estimated costs are to how much you get per month. However, they don't show you what you could get with a Cash Account, only HECM and Home Keeper. For a side-by-side comparison of all three loans, visit www.financialfreedom.com and take a spin on its reverse mortgage calculator.

Checking out payment options

You know how lottery winners get to choose whether they want their money in installments or one lump sum? Well you may feel like you won the lottery when you decide how you want your reverse mortgage funds to arrive. Each loan has its own set of payment options (that's payment to you, from the lender). Listed here are the main payment options, along with which loans offer them. As you read down the list, think about which one would fit best in your lifestyle.

- ✔ **Tenure** (HECM and Home Keeper): If you like the security of having stable, steady monthly checks deposited in your bank account, monthly tenure payments may be for you. The biggest advantage of this option is that no matter how long you have the loan (stay in your home), the lender continues to pay you — even if you've gone beyond what the lender originally agreed to lend you, and even if you live 30 years longer than anyone expected. The downside is that fixed monthly payments don't allow for sudden large expenses and don't adjust for inflation down the road.

- ✔ **Term** (HECM and Home Keeper): A monthly term payment has the security of getting equal monthly checks like the tenure plan, but you decide how long you continue to receive payments. The shorter the term, the more money you get per check. For example, if a lender sets your principal at $100,000 and you want to receive it over eight years, that's about $1,041 per month. If you decide instead to get your payments over five years, you're looking at $1,666 per month. That's a sizeable difference! But remember, once that term is over, you're out of money.

- ✔ **Lump sum** (HECM, Home Keeper, and one Cash Account option): Have you always dreamed of rolling around on a pile of money? Choosing a lump sum means you get the entire amount of the loan in one big check. It's up to you how you want to budget it per month, and it's up to you to make sure it lasts as long as you plan to live in your home. If you have a very large expense that you absolutely must pay in full, a lump sum could do the trick, although a better option is often a line of credit (see the next bullet).

✔ **Line of credit** (HECM, Home Keeper, Cash Account): A line of credit (also called a credit line) works very much like a savings account. You have access to the entire loan amount, but since you have to send in a form to get it, people are often more mindful of how their money is spent than they may be with a lump sum. In addition, depending on the loan, you can earn interest on the money you haven't yet borrowed.

✔ **Combination** (HECM and Home Keeper): Can't decide? Maybe a combination of payment options is your best bet. You can choose how much you want to receive upfront (through a lump sum, line of credit, or both) and designate the rest to a monthly payment. Or work backward — figure out how much you need per month, multiply that by the number of months you expect to stay in your home, and leave the rest in a line of credit. The combinations are virtually endless because they're tailor-made for you.

Discovering the effect of the funds on your finances

Seniors, especially those who have gone through hoops trying to get their fair share of Social Security, pensions, Medicaid, and various other programs, are often concerned that a reverse mortgage may cancel out those benefits. People often ask us if they have to choose between those programs and a reverse mortgage. You should be glad to know that the answer is no. The income from a reverse mortgage has no bearing on your current benefits. What's better, it has no effect on your taxes because equity isn't considered income by the IRS.

Of course, every rule has an exception. Although most people won't have any trouble maintaining their current benefits, some government programs (such as Supplemental Security Income) may include reverse mortgage payments in their income limits. If so, there are usually ways around this. Talk to your counselor and originator about working out a system to circumvent this issue. If you want to err on the side of caution, talk to your tax advisor or financial planner about how your newfound income may impact your finances. In the vast majority of cases, the only effect is a positive one.

Dealing with inflation and interest rates

Any time you're investigating a mortgage, you're sure to have your eye on interest rates. In recent years, rates have been quite low, although they are slowly creeping back up again. What does this mean for reverse mortgages? Just as in traditional mortgages, the lower interest rates are, the more money you can borrow. But unlike traditional mortgages, you don't pay a penny of that interest until the loan is over. It accumulates over time and is paid all at once when you repay the entire loan.

Aside from the initial closing costs and originator's fees, interest can be thought of as the price of borrowing money. The longer you have your reverse mortgage, the more you pay over the years in interest. Rates will fluctuate up and down during your loan — you can drive yourself crazy trying to follow the trends and track rates. But there's really no point. Once you have the loan, the best thing to do is forget about it. You can't control the market, and although you'll see your interest rate on your monthly or quarterly statement, you won't feel its effects until you end the loan.

One financial indicator that you may notice as the years go by is inflation. Think about the cost of your staple items 20 years ago — prices rise on an average of about 1.5 percent per year. It may not sound like much, but when you consider it on a large scale, it makes a big difference. A loan worth $75,000 this year only buys $73,875 worth of goods and services the next year. Why is this important to reverse mortgage borrowers? Unlike income from a job, you won't get a raise for cost of living with a reverse mortgage. That means if you're on a fixed $900 per month payment option, that $900 isn't going to go as far if you hold the loan for 10 or 20 years. A line of credit is a good way to beat inflation since, on an HECM loan, you actually earn interest on unused funds, which will help you keep up with rising prices.

The very savvy among you may see a great opportunity here to get the best of both worlds: stable monthly payments and an easy way to combat inflation. The solution is a combination of payment options. An HECM loan lets you set aside a portion of your principal for a line of credit and then receive the rest as monthly income. You can access the line of credit funds at any time, but by leaving them where they are, you build a greater equity savings. Skip ahead to Chapter 5 to see an example of how this could work for you.

Chapter 2

Deciding Whether a Reverse Mortgage Is Right for You

*Y*ou may have heard about reverse mortgages on the radio or from a friend, and you probably want to know if a reverse mortgage is right for you or someone close to you. While we can't tell you in these pages definitively whether this loan is the answer to your financial wishes — only you and your lending professionals, your counselor (see Chapter 8) and originator (see Chapter 9), can decide that — we can give you a head start. You need to consider several things before you get started on a reverse mortgage, and it's a good idea if you know from the get go whether or not you're a likely candidate. The reverse mortgage isn't free money.
It can be an expensive way to meet your financial needs, and the decision to get a loan shouldn't be taken lightly. For some, a reverse mortgage isn't the answer — and that's what you're here to find out.

In this chapter you can begin to see how a reverse mortgage can impact your life and how to tell if it's a good choice for you and your family. We also give you brief descriptions of alternatives, along with a pre-counseling checklist.

Pinpointing Your Motives

You probably already have a good idea of how you'd like to spend your reverse mortgage money. You may want some material things, such as making home improvements, or you may need the basics, such as paying for food and overdue bills. Whatever your motives for seeking out a reverse mortgage, you need to weigh the costs versus the benefits of getting a loan and make sure that you don't have other options that may better suit your needs.

Before you go to see a reverse mortgage originator (see Chapter 9), sit down and think about exactly why you want this loan, and what you're willing to pay for it. Is your peace of mind worth $3,000 in closing costs? Is your remodeled kitchen going to be worth the extra $12,000 in interest? (See Chapter 4 for a breakdown of fees and potential interest costs.) It's important to weigh these points, because although you get a three-day right of rescission (three days in which to change your mind after the loan closes), most people don't get a whopping case of buyer's remorse in the first three days. You're still too busy making out your "to-buy" list for at least the first month, and by that time it's too late to go back.

So you should not only talk with your family and your counselor (see Chapter 8) about the loan and what that loan can mean for your quality of life, but also read this section to assess your needs and wants, which can give you a good idea of whether you need a reverse mortgage in the first place.

Determining what you need

Human needs can be broken into categories, with some areas carrying more weight than others — like a what-you-need pyramid. At the base of the pyramid, you may place things like food and shelter, and toward the top, less tangible items such as self-esteem and independence. Reverse mortgages can address all of the essential human needs when the mortgage is taken out responsibly and in your best interests. It can help pay for your basic needs, while affording a sense of peace and financial independence that only comes with the security of money in the bank.

As great as that sounds, reverse mortgages aren't a magic solution for every household. Before you start buying up toys and time-shares, create a detailed budget of what you need per month. The things you need depends on how loosely you use the term, but you can consider the things you need as the non-extravagant items that get you from day to day. Food, medicines, health care, a safe place to live, electricity, water, gas, car payment, insurance, taxes — these are all needs that you've probably become accustomed to. Include everything from toothpaste to home repairs to your pet's medications . . . anything you wouldn't be willing to forego.

Preparing a needs budget

To account for your needs, simply look to your wallet. Each of your essential needs has a price, and knowing what you spend your money on is an easy way to focus in on your true needs versus your want-to-haves. Start paying attention to every item or service you pay for, and write it all down in a specially designated note-book or pad that you can carry with you. After a few weeks, take a hard look at your list and circle the expenses that you simply aren't willing to give up. These are the things you personally need. Now consider what your needs alone are costing you per month. It can be a shock to see how quickly it adds up! Check out Table 2-1 for a sample needs budget. Notice that the list of needs isn't strictly food and shelter, but also costs that have become associated with this imaginary senior's standard of living.

Table 2-1	Sample Needs Budget
Need	**Cost per month**
Phone bill	$39.99
Electric bill	$22.00
Cable bill	$45.00
Water bill	$10.00
Car insurance	$115.00
Gasoline	$40.00
Groceries	$150.00
Prescriptions	$67.89
Pet food	$12.50
Pet medication	$35.00
Hair cut and/or set	$45.00
Life insurance	$60.00
Daily paper	$15.00
Postage stamps	$7.35
Weekly lunch with sister	$60.00

(continued)

Table 2-1 *(continued)*

Need	*Cost per month*
Internet connection	$9.95
Club membership	$35.00
Housekeeper	$50.00
Total	$819.68

You can see how quickly these things add up. Now take an honest assessment of your own list. Determine if you can pay for all of these needs now. If not, figure out how much more money you need to meet your expenses. Don't forget to consider cutting back on your expenses to meet your budget (see the section "Paring down your needs," later in this chapter, for more on budgeting tighter).

However, even when you live on a tight budget, your expenses may be more than you can handle. Many people find that their pennies are pinched so tightly they've got "one cent" permanently imbedded in their thumbs, and yet their monthly expenses still come up higher than their monthly income affords. A reverse mortgage can change all that, giving you the extra padding you need to keep your life running normally, without giving up your necessities. If the things you need have become the things you're struggling to get, a reverse mortgage may be able to give you the economic boost you need to make ends meet.

Paring down your needs

When you look at what you spend each month, or even each week, you may be shocked by how much money goes flying out of your wallet. You spend $5 here and $2 there, which all seems perfectly harmless until you realize that you've spent $150 in one month on ceramic toothbrush holders and yet another pair of slippers.

We would never tell someone not to buy the things they really need. By all means, if your feet are cold, buy more slippers. But first, take a peek under the bed and see if you can save yourself a few bucks by using what you already have. We know a woman who moved out of her home after 10 years and found 38 pairs of nearly identical sunglasses throughout her house — she just kept buying new ones each time they were lost. At $10 a pair, that's $380 down the drain.

You may be surprised at how much you can save by simply elimi-nating one small thing. While this is by no means a complete list, here are some simple suggestions to get you thinking about how you can reduce some of your expenses:

- **Try going to the movies less frequently.** If you can't forego having a weekly movie night or several nights a week dedi-cated to movies, try renting or hit the matinees (and don't forget to ask for the senior discount!).

- **Consider getting your hair done every 12 weeks, rather than every 6 weeks.**

- **Assess whether you really need to go shopping for junk at the bargain store every weekend.**

- **Experiment with different, less expensive brands at the grocery store.**

- **Sniff out the bargains.** Check out whether you can find a simi-lar item somewhere else for a better price.

- **Keep track of your things.** If you find yourself repurchasing things because you lost the original . . . for the sixth time, per-haps you can devise a way to make sure the items you lose most often have a special place of residence.

- **Pare down to basic cable** (who really watches all those chan-nels anyway?) and you could save about $400 per year.

- **Make coffee at home every morning** instead of going out to a café and you could save around $900 per year!

Hopefully, this list gets you thinking about your spending habits — perhaps you don't need more money, just less spending! Many sen-iors need to make every dollar count, especially since newly retired people may not be used to living on such a fixed income. It takes some planning and careful spending to make any income, including a reverse mortgage, work for your budget.

 If you can afford your current lifestyle by budgeting a little tighter, you may not need a reverse mortgage for your daily living. Mortgages cost thousands of dollars in fees, interest, and little incidentals. You may be able to skip all that hassle and expense by simply watching your wallet a bit closer. If you think you'll need access to more money in the future (your income is running out or you're expecting big medical bills) you may be able to wait a few years and still save yourself some money. On the other hand, if you need a little extra so that your necessities don't have your wallet running on empty, a reverse mortgage may be just the thing.

Deciphering what you want

We all want something. We may say we're contented or deny that we want anything for our birthdays, but in reality there are always things we want. Oftentimes the things we want are trumped by the things we need, and those glimmering wants are just out of reach. Maybe you're living comfortably now, but can't afford to take that dream vacation or start your own business. Maybe you have quite enough to get by, but don't want to spend your entire savings on remodeling your home to accommodate a first-floor master suite. Or maybe all you want is peace of mind, knowing that although you don't feel you need to live lavishly, you're safe with a steady stream of income. A reverse mortgage can be the answer to getting some of the things you want without strapping for funds in the future.

Reverse mortgages can certainly be a miracle in the form of an electronic transfer for some people, but many others are disappointed that their loan didn't afford them a small fortune. If you had a plan for your money before you even picked up this book, consider whether the things you want could really be funded with the money you'd get from a reverse mortgage as well as whether you'd be able to live out your retirement on whatever's left. A reverse mortgage is not a bottomless cash purse — although you're certainly free to do whatever you like with your money, remember that reverse mortgages can be a costly decision. Enjoy your retirement, but be sure to exercise the same financial discretion you would with any other limited funds.

Checking out the most-wanted list

Reverse mortgages have helped thousands of people get the things they wanted in life. Lender Web sites are full of stories about seniors who took off on motorcycles across the Mojave Desert, paid for college tuition (whether for a grandchild or themselves), or made a point of going out to eat at their favorite swanky restaurant every month. That's part of the beauty of a reverse mortgage; although it's a loan from the equity in your home, you can use the money for whatever you want. There are no limitations, no quid pro quo, nothing to stop you from enjoying that cash to its fullest, greenest, most E Pluribus Unum potential. Just for fun, go to www.financial freedom.com and click on "consumer" then "testimonials" for real-life tales of seniors who got exactly what they wanted. Who knows? That could be you up there someday!

To assess the costs of your wants and how those costs impact your reverse mortgage, follow these steps to create your wants list (Table 2-2 gives you an example):

1. **Write down a list of all the things you really want.**

2. **Record how much each item costs.**

3. **Total the costs of the items.**

4. **Subtract the approximate cost of the reverse mortgage to see how much money you'd have left.**

Table 2-2	Sample Wants List
Want: Two-month trip to Italy	**Estimated cost**
Italy For Dummies	$19.99
Roundtrip plane tickets (2)	$1,200.00
Hotels at approximately $80/night	$4,800.00
Food at approximately $80/day	$4,800.00
Buses, trains, and taxis	$1,400.00
Museum tour	$30.00
Souvenirs and gifts	$2,000.00
Incidentals	$500.00
Subtotal	$14,746.99
Less approximate loan amount	$97,000.00
Total left for retirement	$82,253.01

In Table 2-2's example, the borrowers would have a remaining $82,253 after they took care of their lifelong dream of touring Italy. That works out to about $685 per month if they stay in their home for the next ten years. If you take a look at the needs list in Table 2-1 (see the earlier section "Determining what you need") you can easily see that if this couple has the same kind of needs as reflected in Table 2-1, they are going to need a lot more money if they plan to live on their reverse mortgage alone.

Find out approximately how much you can borrow by going to the National Reverse Mortgage Lenders Association (NRMLA) Web site and clicking on "calculator." From there, just enter your specifications (age, home value, zip code, debts), and the calculator can give you an estimate of what you may be able to get. Keep in mind that it's just an estimate. Until you sign the closing documents, you are really only operating on an assumption.

Of course, you know that with money comes responsibility. You're an adult. You've handled finances before and can most likely balance your own budget. But it can be awfully tempting to overextend your money when you're expecting a check in the mail for $80,000. Don't put a down payment on that yacht until you know what you can actually afford after you consider your needs and wants, or you may find yourself in over your head.

Rooting for single, senior women

Ladies, did you know that you're outliving men nearly three-to-one? It may not be surprising that with men's earlier mortality, our collective higher divorce rates, and fewer women feeling the need to marry at all, single women make up a very significant portion of the senior population in America. It may come as no surprise then that nearly half of all reverse mortgage borrowers are single women. That's right sister, you're not alone.

While it's true that the number of couples who take out reverse mortgage loans are on the rise, you single gals still make up the largest percentage of all reverse mortgage borrowers. Good originators should know this and need to talk to you about your understanding of your own finances before you get started with the loan. That said, they should never talk down to you or treat you like a child — whether you're male, female, senior citizen, or middle-aged, originators must give you the respect that they would bestow upon any other customer.

A large majority of single senior women are widows. Many come from a mindset, as you may have, in which the husbands took care of all the money stuff and the wives took care of the house and children. If your husband dealt with the mortgage process when you bought your current home and you weren't part of it, you may not have any experience with home loans. That system was fine for the times, but today there are a lot of senior women out there who are uncomfortable with financial dealings and prefer to let someone — anyone — else handle it. The light at the end of this unbalanced financial tunnel is that the next generation of senior women will probably be more financially sophisticated. Many Baby Boomer women run their own businesses, hold high-powered financial jobs, and manage households — to them, getting a reverse mortgage will be like ordering pizza.

You may find that the thought of taking out a loan on your own and making such a big economic decision is enough to make your stomach ache and your knees feel weak. It could be love, but it's probably mortgage flu. This is completely normal, but it doesn't give you a license to be removed from your reverse mortgage process. The prescription? Education and great counselors and originators.

One part of the process that will help tremendously is your trip to the counselor's office (see Chapter 8). Counselors are a required step in getting a reverse mortgage. They know that this may not be easy for you, and it's their job to help you feel at ease with whatever decision you make. You can ask all the questions you want, and the counselor won't think any of them are silly.

Keeping Your Options Open

There are some cases in which a reverse mortgage just isn't right for you. There are a few main alternatives that counselors often suggest when a reverse mortgage is too costly, or your profile doesn't fit with the needs of a typical reverse mortgage borrower. If your counselor feels that one may be a better choice for you, take his or her advice to heart. You can always reconsider when your situation changes. Check out Chapter 8 for more information about these options:

- ✔ **Waiting:** In many cases, waiting a few years to get a reverse mortgage really pays off. Since the lender calculates your loan partially based on age, the older you are, the more money you will most likely receive. Interest rates play a big part in determining your loan amount as well — when rates are low, you can probably expect more out of your reverse mortgage. In a low interest rate market, you can figure on an extra $8,000 to $15,000 for every five years you wait, depending on the value of your home. If you can afford to hold off for five years (or more) it's definitely worth it. For example, if you're 65, own a $200,000 home, and are considering an HECM loan, you could probably get about $10,000 more out of your loan if you waited until you were 70. On the other hand, higher interest rates will produce less available funds. If rates seem to be rising, you may want to jump on current rates before they get too high. Either way, don't wait too long — you want to have time to enjoy your newfound financial independence.

- ✔ **State loans:** Some state loans, like the Deferred Payment Loan (DPL), work like a reverse mortgage — they give you money and you pay it back when your leave your home permanently. But there's a catch . . . the DPL can only be used for a specific purpose, usually to repair something dangerous or unlivable in your home, whereas a regular reverse mortgage can be used for anything your heart desires. Another option is property tax deferrals that allow you to forego paying your property taxes for a while. These vary by state; some let you defer your payments forever, some only for a set timeframe. Both of these state loans offer very low interest and very low closing costs (if any). Check with your counselor (for more on talking with a counselor, see Chapter 8) to find out if other state loans exist in your area.

✔ **Selling your home:** This is often the obvious answer to your problems — sell your home, use the money to buy something smaller or simpler to maintain or easier to maneuver around, and live on the excess money from the sale of your house. If you think you'll be moving soon anyway, selling your home is usually the way to go. This assumes, of course, that you want to move, and that your home is worth enough to buy a new home with the equity. If you live in an average town in the Midwest and think you can buy a condo in San Diego with your equity, you're in for a big surprise. Housing prices vary greatly across the country, so do your homework if you plan to retire in another area.

Another non-traditional alternative to selling your home is to work out an agreement in which someone (usually a family member or friend) buys your home and rents it to you for a nominal fee. They get the benefit of the home's appreciation, and you get to stay in your home, collect on the sale of the house, and reduce your payments. Still, some people prefer not to mix family and money, and for good reason. Be sure to discuss this kind of arrangement in detail, and involve a real estate professional if appropriate.

✔ **Sharing space:** Your financial situation might be such that you don't need a huge sum of money for any big vacation or fancy new bathroom. You just need money for the essentials or to supplement your Social Security. Your counselor could bring up the idea of sharing a home with a friend or relative in a similar situation. Do you have a sibling or sewing club friend who is also in need of a little monthly help? Invite them to live in your spare bedroom, charge them a fair rent, and meet your monthly requirements. You may also consider moving in with an adult child. This is an ideal situation for some families, but it can be a huge lifestyle change and is not a decision to be taken lightly.

✔ **Refinancing with a forward mortgage:** Okay, maybe the idea of having a new payment to worry about doesn't thrill you, but if you can reduce your payments, a forward mortgage may help cushion the savings or retirement income you're living off of today. ARMs (adjustable rate mortgages) always have lower interest rates, which means a lower monthly payment.

Keep in mind that because forward ARM interest rates change frequently (usually once per year) what may have been a great interest rate last year can suddenly skyrocket next year. If you're uncomfortable with an unpredictable interest rate, an ARM may not be the best choice for you.

Home Equity Lines of Credit can also be a good option, offering another way to use your equity now. Downsides are that they sometimes have a higher interest rate over the long term; they have a minimum monthly payment (that's you paying the lender); and some have a *balloon payment* built in, which forces you to pay more after a certain time period.

✔ **Public assistance:** Many people think of public assistance as a negative, and would often rather protect their pride than get the help they need. Don't be one of those people. Public assistance is nothing to be ashamed of, and can give you all kinds of breaks on daily expenses. There are meal delivery programs for those who can't cook anymore (whether it's due to inadequate funds or mobility), prescription drug benefits, medical assistance, transportation for those who can't drive, in-home helpers, and many, many more opportunities for help. Several resources aren't being utilized by enough people. You've paid for these public assistance programs through taxes all your working life. This is the time to reap the benefits of your own tax dollars.

A great resource for all types of help is the Area Agency on Aging. They can give you information about some of the options listed here, plus reduced energy bills, tax support, and more. Contact them at 800-677-1116 or online at www.eldercare.gov. Another great resource is a Web site called www.BenefitsCheckup.org. BenefitsCheckup is sponsored by the National Council on the Aging and works by creating a profile of you and your needs and matching it to all the programs out there that may be able to help you. All you have to do is fill out a questionnaire and let the Web site do the work. Your results will include information about each organization and how to contact them to apply for benefits.

Of course, with hundreds of thousands of individual circumstances, your counselor may be able suggest another alternative that's tailor made just for you. The point is: You have options. Just because you're reading up on reverse mortgages doesn't mean you're locked into a loan. Before you meet with your counselor or your originator, keep an open mind to all options so you find what works best for you.

Reverse mortgage, eh?

If you are a resident of Canada, you won't be able to get a reverse mortgage through FHA, Fannie Mae, or Financial Freedom. The answer to "is this loan for me?" is a resounding "no." So what's a Canuck to do? Canada has its own brand of reverse mortgage, called the Canadian Home Income Plan (CHIP), which was developed in 1986, just as the Home Equity Conversion Mortgage was coming into play. The requirements are essentially the same as American reverse mortgages (see Chapter 3 for more on borrower qualifications for American reverse mortgages): You must be 62, own your home, and have sufficient equity. Loans range from $20,000 to $500,000, and repayment isn't due until you've left your home permanently. To find out more about the CHIP loan, email info@chip.ca, visit www.chip.ca, or call 866-522-2447.

Knowing When to Walk Away

If reverse mortgages were the absolute best choice for every homeowner over age 62, we wouldn't need this book. The reality is, a reverse mortgage is a complicated loan with a lot of specifications and calculations that make it supremely perfect for many people, but a very wrong choice for others. Before you decide to visit a reverse mortgage counselor, make sure you're a good candidate for the loan by reading through this section.

Knowing when you shouldn't get a reverse mortgage

As a rule of thumb, reverse mortgages are designed for people who plan to live in their homes for at least five years (but more likely 8 to 12 years). Some senior homeowners are over optimistic about their current living situations, believing that they can continue living in their homes indefinitely, even though their doctor or concerned family has other ideas. Others aren't patient enough to wait a few years to make the loan worthwhile before picking up and moving to Cancun. Of course, if you're on the elder end of the borrower spectrum and need the funds from a reverse mortgage despite the fact that you may only hold the loan for a couple of years, don't let that five-year timeframe keep you from seeking out the loan. Again, only you and your lending professionals know what's right for you, but you'll probably want to think twice about getting a reverse mortgage if any of these apply to you:

✔ **Your home is damaged beyond the point of repair.** Reverse mortgages are great for revamping a few rooms, or making a home more accessible, but they don't work miracles. Unlike the shows you may have seen on TV, you won't be able to tear down your home and build a new one if there are major structural or foundation problems. Dangerous electrical or plumbing may also be an issue. Sometimes it's better to cut and run. You may be able to purchase a new home with the Home Keeper for Purchase (see Chapter 6 for information on this loan), but don't expect anyone to let you stay in a house that's crumbling.

✔ **You're young and have plenty of money.** Just because you're 62 doesn't mean you need to run out and apply for a reverse mortgage. The lenders aren't going anywhere — there's no rush. In fact, as we noted earlier, the younger you are, the less money you'll get from your loan. If you can live off your nest egg for a few years, wait to get your reverse mortgage. Not only will you save money, you'll get more money as well.

✔ **You think you'll want to move out in the next couple of years.** Reverse mortgages get less expensive the longer you have them. Moving out too soon means you'll pay more for the privilege of having a loan, which is less money you'll have for your fun and extravagant lifestyle or for the needs you took the loan out for in the first place. If you stay longer, you win. A reverse mortgage isn't usually the best short-term solution. Talk to your counselor (Chapter 8) and originator (Chapter 9) to get a better idea of costs versus benefits.

✔ **You are ill and don't believe you'll live as long as the lender predicts.** Just like moving out too soon, it doesn't make sense to take out a loan that you know you'll never be able to fully enjoy. Keep in mind, however, that sometimes need overrides financial considerations and the reverse mortgage is still your best choice. The loan may allow you to live out your last years more comfortably than your could otherwise manage. Make sure your counselor (see Chapter 8) explains the pros and cons, and don't be afraid to tell him or her about your condition. They need to know all the facts.

✔ **You have a spouse or other person living in your home who doesn't qualify for a reverse mortgage.** The loan becomes due and payable when the borrower (or last remaining borrower) permanently leaves the residence. That means if you get the loan when you're 65 and your spouse is 57 and you die or move out for any reason, your spouse will be responsible for paying off your mortgage, which often means selling the house. If you can't add all residents to the mortgage, you may want to wait or seek out a different option.

Of course, this isn't an extensive list. With hundreds of thousands of individuals out there who may qualify for a reverse mortgages, there are countless situations that could make a reverse mortgage a less-desirable choice. The only way to know for sure is to visit a reverse mortgage counselor and take his or her expertise into consideration. To find out more about getting a certified counselor, flip to Chapter 8.

Knowing if you're ready

Before you make up your mind about pursuing a reverse mortgage, take a minute to make sure you're starting out on the right foot. Having a strong foundation will make your loan process much easier, both for you and for the professionals involved. Use this checklist as you go through this book to keep track of your eligibility and progress, and make sure every item is checked off before you seek out a reverse mortgage counselor:

- ✔ I am at least 62 years old.

- ✔ I own my own home.

- ✔ I have a good idea of what my home is worth. An appraisal (see Chapter 10) will address this if you don't already know how much your home would hypothetically sell for.

- ✔ I understand how a reverse mortgage works (see Chapter 1).

- ✔ I have or will read up on the reverse mortgage products (see Chapters 5, 6, and 7).

- ✔ I know what my monthly expenses are.

- ✔ I have compared my expenses to what I can expect to receive from a reverse mortgage.

- ✔ I know what I want to do with my reverse mortgage payments.

- ✔ I have talked to my family about reverse mortgages and am keeping them informed about my decisions.

Chapter 3

Having the Right Stuff: Borrower Qualifications

*I*f you think a reverse mortgage sounds like a good way to start heading down a path of financial security, you're ready to see if you qualify. You can relax: The reverse mortgage is one of the easiest loans to qualify for in all the lending world. The basic requirements, which we explain in this chapter, to qualify for a reverse mortgage are:

✔ You must be 62 years old or older.

✔ You must own your home.

✔ You must own a home that qualifies for the reverse mortgage product you choose and live in it full time.

There are certain caveats of course, and lots of fine print, which we expose in the next few pages. In this chapter you can compare your individual living situation with the borrower requirements to see if you'd be eligible for a reverse mortgage.

Finding Out If You Qualify

Almost anyone who meets the basic requirements can get a reverse mortgage. You don't need perfect credit, you don't need a down payment, and you don't need a steady job. In fact, none of those points matter in a reverse mortgage.

Aging gracefully

Though you may feel discriminated against because of your age in some facets of life, reverse mortgages were designed especially for you. In order to receive a reverse mortgage you must be at least 62 years old. No exceptions.

But wait, it gets even better. The older you are, the better you'll do on a reverse mortgage. Why? Because lenders know that the younger you are, the longer they'll have to pay you. Lenders use actuarial charts (just like insurance companies) to guess how long you'll be in your home. The charts aren't a crystal ball, and they're not always right, but they give a pretty good estimation. Then lenders calculate your loan based on your age, your home's value, and whatever the current interest rates are.

Look at Table 3-1 for an example of how your age can work for you in a reverse mortgage. Let's say our borrower, Nathaniel, owns a home worth $235,000 in Jenkintown, PA, and owes no outstanding mortgage debt. He's choosing a Home Equity Conversion Mortgage (HECM) reverse mortgage product and wants a lump sum, giving him all his money in one big check. We'll pretend for our purposes that interest rates don't change into the future (although in real life, Nathaniel's initial loan amount would be affected by rising and falling rates). The table shows how much Nathaniel could expect to borrow if he closed the loan at particular ages. Notice that the older our fictitious borrower gets, the more money the lenders are willing to loan him.

Table 3-1	How Age Affects Your Loan
Age at time of loan closing	*Total loan amount available*
62	$116,754
67	$126,806
72	$137,401
77	$148,796
82	$160,349
87	$171,433
92	$182,354

The typical age for reverse mortgage estimates is 75, because by then you're old enough to get a pretty hefty check but young enough to be able to enjoy your new income. When you see examples of reverse mortgage calculations (in this book and in the world at large) you'll probably notice that the hypothetical borrower is 75. It's not a magic number, and by no means should it be seen as any sort of limitation, but as far as the lenders go it's the perfect win-win age.

There's a disadvantage to this age system, however. If a couple, ages 62 and 75, want to get a loan, you may think they should be able to get a pretty good-sized check since 75 is just about the ideal reverse mortgage age. But that's not the case. For most reverse mortgage loans, the age used to calculate the loan is that of the *youngest* borrower (sneaky, isn't it?). If Nathaniel (age 75) and his youngest brother (age 62) want to live together to save some money, their reverse mortgage will be calculated using his brother's age, which means a lower loan amount. On the other hand, Nathaniel and his brother may find that they can get a larger sum with a Fannie Mae Home Keeper loan (see Chapter 6) because Fannie Mae uses a combination of borrower ages to determine the available funds.

No matter what your age, if you are interested in getting a reverse mortgage, find out what your options are from your originator (see Chapter 9) and reverse mortgage counselor (see Chapter 8). It can't hurt to ask.

Coupling

With divorce rates in America climbing higher and higher, it's amazing that there are any couples left at all. If you're one of these lucky couples, you can count yourselves among a growing trend. Couples are increasingly among the seniors who are taking out reverse mortgages. It used to be that reverse mortgages were largely held by widowed women around age 76. Today, more and more couples, and younger ones at that, are seeking reverse mortgages.

There has also been an increase of couples who get a reverse mortgage when only one individual qualifies. It's perfectly legal: One person is age 62 or older and owns a home that's covered under the loan (see the section "Living Room: Eligible Homes," later in this chapter), and the other is a bit younger. To get the reverse mortgage, however, the loan can only be for the eligible spouse — that younger person will have to be removed from the title. And when the qualified spouse dies or moves out for other reasons the younger will be responsible for paying back the loan in full. This often means selling the home, and it may come at a time when that resident isn't ready to move (or just plain doesn't want to). Most counselors and originators will advise you against this, since this situation can create serious financial stress at a time when the remaining resident is probably stressed enough as it is.

Regrettably, once the loan is closed (it's in progress and you're receiving money) you may not add anyone to it. A change in the borrowers would affect the loan, since it is based partially on your age. The lenders will have figured the loan with the age of the only eligible resident in mind. Adding another person would end the loan and start a new one, meaning that whatever you'd borrowed up to that point would be due at the time that a new loan was issued. In cases where one spouse or other resident is much younger and wouldn't be eligible soon enough to benefit the older person, a reverse mortgage may still work as long as everyone involved knows the responsibility attached to the loan and has a plan for repayment.

The bottom line: Either wait for everyone on the title to become eligible, or look for other options.

Retaining Title

In order to qualify for a reverse mortgage you must own your home. You don't necessarily have to have it paid off completely, but the less you owe, the more you can borrow. This is because the reverse mortgage is based largely on *equity* — the value of your home minus any debts. The money that you borrow is actually a percentage of the equity in your home; the lenders are essentially lending you a portion of the money you'd have if you sold your home. What they don't do is buy your home from you, nor do they force you to hand it over to them when the loan is completed. That's a big misconception, and one that you should put out of your mind right now. Repeat after us: A reverse mortgage doesn't mean the lender gets your house.

Many people operate under the misconception that a reverse mortgage means giving up the title to your home. In fact, the home's title remains in your name as long as you own it. If your name is removed (for example, if you sold your home), the loan becomes due and payable. What's more, everyone who's on the title must meet the rest of the loan requirements. An adult child who helped you purchase your home, for example, would have to be removed before you obtained a reverse mortgage if he or she didn't meet the requirements.

Unfortunately, there are no provisions in reverse mortgages for people who rent their residences, since the money you're receiving is based on equity — no ownership, no equity. If you live in a home that you personally don't own, we're sorry to say that you won't be eligible for a reverse mortgage. It's a shame too, since many people who rent would benefit enormously from the extra income. Restrictions against renters also include people who rent-to-own, since you technically don't own the home yet. Seniors already living in assisted living facilities won't be able to get a loan either unless the home or apartment is owned by the resident (you) and falls under the housing guidelines (see the section "Living Room: Eligible Homes," later in this chapter).

Paying off your current mortgage

Many people think that you can't owe anything on your current mortgage in order to get a reverse mortgage. If that were the case, it would seriously limit the number of people who could qualify, and the reverse mortgage gurus know this. The fact is, you only need to have *some* equity in your home to qualify. Of course, the more of your home you own outright, the more money you'll see from a reverse mortgage since they're loaning you a portion of your existing equity.

Financing your debt

Any outstanding mortgage will have to be paid off before you see your first reverse mortgage payment. The upside is, you can roll that pay-off into your loan amount to be paid off over time. You never have to write that huge check to your last lender, and you don't have to take a big chunk out of your reverse mortgage funds to pay it off all at once.

Here's how it works for Adam, a hypothetical borrower:

1. Adam and his originator fill out all his forms for the reverse mortgage, noting that he still owes $35,000 on his previous mortgage.

2. The lender figures out Adam's total loan amount and agrees to lend $129,000.

3. The $35,000 that Adam owes on his current mortgage is subtracted from the $129,000 leaving Adam with a total of $94,000 to do with as he pleases.

4. Adam lives happily ever after.

Repaying before you borrow

For many people, the idea of giving up some of their loan in order to pay off a current debt just won't fly. If you don't own your home free and clear today, take a look at how much mortgage debt you have. How many years will it take to pay down your existing loan? You may not want to wait that long before reaping the potential benefits of a reverse mortgage. By rolling your current loan into a new reverse mortgage, you'll also save money on future interest payments, which can add up pretty fast.

If you're adamant about paying of your current mortgage before seeking a reverse mortgage, you can speed up the process by paying a little extra each month. Check with your current lender to make sure there are no prepayment penalties first, and then start sending as much as you're comfortable with in addition to your standard payments. Before you put the idea of a reverse mortgage on the shelf while you repay your existing loan, talk with your counselor or originator about your individual situation. You may find that you'd have to wait longer than you're comfortable with, or that you can't afford to send any extra payments. Just remember, if you start paying a higher monthly mortgage to repay your original loan and then change your mind, whatever you've put into it has increased your equity. Every little bit can make a difference.

Generally speaking, you're an okay candidate for a reverse mortgage if you've paid off about 65 to 75 percent of your home, a good candidate if you've paid off 76 to 85 percent, and an excellent candidate if you've paid off 86 to 100 percent. These aren't hard-and-fast numbers, and they'll vary with your age and value of your home, but you get the idea. If you and your counselor play with the numbers and can't find a reverse mortgage solution that works for you due to your outstanding debt, you may find that you have other options. For a description of other loan or income choices that a counselor may suggest, see Chapter 8.

Staying put

Once you get a reverse mortgage the assumption is that you are going to live in your home. That's why you would get a reverse mortgage in the first place. To prove this reasoning, reverse mortgages prohibit you from moving out of your home for more than 12 months at a time. This is how much the reverse mortgage lenders want you to stay in your own home into your retirement: If you move out for whatever reason, you end the loan and it must be repaid. To take it one step further, even if you don't sell the house — if you still own it, but decide to rent it out to someone else and stay with your family or live somewhere cheaper instead — your loan will be due. This applies no matter what the situation is: If you move out and rent it out to your sister, your son, your neighbor's nephew, a total stranger, whomever . . . your loan will end.

This is not to say that you're never allowed to leave your home. You can absolutely feel free to go on vacations, spend a few months traveling, or (although not nearly as pleasant) spend some in-patient time in the hospital. You are also free to move out of your home when you need to, just as long as you understand that when you do, you will have to pay back your loan. As we explain in detail in Chapter 4, your lender will try to contact you about once a year to make sure you're still living in your home. Take these attempts seriously and be sure to respond promptly.

It should stand to reason then, that you can't sell your home either. The loan is due when you don't live at your home anymore, and selling definitely qualifies under that restriction.

Living Room: Eligible Homes

If you're over 62 and own your home, you're over halfway to quali-fying for a reverse mortgage. The next aspect of qualification is your home.

Most houses and units will qualify for reverse mortgages, but there are some, such as the following, that will never pass muster:

- Mobile homes or trailers
- Motor homes
- House boats or yachts
- Multi-family properties with more than four units
- Manufactured homes built before 1976
- Timeshares
- Barns
- Impermanent structures (even if you own the land)

If you do own one of these home types, you are still entitled to talk to a counselor about your options. While reverse mortgages may not suit your unique living situation, other loan programs and assistance opportunities may exist in your area.

If you live in virtually any other type of home, you can breathe a sigh of relief. Your home will probably qualify.

Why just "probably"? If your home needs extensive repairs that the loan won't be able to cover, isn't up to code, or falls into one of only a few ineligibility categories, you won't be approved for the loan. Your appraiser will assess your living situation and make note of anything they see that would keep you from getting your loan (for more on the appraisal, flip ahead to Chapter 10). This section covers the types of homes that are eligible to qualify for a reverse mortgage. There are a few reverse mortgage guidelines that apply to any home type:

- ✔ Your house must be in relatively good condition. Each loan program has its own set of standards, but a good rule of thumb is to follow the FHA/HUD standards (available from your counselor or originator).

- ✔ Your home must be free or serious hazards like lead paint and clear of any damaged plumbing, wiring, or structural elements. Your reverse mortgage may be able to pay for repairs, but it won't pay for a whole-house renovation.

- ✔ You must live in your home full time. You can come and go as you please, but if you're gone for more than 12 months, your loan may become due.

- ✔ If you own a rental property, you can move in and reap the benefits of that built-up equity. It doesn't matter how long you lived there before, only that you live there as long as you have your reverse mortgage.

Single-family homes

A single-family home is any home that is detached from other dwellings. Does your home sit on a plot of land that you own, with no other homes touching it? Then you probably live in a single-family home.

Single-family homes is the simplest category for loan purposes, since there are very few rules about what kind of single-family home is eligible. One-story, two-story, big, small, pool, no pool, garage, no garage . . . as long as it stands alone, it counts. Unless you built your home yourself and didn't follow building standards, you should be fine. Your home will need to meet Housing and Urban Development (HUD) minimum property standards, which are pretty straightforward (how wide your stairs must be, where your utilities are located, and things like that). The rules are standard, and while your state or county may have specific housing regulations, everyone has to adhere to HUD.

Heavy metal mamma

One thing you should be aware of is lead paint. Many people in older houses don't even realize that their walls are teeming with heavy metals. Lead paint has been linked to several heath problems, ranging from such banal complaints as headaches to much more serious issues, like cancer and nutrient malabsorption. If your home was built prior to 1978 (when they stopped using lead paint) your appraiser will look for signs of it. Simple tests can determine if the paint in your home is harmful and if so, you may be required to fix the problem before they'll give you a loan (or promise to fix it afterward). You'll see a note about lead paint in your appraisal report, as well as your loan application — that's how serious it is. The lenders really want to make sure you're safe.

Condos and townhouses

If your house touches someone else's, you most likely live in a condominium or a townhouse. The difference is that townhouses have two stories within the unit, with no other home above or below it. Loans may also lump planned unit developments (PUDs) and co-ops into this category. They're all basically the same idea: at least two homes that share at least one wall. Most condos and townhouses will qualify easily. Each loan product will have different rules governing what kind of condos and townhouses are allowed under their terms. Skip ahead to Part II to read more about housing eligibility for each loan option.

Some loans have rental limits. Many condo and townhouse developments welcome renters — but if your neighborhood allows more than a certain percentage of rentals within the community (it differs depending on the loan program you choose), your home (even though you're not renting it out) may not qualify. Talk to your originator or counselor to find out if your home meets the rental requirements.

In addition, your unit will have to pass the same safety tests as the single-family homes. This isn't to say your home has to be a pristine, unlived-in museum, but it does have to be a safe place for you to live.

Manufactured homes

Some manufactured homes aren't eligible, but there's a loophole. If your manufactured home was built after June 1976 *and* you own the land it's permanently affixed to, your home may be eligible. Manufactured homes are tricky business when it comes to any type of loan — reverse or not — because they may not meet certain criteria, and more often than not they depreciate in value just like your car.

Lenders are understandably wary to let you borrow against your equity in a manufactured home, since that equity is usually either static or declining. Historically, manufactured homes are a wonderful choice for people who want to own a piece of the American dream and stop paying rent to someone else, but they have never been a stellar real estate investment. The upside is that if you bought your manufactured home a decade ago, chances are that it is worth slightly more today than it was then. But chances are better that it hasn't gained or lost value. Not a significant amount anyway.

What lenders are afraid of is that the wear and tear on your manufactured home will render it less valuable than the day you get your reverse mortgage. If they lend you $30,000 on a manufactured home valued at $50,000 and it depreciates to $25,000 over the years, they'll never recoup their money. They'll have lost $5,000 and that is something that big corporate lenders don't like any more than you do.

Generally speaking, only HECM (see Chapter 5) and Home Keeper (see Chapter 6) will lend to borrowers who own manufactured homes. They make up for the risk of depreciation by charging a mortgage insurance premium (on an HECM) or simply loaning you less money (on a Home Keeper). Since Financial Freedom (see Chapter 7) has a $75,000 home value minimum (and isn't ideal for anyone with a house worth less than about a half million dollars) they will rarely if ever lend money to a manufactured home owner. Keep in mind that even the HECM and Home Keeper aren't a sure bet. Talk to your originator or counselor about your eligibility if you live in a manufactured home. An always growing number of seniors are finding that manufactured homes are an affordable way to own a home and stay within their budgets. The reverse mortgage lenders are slowly starting to realize this and are very gradually accepting them for the legitimate houses that they are.

Multi-family homes

Multi-family homes are known by lots of different names; most often they're duplexes, triplexes, or fourplexes (don't get us started on the grammatical incongruousness of "fourplex"). For those savvy real estate investors who purchased a multi-family residence, don't feel left out. As long as you live in one of the units full time, your property may be eligible. What's even better is that there's no rule as to how long you have to live at your residence before you take out a reverse mortgage. If you're thinking of getting a reverse mortgage on a multi-family property that you use as an income source, get packing and move into one of those units. Just make sure it's someplace you can see yourself living for several years down the road.

Of course, "slum lords" need not apply. Your multi-family home must be up to FHA/HUD standards in every way. Every unit must be safe and sound, and every unit is subject to inspection. The only major caveat to the multi-family home is that it can't have more than four units. The good news is that your entire property — every unit — is calculated in the loan value. It wouldn't make sense to treat it like a condo since you own the whole place. Not every loan product has multi-family homes under its mortgage umbrella, so talk to your originator and counselor about your options.

Not to dissuade you from a reverse mortgage altogether, but if you own a multi-family residence and you're hurting for ready cash, you may be better off either selling the property or raising the rent on the other units — just make sure you're asking a fair and reasonable rent (fair for you and the tenant).

Reverse mortgages are designed to last about seven years on average. Will you still want to be responsible for those other units in seven years or more? Of course, you're free to end your loan by selling your home at any time, but selling too early can make your loan more expensive in the long run. Or short run, as the case may be.

Second homes

Reverse mortgages only allow you to take out a loan on one home at a time, but they don't say anything about how many homes you can own. In fact, your second home may be the perfect solution to the question of where you'll go if you decide to move out of your home and end your loan.

Remember that you must live in your home full time to be eligible. For those lucky ducks who have two or more homes to spend their time in, you can still get a reverse mortgage . . . but only on one of your homes. Most people who own a second home have it for a getaway and don't spend their time equally in both homes. One house is a primary residence and the other is secondary. It's your primary residence exclusively that can have a reverse mortgage lien on it. You may have to choose which house you want to use the reverse mortgage for if you use each one for half the year.

The decision can be as easy as choosing the one with the higher value, or the one with the best weather. Either way, the one you choose will be your primary residence for the next few years.

Whether it appears clear which home you actually live in, or you do truly spend your time exactly equally between homes, the originator and lender will base their loan assessment on the address found on your driver's license or other legal identification. Since no one can hold more than one valid driver's license or other similar identification, it will become clear very quickly which house you actually call home. If you want to use what was your secondary home as a retirement residence and get the reverse mortgage on that property, you'll need to update your identification (it's easy, just call your department of motor vehicles).

Of course, just because you named one house as a primary residence doesn't mean you have to abandon the other. What's the use of getting that extra cash if you can't use it to travel to your favorite destination? Remember, you can't be away from your primary home for more than 12 months at a time. Lenders figure that if you can stay away for that long, it probably isn't your primary residence.

You know that you can only have a reverse mortgage on one of your homes, so you must choose which one to mortgage. But if you think you and your spouse can each take your name off of one of the home's titles and both get reverse mortgages on separate houses, thereby doubling your income, don't. It's illegal, and you don't want to spend your golden years in the slammer, do you?

Chapter 4

Repaying Your Loan

In This Chapter

▶ Figuring out repayment

▶ Finding a repayment option that suits your situation

*Y*ou've probably been paying a lender every month for your traditional "forward" mortgage for the past 40 years. As you paid, your balance went down while your equity (the amount of money you would get from the sale of your home after all mortgage debts are repaid) went up. Your reverse mortgage is just the opposite: It pays *you* every month (or however you choose to receive your money) and *increases* your loan balance as your equity *goes down.* It sounds like the perfect plan: Live in your house, get money instead of paying it, never have to worry about a mortgage repayment. Well, almost never. There comes in life an end to all things, and your reverse mortgage is no exception. In this chapter we tell you how you repay your loan and when that repayment is due. We also give you some tips on how you and your family can prepare for that day before the time comes.

Getting the Loan Repaid

We've said it before and we'll say it again: The reverse mortgage is not free money. When you take out a reverse mortgage, you are essentially borrowing ahead of time the money you'd get if you had sold your home, without actually having to sell it. The key word is *borrowing.* They hand you a portion of what your home is worth today, and you agree to pay it back at a later date. It's not a gift; it's a loan. In addition to repaying the portion of equity you've borrowed, you'll also pay a few thousand dollars in fees, plus interest. No matter which reverse mortgage product you choose, your loan will have to be paid off sooner or later — luckily, it's usually later.

The idea of repaying a loan that came out of the equity in your home may seem a little confusing at first for you and for your family, but the facts are actually pretty straightforward.

Figuring out when it's due and who has to pay it

Any reverse mortgage becomes due and payable when you meet any of these circumstances:

- ✔ **You permanently move out of your home.** If the mortgage comes due because you've decided to move out, you will be responsible for paying back the loan at that time and will have to wade through the repayment process. In cases where you're being moved to assisted living, it's common for a durable power of attorney to take over and worry about this matter for you.

  You can only have a reverse mortgage on one home at a time. Seniors who have two homes (for instance, a summer home and a winter home, or a cabin by the lake) will have to choose one as their permanent residence for reverse mortgage purposes. You can, of course, still spend your winters at your second home in Tahiti or summer in Cape Cod, but if you choose to retire to the one that you have *not* claimed as your primary residence, your loan will come due.

- ✔ **The last borrower dies.** If the loan is due because the last surviving borrower has died, the responsibility of payment falls to your heirs (or whomever you've named in a trust or will). They have several options available to them that are covered further in this chapter, and in more detail in Chapter 13.

- ✔ **You fail to pay property taxes, fall behind on home owners insurance payments, and/or maintain the home (although this rarely happens).** You will also be held accountable for repayment if you neglect your home. This isn't a subjective matter, where one person thinks your creaky staircase is unacceptable and another would let it slide. These are serious problems, like a hole in your roof or a backed-up sewer line. This requirement also includes keeping up with your property taxes and insurance, which are necessities for any homeowner.

When two or more borrowers exist on a loan and one has to move out (for assisted living or personal reasons, for example) the loan will not need to be repaid. Only when the last borrower permanently leaves the house will the loan come due.

When your loan is due, the whole entire kit and caboodle must be paid at once. There are no installment plans, so you (or your heirs) need to have a plan in place for paying the loan back in full. This is why many people choose to sell their homes — you'll easily earn enough on the sale to pay the balance, and may have some left over to do with what you wish.

Contacting the lender

If your lender estimates that you'll keep your loan for 10 years and makes payments to you reflecting that timeframe, you may think you have to start paying back the loan after 10 years. In fact, as long as you continue to pay your property taxes and keep up the home in good condition the lender can never demand payment from you until you no longer live at that address.

Many seniors wonder how the lender will know when the last borrower has moved out or died — it's not as if they peer through your hedges at you, or check the resident lists at the hot new retirement communities for your name. Technically speaking, it is *your* responsibility to let the lender or servicer know that you've left your home for good. Obviously if the loan has become payable upon your death, it may be a little tricky for you to alert them. It's a good idea to let your family know that part of settling your estate includes letting the lender in on your passing, but often family members are too consumed by your absence that they let it slip by the wayside. The same is often true if you are moved to assisted living or another facility and aren't in a state of mind to alert the lender. This doesn't mean that you can unintentionally get away with never repaying your loan. They'll find out sooner or later that you are no longer at home.

In fact, the servicer of the loan has the responsibility of making sure that the owner is still occupying the property. Are they hiding in that unmarked van outside your house all day just to be sure? No, believe it or not they thought of a much easier way. The servicer will send you a letter, or call once per year just to say "hi." A letter will request a response (probably a note to sign or a short form to fill out) asking you to verify that you do, indeed, still live in your home. Simply fill it out and send it back. They even come in pre-addressed envelopes more often than not, so the effort is very minimal.

If you don't answer the letter, or the person who answers the phone reports that no one with your name lives there, the servicer will probably try to reach you by another method just to be sure (if they called, they may try a letter the next time or vice versa).

Servicers don't want to be too hasty, just in case your letter was lost in the mail, or your grandchild picked up the phone and didn't know that your name isn't Grandpa.

In cases where the servicer still can't reach you, the next step is to follow up with a call or letter to your *alternative contact.* When you fill out the pile of forms needed to apply for the loan, one of these will be an alternative contact form, on which your lender will ask for an alternative contact person who they can reach for just such an occasion. This should be someone stable, who you know well, and who isn't likely to move in the next few years (if they do, make sure you let the originator and/or servicer know). Alternative contacts are usually family members, friends, or neighbors, but they could also be attorneys or other professionals (just be sure you get their permission first).

If you get a letter or call from the servicer, return it right away! Otherwise, they'll start to assume the worst.

Settling your tab

You've seen a lot of varying numbers up to this point — value of home, value of loan, loan balance, interest rates, servicing fees, and more — and each loan has a different formula for calculating each facet of the loan. So how will you know how much you owe? The quick answer is: Your lender will send you a bill. In fact, you can estimate what you'll owe based on the statements your servicer will send you on a regular basis (usually monthly or quarterly). To get the total figure, your lender and servicer total five main elements:

- ✔ **Principal loan amount:** The principal is the total base amount that the lenders have established for you to borrow. They guess how long they expect you to stay in your home and come up with a reasonable dollar amount for your available funds. This is a clean, unaffected number, a foundation on which the rest of your loan costs grow.

  Once the lenders determine that amount, they simply have to keep paying you if you've chosen a monthly tenure payout, no matter how long you decide to stay in your house over and above the number of years they guessed. A possible downside to this otherwise positive benefit is that your loan balance (what you owe) will increase as the lender adds monthly payouts to your tab beyond the original estimated total loan amount.

✔ **Accrued interest:** Each loan product has its own way of creating the interest rate for that particular loan. That rate is multiplied by your loan balance each *term* (the length of time it takes for your rate to change — we give you details on when the change occurs for each loan in Chapters 5, 6, and 7), and that amount is added to your total due. Each term until the day the loan comes due, interest will continue to be added to the total amount you have borrowed up to that point.

✔ **Origination fees:** Your originator charges you a fee based on the particular loan type's allowances (see Chapters 5, 6, and 7 for details on each loan type's origination fees).

✔ **Closing costs:** Your closing costs cover things like your appraiser, flood inspection, and other additional tasks. (See Chapters 5, 6, and 7 for details on each loan type's closing costs.)

✔ **Servicing fees:** The servicing fee is also controlled by the type of loan and pays the servicer monthly to cut you a check and to generally make sure everything is still running smoothly with your loan. (See Chapters 5, 6, and 7 for details on each loan type's servicing fees.)

Your origination and servicing fees, plus closing costs, are bundled up into your loan balance and charged interest as well.

If you can afford it, you may as well pay these costs up-front (before you start receiving money) since the interest will have you owing much more for them in the long run.

The total loan balance is the culmination of all the above factors. If at any time you have questions about what you owe or are confused about the statement your servicer sends, call them or your originator and ask. Most people have questions about their statements at some point, and your servicer or originator will be happy to help you sort it out.

How much your personal loan will finally come out to is really anyone's guess. Unless you have a definitive timeframe in mind (seven years in this house and then off to assisted living, for example) there's no way to know when the loan will come due or what the loan balance will be until it actually ends.

Sometimes your home will have decreased in value over the years, and the loan balance will come out to more than you could ever hope to sell your home for. If your loan balance comes to $100,000 and your home is only worth $70,000, don't fret. In these cases, you can never owe more than your home is worth. What happens to that $30,000 difference? The lender simply has to absorb it.

They will never foreclose or force you out of your home. That's part of the beauty of the reverse mortgage . . . even the idea of losing your home is reversed!

Understanding the TALC

If you feel a little wary of getting a loan for an unknown amount, there's a silver-plated lining. Your originator is required to give you a Total Annual Loan Cost (TALC) estimate before you sign on the dotted line. It takes a stab at calculating, on average, how much your loan will cost you per year. Of course, you don't actually pay anything until your loan comes due, this just helps estimate what you'll pay at the end of the loan: the yearly cost multiplied by however many years you live in the home.

Although a TALC disclosure is designed to give you a pretty accurate look at what you can expect to pay each year for the life of the loan, it can be very misleading. Here's why:

- ✔ The TALC disclosure's estimation includes all prorated closing costs and other fees, under the circumstance that you take half your money as a line of credit and then don't touch the rest. However, nearly no one would choose that payment option.

- ✔ The TALC isn't a crystal ball — it can't tell you how long you'll live in your home or what will happen to home values in that time, so it's really just a guessing tool.

- ✔ The TALC designers forgot to figure in changing interest rates, monthly payments versus credit lines, how much you'll want to withdraw, and growing credit lines.

Two seemingly identical loans could end up costing a lot more (or a lot less) if even one of the above variables change, but the TALC would suppose that they would have the same yearly costs.

Although the TALC misses out on a lot of factors, don't discount it altogether. You can use it loosely as a tool to plan ahead, especially if you mean to move within a certain timeframe, or plan to follow the TALC assumptions of only using half of your line of credit.

Knowing When to Repay Your Loan

You need to be comfortable with the amount of money that will eventually have to be repaid to the lender and confident that the costs involved are worth the benefits of the loan. How you pay for it is up to you, as well as when you choose to end the loan.

Try to decide before you obtain a reverse mortgage which of these methods you want to use to pay off the loan. Use the section below to decide and plan ahead so you can save yourself a lot of headaches later.

Paying as you go

Borrowers who opted for a line of credit or lump sum usually have the option to repay the loan "as they go." (See Chapters 5, 6, and 7 for more on lines of credit and lump sum options for each loan type.) This type of loan that can be paid back as you go is called a revolving or "open" credit line. You can keep paying and borrowing the same money over and over — for instance, if you withdrawal $1,000, you can pay it back the next month and then have that $1,000 available again to withdraw. Thus it revolves back and forth from the bank to you. However, if you choose to pay back your mortgage throughout the life of the loan without withdrawing that money again, you'll save yourself (and your heirs) from having to repay that money later.

Although two of the Financial Freedom options (see Chapter 7) don't allow this for the first five years, you are free to pay any amount back you choose at any time after that point (up to the total principal). But be careful . . . some loans don't allow you to repay the full amount, or if they do allow it they consider the loan ended at that point, which means you can't borrow any more money. (See Chapters 5, 6, and 7 for more specifics on each loan.)

You may enjoy these benefits to paying as you go:

✔ **Lowering your loan balance also lowers the amount that is charged interest.** You will only pay interest on money that has been borrowed and not yet repaid. If you have borrowed $20,000 and pay back $5,000, you will only be charged interest on $15,000 from that point forward. Every time you send in another repayment, your loan balance goes down and you're charged interest on less and less of your loan.

✔ **You can lower your final payable loan amount.** If your loan closes due to your death, your heirs will thank you for having the foresight to reduce their inherited debt. In fact, some families work out a system of repayment in which the heirs help pay back the loan as you go so they aren't faced with a large debt when you're gone. They may contribute $50 or $100 per month (or whatever they can afford) toward the loan balance. In families with several heirs, the burden can be distributed among all of them, allowing the loan to be paid back faster.

Paying as you go isn't an option for everyone — lots of people need every last penny of their payment during the life of their loan — but if you have some money left over at the end of the month, you can deposit it back into your available funds to lower the costs at the end of the loan. If you're on a line of credit and take out $800 to buy a new dress for your daughter's wedding, but only end up spending $600, put that remaining amount back in your account. Think about how much more money we all tend to spend if we have cash in our pocket versus money in our savings account — replace unused funds instead of keeping it at your quick disposal, and you'll save more than you expect in the long run.

If you have the means to pay back a little as you go, and your loan allows it, this could be a good start toward paying off your reverse mortgage.

Moving out

If you've chosen to move out of your home for any reason (for instance, relocating to a retirement home, moving into an assisted living facility, or living with a friend or family member) your loan will become due and payable. Selling your home when you move out is the easiest option and the most popular choice for repayment.

A reverse mortgage doesn't mean that the lender owns your home, or that you automatically lose it at the end of your loan. You still hold the title to your home, and selling it to repay the loan is just one option.

Here are the benefits to selling your home:

- ✔ **You won't ever have to take money out of your pocket to pay for the loan.** Even if your home value drops below the total loan balance, you will never owe more than the value of your home. For instance, if your loan and total fees, including interest, total $83,000 but your house sells for only $75,000, the lender will absorb the difference.

- ✔ **You may have money after the sale to pocket even after the loan is paid.** If your home is worth $300,000 at the time the loan ends and your loan came out to a balance of $132,000, you or your heirs could sell the home, pay off the debt, and be left with $168,000 in your pockets. For that much money, you can probably buy your retirement condo debt free! It's also a nice gift to leave to your family — who couldn't use that kind of money?

You may be especially wary of selling your home if it has a special sentimental value. Maybe a family member built it by hand, or it's the home your children were all raised in. If you know for certain that someone in your family will want to live in your house after you've moved out, then by all means, don't sell. Or better yet, sell it to that person. Your heirs should be thrilled to be able to purchase your home, and you'll love being able to see them enjoy it while you're still around. Talk to your heirs about this early on, so you don't have to make a snap decision later.

In most cases, you won't need to hang onto a second home, although it's perfectly natural to want to keep it around in case you don't like your new location . . . natural, but not a smart move financially. Why pay off a loan from your own savings, plus the new mortgage or rent, when you can take care of it all by selling? Selling your home is a decision only you and your family or financial advisor can make, but it is by far the simplest way to pay back your loan.

Selling your home may be a good choice for you if you are going to move out anyway (whether you are buying a new home, going into assisted living, or moving in with family) or have exhausted your reverse mortgage funds and need to find a new source of income. The loan is easily repaid and you may even be left with extra money from the sale!

Moving on

The other common way for a reverse mortgage loan to become due and payable is when the last borrower on the loan dies. This is a topic that many people prefer to avoid, as the prospect of planning one's own death can seem a bit too macabre. Many times the borrower is fine with the idea, but their children are uncomfortable thinking about their parent's eventual death. The key is to deal with your family in a sensitive manner, and regardless of their protests, make them understand that they need to know how to repay your loan.

Preparing your family for repayment of the loan is critical because there are no provisions to pay the loan back in installments. Technically, it won't be you personally who has to worry about repaying the loan, so you need to be sure that your family knows what is expected of them, how to pay off the loan, and how you want your remaining money spent. Your heirs have several options for paying back the loan:

- ✔ **The heirs can pay back the loan with their own cash.** Keep in mind, however, that your family may not have enough ready cash available to pay the loan in full, so the other options listed below are likely more realistic.

- ✔ **The heirs can sell the home.** If they don't have a sentimental attachment to your home, most family members will choose to sell the home. It will repay the loan, and they can keep any money left over from the sale (be sure to give instructions for that possibility in your will).

- ✔ **You can leave part of your estate (your other valuables, money, and investments) to pay off the loan upon your death.** Just as you would for any other financial arrangements post mortem, make sure that your wishes are clearly defined to your family. If you have enough assets and your family doesn't wish to sell the home, this can be a nice alternative.

- ✔ **The heirs can take out a forward loan (a regular mortgage) on the house to pay the lender immediately and then rent out your former home to help cushion the costs.** Your family can cash in on renters until they're ready to use your home for their own personal purposes.

Your heirs are not selling your home to the lender. They're selling it to the next family member who wants to live there, and then using all or a portion of the proceeds from that sale to pay back the loan.

Note that the loan is payable when the last borrower is gone, not the last resident. This is why it can be so important that anyone living in the home is named on the loan. Obviously, this doesn't include people who don't qualify, but if a couple aged 64 and 56 are looking into a reverse mortgage, it would serve them well to wait at least six years (until the younger person is 62) before taking out a loan.

There is a certain appeal to gettin' while the gettin' is good and signing off on a loan as soon as someone in the home turns 62, but this can be dangerous to the younger borrower if something should happen to their elder housemate. For example, if the older borrower dies before the younger borrower, the surviving resident can be responsible for paying back the entire balance. If that person wants to stay in their home, they'll have to take out a whole new loan to pay for the reverse mortgage or hope that there is enough money saved up to pay it out-of-pocket. This can also be troublesome if the sole borrower has left the home to other heirs, because they may wish to sell the home to pay off the debt, leaving the remaining resident displaced.

Planning ahead for your assets

Although it doesn't happen too frequently, some borrowers die leaving no heirs whatsoever (it's rare because lost relatives almost surely show up when they hear that they may be the recipients of your money). In this case, the lender would get the title to your home, and after they are repaid, the state you live in would take over and handle the settlement of your estate.

What would the state want with your estate? Why, to sell it of course. Once they've put your house on the market and sold off all of your worldly possessions in order to pay back the loan, any leftover equity (money from those sales) will also be managed by the state. That leftover balance could potentially be quite large, depending on home prices and the value of your loan.

In the event that the opposite has occurred — your home value has turned out to be much less than the value of the loan — the lender or servicer has the right to step in and sell the property. This is the only time when a lender or servicer would have this right!

This is why you must have a plan for your assets after you die. Whether you want your money to go to the Louvre's restoration fund, public radio, or the National Kitten Appreciation Club, you need to have your wishes in writing for exactly the reasons mentioned above. Otherwise, your estate will be used as the state sees fit. While the state may use your estate for noble causes (paving roads, paying county clerks, buying pads of tickets for traffic cops), you will have no say in what your money is used for. This is why you must specify your wishes in a will.

In your will, you can elect any organization, charitable or otherwise, to receive any leftover money after your reverse mortgage has been repaid. You worked hard for

(continued)

(continued)

your estate, no matter what size it is, so make sure it goes to someone who can really appreciate it.

You should know by this point that the lender or servicer never has rights to your home as long as you hold the title (which is always until you personally give it up under your own wishes, or die, leaving the title to someone else). But, if you should die and leave no heirs, the title will go to the lender or servicer, since it's their loan that needs to be repaid. Just remember — how you pay your loan is your decision, but it will always help to plan ahead and make your wishes known.

Part II
Going Shopping: Product Options

The 5th Wave   By Rich Tennant

"Your son's resume is very impressive, but we can only lend you money on the equity of your house, not on the equity of the person you raised in the house."

In this part . . .

*W*e highlight three main types of reverse mortgage products in this book. Part II goes into detail on all three, in three individual chapters — the Home Equity Conversion Mortgage, Home Keeper, and Jumbo Cash Account — with tips on which may be right for you, qualifying, costs, interest rates, and how to choose a payment plan.

Chapter 5

Following the Crowd: The Home Equity Conversion Mortgage

In This Chapter

▶ Figuring out the Home Equity Conversion Mortgage

▶ Making sure you meet the requirements

▶ Paying loan fees

▶ Getting a mortgage insurance safety net

▶ Choosing your payment type

*I*n 1989, when most people were exercising with Richard Simmons and donning extra-puffy shoulder pads, the U.S. Department of Housing and Urban Development (HUD) was busy creating the Home Equity Conversion Mortgage (HECM), America's first widely accepted reverse mortgage. Although there had been prior attempts at developing other "reverse flow" loans, they were costly, uninsured, and left little to be desired for the hundreds of thousands of seniors who could have really used them. Luckily for you, HUD stepped up and worked with the United States Congress to establish the HECM (you may hear your originator or counselor refer to this as the "heck-um"). This chapter explains the HECM loan, what the qualifications and lending limits are, how your interest rate affects your loan, how mortgage insurance can protect your investment, and how you can receive your payments.

Getting to Know the HECM

Up until now, you may have only imagined the Federal Housing Administration (FHA) as a far-away entity that regulates low-income housing and mortgage rates. In fact, the FHA (which is a division of HUD) oversees all aspects of housing in the country and is designed to protect you, the homeowner. When HUD and Congress developed the HECM, their goal was to help people over 62 live comfortably without the fear of going broke from medical bills, not to mention an economy that encourages inflation rates that escalate faster than most people's pensions and retirement funds can grow.

The FHA insures HECM loans, which means that your loan is federally insured. If your originator suddenly goes out of business or your home loses value, it's the FHA to the rescue. Just imagine a government agency where they all wear red spandex and flowing capes, but instead of being able to leap tall buildings in a single bound, they protect your mortgage.

HECM loans are the most popular in the country — they're available in every state (plus Puerto Rico) and have "set the bar" for all other reverse mortgage products. In fact the other two reverse mortgage options we will discuss in Chapters 5 and 6 are modeled on this trendsetter. According to most sources, up to 95 percent of all reverse mortgages are HECMs. It's true that they are the most widely publicized, but people like them because they usually offer more cash in your pocket. In fact, many forward mortgage originators are only familiar with the HECM loan (which is another good reason to work with an approved reverse mortgage originator).

As in all reverse mortgage products, your HECM loan does not come due until you leave the home permanently. You will never be foreclosed on, and they will never ask for payments before you move out or die — all you have to do in return is pay your property taxes and homeowner's insurance, and keep up the maintenance on your home (things you should be doing already). In fact, if you live in the home longer than the lender originally guessed you would, they must keep paying you the same amount until you leave the home. If you ever needed a good reason to take better care of yourself, this is it: The longer you can stay in your home, the more money they'll lend you (when you choose the monthly payments; see more on this later in this chapter in "Receiving monthly payments").

Meeting HECM Requirements

Each reverse mortgage product has its own idiosyncrasies that make it unique. While all reverse mortgages have the same basic eligibility requirements, the HECM has some additional points to consider, such as disbursement options (how you get paid), additional costs, meeting with a HUD-approved counselor, and lending limits.

There are, however, some common traits among all reverse mortgages. As a reverse mortgage borrower, you must:

✔ Be at least 62 years old (see Chapter 3)

✔ Be a homeowner with at least some equity in your home (preferably all or mostly paid off) (see Chapter 3)

✔ Live in your home full time (see Chapter 3)

✔ Own a home that qualifies (see Chapter 3)

Anyone in a household who is listed as a homeowner on the title is eligible for an HECM loan as long as that person meets the requirements listed above. However, the FHA will calculate your loan based on the youngest homeowner. It could be worth about $5,000 to you to wait a few years before getting your loan, because in most situations, the older you are, the more money you'll be able to borrow (if interest rates are extraordinarily high, this may not be the case). If your spouse or any other resident is too young to qualify you can still get a reverse mortgage in your name only, but there are consequences. When you die or move out for any reason, your loan will be due and the person remaining in the home may be responsible for your debts. Talk to your counselor about the ramifications of getting a loan too early (see Chapter 8).

Standard reverse mortgage housing requirements (see Chapter 3) apply to the HECM, with one minor exception: If you live in a condominium, it must be FHA approved. Talk to your counselor (Chapter 8) to be sure that your home qualifies.

Checking out lending limits

The HECM is a great loan — don't get us wrong — but if you own a home with a higher value than the national average, this may not be the loan for you. While they cover a wide array of home types, HECM mortgages have the lowest lending limits of all the reverse mortgage options. The upside is you can still get more cash out of an HECM loan than the other major products. Lending limits (called "203-b" limits, because that's where they're found in the National Housing Act) are based on HUD's statistics regarding average sales prices in various counties.

For your personal lending limits there are three main variables:

✔ your age — or the age of the youngest homeowner

✔ the value of your home

✔ current interest rates.

We discuss these variables in the sections that follow.

Factoring in your age

Just like when you bought your life insurance policy, an actuarial table will be used to guess how long you'll live and, in this case, how long you'll live in your home. The lender will determine your loan partly based on this information. The good news is, HECMs typically have very generous actuarial tables. They also only base your life/home expectancy on your current age, nothing else. You could be a professional sword swallower and they'd estimate your lifespan with the same table as they would an avid knitter if your ages were the same.

Under an HECM, a married couple would get the same amount of money as a single person because they base your household's payments on the youngest borrower. Other loans, like the Fannie Mae Home Keeper, give less money to a married couple because studies show that married people live longer, and the longer they think you're going to live, the less money they'll lend to you.

Getting ahead of the game

For a calculator that will give you a ballpark estimate of how much you can borrow, visit the National Reverse Mortgage Lenders Association's Web site at www. reversemortgage.org and click on "Reverse Mortgage Calculator." Simply enter your age, home value, and any outstanding debts you have, and they'll tell you how much you can expect. At the bottom of the estimates page, click "Loan Summary" to find out how they came up with your loan amount. This is a great way to get familiar with typical loan amounts and the math that's involved. When your originator figures your total loan amount, he or she will be looking at a screen that's similar to the one you'll see here. You may want to print this page to take with you when you see your counselor, who can give you an idea of how close this computer-generated loan is to reality.

Taking into account your home's value

The area you live in affects the value of your home and will also affect the lending maximums in your county. Consider housing prices in your town. A three-bedroom, 2,500 square-foot home in Topeka won't generate as much equity as the same house in Miami, because cost of living in different areas pushes housing prices up or down. FHA has set specific lending limits in relation to defined counties — they realize that two identical homes with identical borrowers would have different values in different areas and capped lending limits accordingly.

When you apply for any reverse mortgage, an appraiser will visit to determine you home's value (see Chapter 10) but for now, don't worry too much about the actual value of your home. Instead, think about housing prices in your area. Are they unusually high? Low? Just right? Rural neighborhoods and smaller towns typically have a lower cost of living (and therefore lower average home values) and fetch a lower lending limit, just as homes in urban areas often carry a much higher selling price and thus higher lending limits. For example, Los Angeles County will have higher lending limits than Southern Arizona's Pima County because housing prices in Los Angeles are so much higher.

It sounds like an oxymoron, but HECM loans have set a low maximum lending limit, as well as a high maximum lending limit. Low maximums are for lower-home-value areas and higher maximums are for higher-home-value areas. There are also countless lending maximums in between for different costs-of-living in counties nationwide. Though it changes every year, the 2005 low maximum was $172,632. If you live in a higher-cost urban area, your ceiling for 2005 would've been $312,896. These figures aren't pulled arbitrarily from the air. They're based on home value averages across the country. HECM lending limits may or may not be close to your actual home value, but they should be in the ballpark of your county's average. Ask your originator (Chapter 9) what your county's lending limits and county housing price averages are.

The maximum does not mean that only people within those lending limits can get an HECM loan. All it means is that regardless of the actual value of your home, the FHA will never loan you more than that maximum. But (and this is a big "but" so pay attention)

you will almost always get more cash from an HECM if your home value is near your county's average home value. If your home value falls within about $100,000 of the maximum lending limit, you should seriously consider the HECM loan. If you're looking at these figures and thinking "My next-door neighbor's house just sold for five times that!" skip ahead to Chapter 7, to read about Jumbo Cash Accounts.

The FHA always calculates your loan amount on the lesser of *either* your home value *or* the FHA maximum. Therefore, in a high-cost area in 2004, the most you could ever borrow is $312,896, even if your home is worth $300,000. If your home is worth $150,000, they would base your loan amount on the home value because it is *less than* the FHA maximum.

Your originator will also let you know what the current HECM lending limits are when you begin the loan process. Because limits vary from county to county, check the HUD Web site's maximum lists for the most up-to-date information in your area (https://entp.hud.gov/ idapp/html/hicostlook.cfm). Don't worry about your originator giving you a lower loan limit than you think you deserve. FHA gives them a free software program that calculates your particular loan amount automatically. The originator actually has very little to do with the amount you can receive.

Checking out current interest rates

Another factor in determining your loan amount (aside from your age and home value) are current interest rates. As interest rates go up and down, the amount you can borrow will change, just as it would in a forward mortgage. When you sign off on your mortgage (Chapter 11) the interest rate at that moment will be figured into the equation that determines your loan amount. The lower the interest rate, the more you'll be able to borrow.

Understanding ARM rates and margins

HECM interest rates are adjustable-rate mortgages (ARMs), and it's up to you to decide which type of ARM you want. An ARM means that the interest rate changes regularly — either every month or every year. Usually it only changes by a fraction of a percentage point at a time. It may go from 4.27 to 4.60 percent, nothing that you'd really even notice. It's the change over time that really impacts your loan. Let's say that on the day you get your reverse mortgage, interest rates are at 4.25 percent and your total loan amount is $90,000. If your rate stayed the same over the entire course of your loan, you'd eventually pay 4.25 percent for every year that you had the loan. With an ARM, your rate could jump up to 10 percent at some point down the road, and until it changes (for better or for worse) that's the rate you'll be charged. Every mortgage will charge you interest; if you're comfortable with rates that fluctuate in exchange for generally lower rates than you could get with a forward mortgage, an HECM may be right for you.

Interest is added to your *principal* loan amount — the amount the lender will actually let you borrow. When you get a loan for $50,000 you need to remember that when your loan comes due you can't just hand over a check for $50,000; there will be interest added that could amount to several thousand dollars. While the interest rate won't affect your payouts, it does affect how much the lender will initially calculate for your total loan amount, and how much you'll pay at the end. Pay attention to interest rates if you like, but don't let them stress you out. You probably won't even think of them again after you close your loan.

The interest rates for an HECM are based on the one-year U.S. Treasury Securities rate, a percentage figure that changes weekly. Originators add that one-year Treasury Security rate to a *margin* to get your interest rate. The rate margin is just a fancy way to say "how much we can tack onto your rate." The FHA puts these margin limits in place to keep originators from charging ridiculously high rates, or ridiculously low ones . . . it forces everyone to play fair. The higher the margin, the less cash for you. The lower the margin, the more cash for you. Remember, the rate doesn't change your payments, but it does affect how much you can borrow at the outset.

When you speak to your originator, you will be given the choice of a monthly or yearly ARM.

Betting on the monthly ARM

The monthly ARM is by far the most popular, because it usually gives you more cash in your pocket up-front and a lower interest rate. For example, when the annual is at 5.60 percent, the monthly is probably at around 4.00 percent. The monthly ARM tends to be much lower than the yearly because it changes so often, but it has the potential to rise faster than a yearly ARM — you're assuming the risk of higher rates over time in exchange for a lower initial rate.

Here's the really good news: The monthly ARM can never (ever, no matter what) go up more than 10 percent over the entire life of the loan. Remember in the late 1980s and early '90s when interest rates were at nearly 15 percent? If you had gotten an HECM loan then (you would have been one of the first!) and your originator locked in an initial monthly rate of 3.20 percent, no matter how high the rates went for the rest of the country, yours would never have gone up more than 13.20 percent. Even if you kept the loan for 15 years and rates miraculously skyrocketed every year that you had the loan, you'd still come out ahead. And quite frankly, the chances of another rate hike like the one back then aren't likely. We heard a lot about "historically low rates" in the early 2000s, but in reality, those rates were more in keeping with the average. People had just become accustomed to high rates.

It's also good to keep in mind that what goes up must come down. Even if rates shoot up in the first couple of years after you get your HECM, they will almost invariably go down and even out throughout the life of the loan.

Advantages to a monthly ARM include:

✔ You get a lower margin, which usually means a lower rate.

✔ Your rate will never go up more than 10 percent over the life of the loan.

✔ You receive more cash because you'll usually have a lower initial rate.

A disadvantage to think about is that rate changes often, with no cap on how much it can change per month/year. Although the rate will never be more than 10 percentage points higher than your original rate, the difference from month to month can seem alarming if it changes from 4.70 percent to 11.50 percent over the course of a few months.

Looking at the annual ARM

The monthly ARM isn't for everyone. If you don't have a strong poker face to ride out higher interest rates, you will probably enjoy the security of an annual ARM. Just as its name implies, the annual ARM will only change once per year. If you lock in a great low initial rate and then rates go up, you can smile smugly knowing that you're safe from an abrupt rate change for at least a year.

Fortunately, you are protected by a couple of very generous rate caps. Remember how the monthly ARM had a rate cap of 10 percent over the life of the loan? Well the annual does it one better and caps the rate at 5 percent above the original rate. So if your originator locked in an annual rate of 4.20 percent, no matter how long you keep the loan, you would never pay more than 9.20 percent. However, unlike the monthly ARM, if rates go down throughout the year, you won't be able to take advantage of them until your next annual rate change.

What's even better, your rate can't be raised more than 2 percent per year. Let's say that rates begin to rise again, and one year later the loan you locked at 4.20 is now going for 7.30 percent. You are safeguarded — your interest rate will only go up two percent, to 6.20.

Advantages to the annual ARM include:

✔ Retaining peace of mind from a year-long fixed rate.

✔ Rates can only go up 5 percent over the life of the loan.

✔ Rates can only go up 2 percent per year.

Disadvantages to think about include:

✔ You receive a lower loan limit because interest rates are generally higher.

✔ You can't take advantage of lower rates if they drop throughout the year.

Paying Up

Although you don't actually have to pay the loan back until you move out permanently, there are some fees that work their way into your reverse mortgage. When you got your original mortgage, you probably had to pay all of your fees up-front, even before you got the keys to your new home. A reverse mortgage works a bit differently — most, if not all of your fees are rolled into your loan, which your originator may call *financing*. (The only fee you may not be able to finance is the appraisal fee, but your originator can advise you about that when you discuss closing costs.) Those amounts are added to the total you will owe on your loan. The FHA knows that most people aren't in a position to write checks that large — an even distribution makes it simpler for everyone involved. Instead of paying $5,000 up-front, that amount is added to your loan balance and is paid back when you repay your entire loan. Increasing your loan balance with closing costs will lower your payouts very slightly if you choose to receive monthly checks, because your total available loan amount is decreased.

Typical closing cost amounts are below, but remember that they may vary from city to city, or even from originator to originator:

✔ **$2,000–$5,806 for origination fees:** The FHA states that an originator can charge you no more than 2 percent of either the total lending limit or the home's value (whichever is less), *or* $2,000, whichever is greater. We've calculated the maximum origination fee based on the 2005 lending limit, $312,896.

✔ **$20 for a credit report:** Originators use the information from your credit report to determine whether or not you have any outstanding federal tax liens (if, for instance, you didn't pay your taxes and the government has a claim on your home) or other judgments. You will most likely already know if you have outstanding debts, but a credit report keeps everything on the "up and up."

✔ **$20 for flood certification:** If you live on a federally designated flood plain, insurance and repair costs may affect your loan. If you live in an area like this, you would have had to have a similar certification on your previous loan.

✔ **$50 for a courier:** Just as it sounds, this is what the originator charges you to cover the costs of mailing things with regards to your loan. It's so costly because they send everything by overnight mail. Why overnight? You want your loan processed quickly, don't you? Your documents may travel to three or four different offices, which can mean weeks of waiting time by regular mail.

✔ **$50–$100 for recording:** Your county needs accurate information about all housing-related information, including Deeds of Trust and mortgages. Every loan (also referred to here as a *mortgage lien*) must be recorded at your County Recorder's office, and this fee covers the charge to do so.

✔ **$75–$150 for document preparation:** This is really an arbitrary service fee, because it doesn't actually cost a specific dollar amount to fill out paperwork, and it isn't based on a per-page or per-hour system. Some originators outsource this work and may charge you exactly what that firm charges them. Others rely on an in-house processor to do it, who gets a salary that has nothing to do with this fee. Either way, it's a relatively inexpensive service.

✔ **$100 for pest inspection:** Because your home has to be structurally sound in order to receive the loan, pest inspectors will be deployed to test your home for things like termites and other destructive bugs. If they find a problem, your home will be debugged and you may need a follow-up inspection. Some charge a secondary fee for the follow-up inspection, and some only charge you once.

✔ **$400–$600 for closing/settlement:** This fee covers the title search and any incidentals associated with the closing of the loan. The title search shows who is currently on the home's title (who legally owns the home) and whether there are any outstanding liens on it, like past mortgages you have yet to pay off.

✔ **$250 for the survey:** Six years ago, your neighbor built a fence that was two feet over on your side of the property line and you've been fighting about it ever since. Well, you'll finally get your justice. In some states, a surveyor will come to your home and establish the official boundaries for your property. Start practicing your "I told you so."

✔ **$300–$400 for an appraisal:** As with all FHA loans, your home must be in good condition before the loan can be approved. The appraiser will check for structural defects (leaky roof, cracked foundation, and water damage, among others), as well as make sure the property is up to code. If not, you'll need to make the changes (completed by a certified contractor) and submit to a re-exam. Don't worry if you can't afford to make the changes right away — the FHA thought of that, too. These costs can be bundled into your total loan, giving you up to one year to fix your home's glitches.

✔ **Varying fee for title insurance:** Your fees will include title insurance, which is designed to protect both you and the lender. The cost depends on the size of your loan (the higher the loan amount, the higher the title insurance premiums). Usually your originator will arrange this for you. All you have to do is sign on the dotted line.

✔ **At most, $30 per month for an annual ARM and $35 for a monthly ARM for servicing fees:** Servicing fees cover all the after-close costs. Servicing refers to all of the tasks the lender has to do once you're receiving payments. This could be menial paperwork like sending out your monthly statements, or more involved chores like making sure you keep up your end of the bargain and pay your property taxes, and that you still live at the same address.

The servicing fee is a bit different from the others, in that the lender *sets aside* the servicing fee. When calculating how much to set aside, the lender multiplies the monthly fee ($30 or $35) by the number of months they expect you to live in your home. A 75-year-old borrower who was projected to live to be 86 would be charged for about 132 months, for a total servicing fee between $3,960 and $4,620. This amount is deducted as a whole from your total available loan funds and the whole projected fee is set aside, interest-free, until the monthly fee is added to your growing loan balance each month.

✔ **Varying fee for Mortgage Insurance Premiums (MIP):** You will never owe more than the value of your home at the time the loan is due, whether you outlive your loan or not. Everyone hopes that home values increase over time. But real estate is a rocky business, and things don't always go as planned. The FHA protects you if, instead of increasing, your home's value has gone down. For example, if you borrow a total of $97,200 and your home only sells for $85,000, you are only liable for the selling price. The FHA is able to absorb that loss because of MIP. MIP also protects you if you outlive your loan by several years; the amount you owe will never exceed your home's value, no matter how much they've let you borrow above and beyond your home's value. In addition, the MIP makes sure you still receive your check, even if something happens to your lender or originator. See the section "Investing in Mortgage Insurance Premiums (MIP)" for more information on this topic.

Investing in Mortgage Insurance Premiums (MIP)

For years people were skeptical about the reverse mortgage because there was an underlying myth and fear that once you signed the papers, the bank owned your home. Seniors were afraid that if they moved to an assisted-living or retirement home and their home had gone down in value, they would owe ridiculous amounts of money on their loan (remembering that the loan comes due if you move out permanently). Adult children worried that if their parents should die, they would be left with the burden of coming up with the cash to pay back their parent's loan. The FHA thought of all that, too, and created Mortgage Insurance Premiums (affectionately called MIP) as a protection for you, for your heirs, and for itself.

Let's say you have an HECM loan on a $245,000 house, worth a total of $215,000. Time goes by, the economy changes, real estate takes a turn for the worse, and today, your home is only worth $145,000 — quite a significant drop. This also happens to be the year that you decide to move in with your daughter and her family, so you loan comes due. How will you pay the $70,000 difference? The answer is simple — you don't. Not directly anyway. Technically, you pay for the difference in the form of MIP.

The MIP is broken down into two parts:

1. The FHA collects 2 percent of your home's value or the loan limit (whichever is higher) in order to insure that it's not left high and dry if your home value decreases, and you aren't left responsible for more loan than you bargained for.

2. The FHA also adds 0.5 percent to the interest rate that is charged on your loan balance per month (in other words, just the amount that you have already borrowed).

The MIP also protects you no matter what happens to your originator or lender. All HECM originators must be approved by FHA and have to stick to a strict set of guidelines and a code of conduct. To our knowledge, no FHA-approved lender has ever been unable to send a borrower his or her check. But in case it ever happens, MIP is there to protect your loan. It may be that the source went out of business, and it may be a simple error — whatever the reason, your MIP guarantees that the FHA will continue to pay your loan.

In order to get mortgage insurance on an HECM, you and your originator will fill out the *HUD Addendum to Uniform Residential Loan Application.* In fact, anyone getting any kind of HUD loan, whether it's a reverse mortgage, VA (Veteran's Affairs) loan, or another FHA variety, is required to apply for mortgage insurance. The form itself is fairly straightforward, but because it wasn't specifically designed for use with reverse mortgages, it has some questions that simply don't make sense for the HECM loan. The main components are:

✔ Your name, address, and property address (which will be the same under the rules of the reverse mortgage)

✔ The name and address of the lender

✔ Your status as a homebuyer (whether you're a first-time homebuyer or not, and you're obviously not)

✔ A certification from you that you have or have not owned or sold another home with an FHA mortgage (what does it matter? Who knows?)

✔ A statement that you understand the appraised value of your home

There's a lot of fine print, so ask your originator to explain it all if you're unable to read it clearly. Make sure you verify that all the information is correct as you understand it before you sign.

Cashing In

There are several payment options to choose from, each with its benefits and downfalls. Take a look at the options here and compare them to your comfort level when it comes to your money and how you control it.

Don't worry if you feel like you've made the wrong decision after your loan has started. You have the right to change your mind about payment options at any time throughout the loan (but you will be charged a $20 nominal fee).

Receiving monthly payments

If you prefer to receive a regular, pre-determined check, monthly payments are probably for you. You will get the largest loan principal available with monthly payments, and it offers a peace of mind to many seniors, knowing that they can count on a steady income.

You can choose from two monthly payment options: "term" or "tenure." Both offer equal payments per month, but have significant advantages and disadvantages to consider.

Timing terms

A term loan is one in which you choose how long you will receive payments.

Check out the following advantages:

- **Receiving a larger check:** You can get a larger check per month if you choose a term loan because, if you pick a short term, your money is condensed into a shorter timeframe instead of being spread out until you move out of your home.

- **Controlling your income:** You choose how long you want to receive payouts. If you know you are going to move into a new home or go into assisted living in 5 years, you can get your entire loan amount in that time.

But don't forget to consider the following drawbacks:

- **Getting less money total:** Lenders tend to allot a lower total loan amount to term borrowers because they are giving you more money in each check (since it's condensed into a few years) than they would with a tenured monthly payment (see "Securing monthly payments through tenure.").

- **Gambling on your term:** The shorter your term, the bigger your monthly payouts will be. For example, if you plan on a seven-year term and are only able to stay in your home for three years, you will have received smaller payouts that were based on a longer term than if you had chosen a shorter term to begin with. Planning ahead is essential to a term monthly payout.

✔ **Losing your monthly check:** Once your term is up you stop receiving payments, no matter how much longer you live in the home, because you've used up all your money. The loan still does not come due until you have permanently moved out of your home, but your well will have run dry.

If you fit into the following situations, a term loan may be the best choice for you:

✔ You have high monthly costs now but expect to have lower costs in a few years, and you know you can put aside some of your money as a cushion for the future.

✔ You know for a fact that the day you turn 80 (five years from now) you're moving to an assisted-living apartment in Florida. You could plan ahead and receive higher payments for that period of time — those payments could be used in part to get your affairs in order, pay for movers, and buy lots of sunscreen.

Securing monthly payments through tenure

You may prefer the monthly tenure plan instead, which pays out monthly until the last surviving homeowner dies or moves out.

Some advantages to tenured payouts include:

✔ **Maintaining a sense of security:** You have the security of knowing that you'll never be without a check; the lender must continue to send checks until the last remaining borrower moves out permanently.

✔ **Receiving a higher total loan amount:** You'll almost always get a bigger loan over time with a tenured monthly payment, because although you get less per month, you'll get more over the life of the loan if you keep it for at least as long as the lenders estimated you would.

But check out the following drawbacks:

✔ **Losing some financial independence:** If you are planning a trip or need to remodel to move your bedroom to the first floor, the few hundred dollars you get per month isn't going to cover it. You either need to be able to save some money from your check each month, or already have savings built up, and simply use your monthly payments for daily living expenses.

✔ **Unchanging tenure payments:** At first, you may think the fact that your payment amount never changes is a good thing, but as the cost of living (inflation) increases over the life of your loan, your check doesn't increase with it. So your money is worth less by the last few years of your loan, especially if you got it in your 60s, when it's likely you'll have a 20-year loan. Take a minute to think about the prices of things 20 years ago compared with today. If you had received an HECM when they were first made available (1989) and had a monthly payment of $600, it would only be worth about $300 in today's economy. The value of your dollar would have decreased by half! If you are older, however, and only plan to have the loan for a few years, inflation isn't as much of a consideration.

A tenured monthly payout may be the right choice for you if:

✔ You are concerned about running out of money. A tenured payout plan lasts as long as you do, so there's no fear of being without a steady income.

✔ You don't know how long you may be in your home and don't want to risk underestimating with a term payout.

✔ You don't foresee any large expenses in the near future, or feel confident that you can save some of your payout each month to plan for upcoming bills.

Banking on a line of credit

A line of credit (also called a *credit line*) works like a bank account. At the beginning of your loan, the entire available funds are sitting in your account. You choose when to make a withdrawal and how much you want at a time, and you're only charged interest on the portion you have actually received.

Credit lines are not permitted in Texas — if you live in the Lone Star state, you have to choose either monthly payments (see "Receiving monthly payments," earlier in this chapter) or a lump sum (see "Choosing a lump sum," later in this chapter).

One of the niftiest things about the HECM line of credit is that your available funds actually grow like a savings account! Even better, the line of credit grows faster than most conventional savings accounts, so it works to your advantage to keep as much of your money as you can in the originator's "bank" rather than your own.

The rate of your loan's growth is based on this equation: your current interest rate plus 0.5 percent, all divided by 12 (because it accrues monthly). If, for example, the interest rate on your loan is 6 percent, the math would look like this:

1. 6 percent + 0.5 percent = 6.5 percent

2. 6.5 percent / 12 months = 0.54 percent

3. 0.54 percent = your percentage of growth

Your quarterly loan statement, which tells you how much you've borrowed up to that point, will highlight the interest you've earned on your unused funds.

You may be thinking that 0.54 percent doesn't sound like much, and it isn't if it was growing on $100. You would only gain 54 cents. But with a reverse mortgage, we're talking about large sums of money. If your loan amount is $100,000, using the example of a 6 percent interest rate above, you've earned $540 your first month for a new total of $100,540! Credit lines compound monthly, which means that every month your money will grow, and every month the rate is applied to the new total. So, if you don't withdraw anything from that $100,540, you would earn interest based on the above calculation on this new total ($100,540, not the previous amount of $100,000), which comes out to about $543 the next month. Each month after that, the new total would go through the same calculation, and after just one year, if you didn't withdraw any money, you would earn $6,672!

The line of credit is a good choice if you have a monthly budget in mind and have taken into account large or unexpected costs, like vacations or medical bills. Like the monthly term loan (see "Timing terms," earlier in this chapter), when your account runs dry, that's it — no more money. It's also an idea source of money for starting your own business or making a solid investment. It requires some planning ahead, but getting a credit line is a great way to manage your HECM payments.

Choosing a lump sum

If you know you're going to need all of your HECM funds to pay for a very big expense all at once (and immediately following your loan closing), a lump sum may be the way to go. This would also be a good option for people who have a savings account of their own, but would rather take out a loan to pay for a specific need, like starting a business. This is *not* the best option if you just want to make a large purchase (like a car) or want to invest your money elsewhere.

A lump sum could come in handy, however, if you had to have a medical procedure that will cost about the same as your loan amount, your insurance wouldn't cover it, and the doctor refused to take installments.

If you take a lump sum, you are charged interest on the entire amount right away. You'd also better have a backup plan for future finances, since once you receive the whole loan, you're tapped out. Again, you don't have to repay the loan until you move out, but you should have enough money to get you through to that point after you've spent the lump sum.

Some people decide to take the lump sum and invest it in their bank's CDs or play the stock market. It's true that some investments will pay off big time, and yes, the average life of a stock pays you pack around 8 percent. But there are several reasons why using your lump sum as an investment isn't such a hot idea:

- ✔ You will probably be paying a higher interest on the lump sum than you are earning on your investment, which just means you're losing money.

- ✔ Most investments and savings accounts opened with lump-sum funds won't have as high or as steady of a return as the interest on the credit line.

- ✔ If you throw all of your money into the stock market and it takes a big dip, you could lose it all without sufficient time to wait it out and earn your money back.

- ✔ A five-year bank CD with a rate of five percent (which is very generous and not too common) will still earn you less than a credit line with the same rate because the credit line com-, pounds monthly.

- ✔ If you use the lump sum to make a down payment on a $300,000 yacht, not only are you charged interest on your HECM loan, but the yacht dealer will charge you interest on your purchase.

Going with combinations

If more than one of the HECM loan options sounded like the perfect solution to you, maybe what you really need is a combination of two or more payment options. Are you the type of person who can never order off the menu? Do you have a better idea about how your payments should be structured? You're in luck — the FHA wants this loan to work for you. Your originator can guide you through tailoring your payments to your individual circumstances.

Many HECM borrowers choose to receive a credit line or lump sum, plus monthly payments. You don't get the full credit line/lump sum *and* the full loan's worth of monthly payments (that's just wishful thinking). Instead, you break your loan apart into sections: a portion goes into a credit line and/or lump sum and a portion will be distributed monthly. This is so popular because you get the best of both worlds: the security of a monthly check, and the freedom of a larger available account.

When you receive monthly payments in addition to your back-up credit line, you are also protecting yourself from some of the effects of inflation, because even though your monthly payments stay the same, your available funds keep growing. If you can live on your monthly check and leave the credit line pretty much alone for a while, you'll have a nice surprise when you finally decide to use it — extra money!

You can also choose to get a credit line and lump sum, without the monthly payments. This is ideal if you have a large expense that must be paid off in one fell swoop but want to keep earning interest on the remaining balance. You could take a month-long cruise to Alaska and pay for it up-front, and by the time you got back you'd have earned another interest payment on your available funds!

Chapter 6

Figuring Out the Fannie Mae Home Keeper Loans

*I*f you read about the Home Equity Conversion Mortgage (HECM) in Chapter 5 and are discouraged by the low lending limits, then the Fannie Mae Home Keeper loan may be for you. You will see a lot of similarities between the HECMs and Fannie Mae loans in this chapter, but there are significant differences as well. Fannie Mae offers many of the same features that the HECM provides, but because Fannie Mae is a private company, it can afford to have higher maximums and lower fees. (For those lucky few whose home value is substantially higher than the FHA or Fannie Mae lending limits, a jumbo loan may be your best bet. We show you in Chapter 7 how larger loans make reverse mortgages possible for higher-valued homes.)

There are two variations of the Fannie Mae loan: the Home Keeper and Home Keeper for Purchase. They work very much like the HECM (see Chapter 5), in that you will receive payments over the course of the loan, and you will not owe anything on the loan until you die or permanently move out of the home. The difference between the two Fannie Mae loans is just as you may have guessed: Home Keeper is for those who wish to stay in their current home, and Home Keeper for Purchase helps seniors who want to use their equity to buy new homes.

While Home Keeper loans are not secured by the federal government, they *are* backed by Fannie Mae — if your lender fails to pay you for whatever reason, Fannie Mae will step in to make sure your loan is doled out as usual.

In this chapter we show you all the ins and outs of the Fannie Mae reverse mortgage and show you how it differs from the other two major loan products.

Buying a New Home

For years, seniors who planned to use the equity from their house to get some ready cash through reverse mortgages were essentially forced to stay in their current homes, even though their lifestyles warranted a change. Many people were understandably unsatisfied with this arrangement. After all, the way you live in your retirement can be drastically different than your working lifestyle, and your home will probably reflect that. If you've been thinking about getting a reverse mortgage because you want to take advantage of your equity, but you'd rather live somewhere else, the Home Keeper for Purchase may be for you.

Here's how it works: If you own your home free and clear, you can use the equity that you've built up over the years to help pay for your new home, without ever having to make a mortgage payment until you permanently move out of that new residence. If you don't own your home debt-free, but you're close, Fannie Mae allows you to work the remaining balance into your new loan (finance it) by taking out a sum of money right away and using it to pay off the remainder of your existing mortgage. The downside is that, unlike a regular reverse mortgage, you won't receive payments. You won't have payments of your own to make either, which may make this option worth it to you.

You are free to buy the home of your dreams with a Home Keeper, whatever it may be. Some people upgrade, but many use the loan to get something more practical. Typical Home Keeper purchases include:

- **Wheelchair-accessible homes:** This is especially useful for people who currently live on property that features lots of stairs, hills, rocky terrain, or small doorways. Many homes are built today with the standard wheelchair turning radius in mind, and some include electric or hydraulic countertops that can actually lower to a comfortable height (and then raise back up again).

✔ **One-story homes:** Usually ranch-style homes or one-story designs allow for single-level living. No more climbing stairs or rummaging around in a dark and smelly basement. This can also be safer — that's just one fewer sets of stairs to fall down.

✔ **Smaller homes:** Many seniors still live in the homes they raised their children in, which is often more house than they need. A smaller house can be a lot easier to maintain, and less expensive (heating and cooling costs alone would make a huge difference).

✔ **Warmer climate:** Who wants to shovel snow when there are beaches and sunny desserts to frolic in? Seniors moving to warmer climates may be a bit of a cliché, but come on . . . you know you've been thinking about it.

The Home Keeper for Purchase can be a wonderful solution to many housing problems, but it isn't always the best answer for everyone. Your counselor can run your financial needs through the Home Keeper for Purchase calculator to help you decide if this is a loan you want to pursue. There are a few things to keep in mind before getting a Home Keeper for Purchase:

✔ You will often receive less money than you would with a regular Home Keeper loan.

✔ Any outstanding mortgage debts must be paid off (either by you or by the loan) before you can apply the money to a new home.

✔ Your loan is for the purchase of a home only — you won't get a monthly check, line of credit, or additional lump sum to go along with it.

Making a down payment

Before you can apply for a Home Keeper for Purchase loan, you have to be able to prove that you have a sufficient down payment for your next home. What counts as sufficient will vary depending on your age and how much you need to borrow. The younger you are, the more you'll probably have to pay out-of-pocket as a down payment. For example, people who run out to get a reverse mortgage on their 62nd birthday will probably have to pay upwards of 70 percent of the down payment out of their own savings. However, a 90-year-old will only be responsible for paying about 30 percent of the total down payment — yet another good reason to wait a few years if possible to get your reverse mortgage.

Like a forward mortgage's down payment, your funds can come from any of three major sources:

- ✔ Your savings
- ✔ Your investments
- ✔ The proceeds from the sale of your home (if the down payment is more than Fannie Mae will lend you)

Figuring out what you can afford

One of the greatest benefits of a Home Keeper for Purchase is that you may be able to afford a slightly higher valued home that you wouldn't ordinarily be able to buy. Because reverse mortgages don't base your loan on credit scores or income levels, the two factors that usually drag a loan value down, you may be able to get more money out of the Home Keeper for Purchase than you would with a regular forward mortgage. But don't start touring mansions quite yet. The operative words here are "may" be able to afford a "slightly" more expensive home. The Home Keeper isn't going to get you into a lakeshore condo if you're currently living in a one-room shack, but with the right equity and a decent down payment, you may be able to move up a little in the housing world.

You may want to use this extra boost to buy a lovely little retirement home, or go all out and get the most house for your money. Either way, remember that if you get the loan when you're relatively young and have to throw a significant portion of your existing savings into a down payment, you're going to be hard-pressed when it comes time to put food on the table since the Home Keeper for Purchase does not continue to pay you over the life of the loan — it lives up to its name and is "for purchase" only. People are making a habit of living beyond their means these days, but you can control your future finances by declining to buy a home that you really can't afford. A good counselor and/or originator will help you sort out your finances so that you can clearly see what you can reasonably afford.

Before you get your heart set on a Home Keeper for Purchase, do some investigating. Find out how much equity is in your home, how much homes cost in the area you want to live in, and what it would cost to modify the home you're in now. It may make more sense for you to sell your home on your own and buy a new one in the traditional way, or to get another type of reverse mortgage to make improvements on your existing home. If home prices are much higher where you want to live, you may be in for a rude awakening when you try to apply your equity. If you're no good with math, ask a friend or family member to help you sort out the numbers, or take your concerns to your counselor (more on how to prepare for a counselor session in Chapter 8).

Meeting the Requirements

Home Keeper and Home Keeper for Purchase have the same requirements (which makes perfect sense, since they're from the same company). You must:

- ✔ Be at least 62 years old
- ✔ Be a homeowner with at least some equity in your home
- ✔ Live in your home full-time
- ✔ Own a qualified home (see "Qualifying homes," later in this chapter)
- ✔ Meet with a Fannie Mae-approved counselor

Anyone on the loan must meet these requirements. Fannie Mae Home Keeper loans can have up to three borrowers in one home, although this is unusual (loans are more commonly made for singles and couples). Loans with three borrowers are often a couple and an adult child who all meet the above requirements, but could also be siblings or friends, as long as every borrower qualifies. Keep in mind that you don't have to meet all of the eligibility rules to live in the house — you only have to meet all the requirements to be named on the loan.

You must meet with an approved reverse mortgage counselor before you can get any reverse mortgage loan. Counselors are there to guide you (but not choose for you) and help you distinguish between your choices. What's a little different about the Home Keeper requirement is that Fannie Mae recommends that you see a non-profit HUD counselor *or* a Fannie Mae counselor. But don't worry — all counselors, no matter their affiliation, should give you a fair, unbiased view of all your loan options. Although they must use Fannie Mae approved "curriculum" in your counseling session to explain the Home Keeper loans, you can expect the counselors to give you an honest assessment of your financial situation and present all of your options equally. For more on finding a counselor, go to Chapter 8 and read up on your counselor options.

Qualifying homes

Housing options are almost the same as the HECM qualifying homes, although Fannie Mae can be somewhat strict about meeting housing requirements. To qualify for a Home Keeper loan your home must be either:

- A single-family home (one that is detached from other people's homes and is constructed on a permanent foundation)

- A condominium

- A home in a planned unit development project, townhouse, or manufactured home that meets Fannie Mae requirements

To find out if your condo, planned unit development (sometimes referred to as PUD), or other non-traditional home is eligible for a Home Keeper loan, ask your originator. Local originators will probably know right away, but out-of-towners will probably need to look up your community on the Fannie Mae Web site. Why not get proactive and do it yourself? When you're dealing with such a big financial decision, you should be (or at least feel) as prepared as possible every step of the way.

To find out if your condo or other PUD is eligible under Fannie Mae, go to www.efanniemae.com. Toward the bottom of the page you'll see "Single Family" in orange letters — click on "origination and underwriting" directly below that. Then under "Reference Tools and Information" click on the first option, "Accepted condo/co-op/PUDs." Here you'll find state listings; just click on your state and find your development in the alphabetical listing. Print out the listing to take with you the first time you meet with your originator. Just imagine how impressed they'll be that you found this all on your own!

Making necessary repairs

If you think you're off the hook because your home fits into one of these categories, just wait. In addition to these restrictions, Fannie Mae states that your home can't have more than 15 percent of the property value in necessary repairs. If your home is worth $100,000 but has a leaking roof, poor plumbing, and termite damage that will cost $18,000 to replace, your home won't be eligible until the repairs are made (or make some repairs to reduce the cost to less than $15,000 in this case). You may be surprised how fast those little repairs can add up. Keep in mind, too, that these are *necessary repairs* — we're not talking creaky floor board, but rather a stove that leaks gas or other dangerous problem.

Holding homes in trust

Many seniors' homes and other property are held in a *trust* to protect their assets. The deed to the house is owned by your trust, and generally speaking, the senior is both the trustee as well as the beneficiary. It's also common for an adult child or someone else you've designated to act as the trustee on your behalf.

Fannie Mae allows for a Home Keeper mortgage in some cases when a home is held in trust. The trust will have to meet certain guidelines to be acceptable for Home Keeper (or the HECM program for that matter). The guidelines are:

✔ The trust must be an *intervivos* (living) trust, which means that you created the trust while you were still living.

✔ The trust must be *revocable* (able to be canceled). There are times when a married couple creates a revocable trust that becomes irrevocable when one of them dies. This would only be acceptable if the trust became partially revocable and the property remained in the portion of the trust that can be repealed.

✔ The trust must have the right to *encumber* (get a mortgage on) the property. If your adult children hold the trust but you don't want them to be able to mortgage your home, you can remove this encumber clause. But until the trustee has a right to get a loan, Fannie Mae won't allow the house to be mortgaged.

✔ The beneficiaries of the trust must be the only borrowers. Anyone else on the trust would only be beneficiaries after the death of the borrowers.

Be prepared to provide a copy of the trust agreement and any amendments to the originator so it can be reviewed to make sure it's acceptable. Your personal attorney or financial planner should have a copy if you've misplaced it.

It will be your responsibility to obtain bids for the costs of any required repairs from a licensed contractor and submit those bids to the originator. Many people don't have the money needed to complete big repairs up-front, so Fannie Mae allows repairs to be completed after your reverse mortgage closes. Funds to pay for those repairs will be reserved and held in your line of credit until the repairs are completed and inspected. Generally the repairs will need to be completed within six months.

Reaching Higher Borrowing Limits

The big question is always, "how much can I borrow?" You'll be pleased to find out that Fannie Mae loans have much higher lending limits (the maximum amount Fannie Mae will lend) than the HECM (see Chapter 5), and Fannie Mae does not set a prescribed lending minimum. In 2005, the maximum lending limit was $359,650, a whopping $46,754 higher than the HECM's highest lending limit, and an incredible $187,018 higher than the HECM lower end of the lending maximums. That can make a huge difference if you live in a higher-valued home, no matter what loan maximum you fall under. However, don't be fooled into thinking that you'll automatically get the full $359,650. There are factors that contribute to the calculation of your loan, just like you found in the HECM:

- ✔ **The national home value average:** What does it have to do with you? Fannie Mae uses an *adjusted property value* (your actual home value as compared to the national average home value) as a starting basis for your total loan amount. If your home's actual value is at or above the national average, you can expect to get more from your reverse mortgage than if your home value was significantly lower.

- ✔ **Your age:** Generally speaking, the older you are, the more you will be able to borrow. The age consideration in Home Keeper reverse mortgages is based on the combined ages of all borrowers on a particular loan.

- ✔ **Interest Rates:** Home Keeper loans are based on a monthly adjustable rate mortgage (ARM). The lower interest rates are when you initially get your reverse mortgage, the more you will be able to borrow.

Adjusting expectations

Fannie Mae calculates an *adjusted property value* to figure out how much of your home value it can actually let you borrow. Your adjusted property value doesn't necessarily (if ever) equal the actual value of your home, nor does it equal the amount you can ultimately borrow. Adjusted property value is just a basis to determine your loan amount. Fannie Mae compares your home value to the national averages and determines your *principal* amount (the actual dollars borrowed) partially based on that comparison (along with age and interest rates). Any home with a total worth above the maximum value will probably be assigned a $359,650 adjusted property value. As a home value creeps further away from this number (lower than the national average), the amount that home owner could borrow goes down as well.

Fannie Mae bases its lending limit on the national average home price. Combine all the home values in America and divide it by the number of homes, and you've got the magic number: $359,650. This means that about half of America's home values will fall below that number, and about half will be above it.

HECM limits change depending on the county your property is in (see Chapter 5), but Fannie Mae's adjusted property value of $359,650 is the same all over the country. If you live in an area with a lower HECM maximum but own a home with a much higher value, the Home Keeper loan may be able to put more money in your pocket.

Considering age

The next-largest factor in your loan limit is your age, and the Fannie Mae rules may surprise you. The older you are, the more money you can ultimately receive. This is because a younger borrower suggests that the lender has to spend more time *servicing* the loan since they will probably have it longer than an older borrower, and the loan would accumulate more interest. Of course, this is not always the case, but Fannie Mae has to hedge its bets.

Fannie Mae includes the following considerations when looking at borrowers' ages:

✔ **Marital status:** Fannie Mae relies on actuarial tables that take your marital status into account. Instead of drawing on one person's age, it considers both borrowers' ages as it calculates the loan.

If you're married, you're about to get some good news and some bad news. The good news is, you're statistically going to live longer than an unmarried person. The bad news is, you're not going to get to borrow as much as a singleton would. Studies have shown time and time again that married people have lower blood pressure, better overall health, and a more positive state of mind, leading to longer, happier lives. (Incidentally, the same is true for dog and cat owners, healthy eaters, and people who do yoga, but so far Fannie Mae hasn't caught on.) What this means for you is that a single 75-year-old man will get more out of his equity with a Home Keeper loan than a 75-year-old couple. Still, don't let this discourage you from getting a Fannie Mae loan — the generally higher loan limit may be enough to sway you in the Home Keeper's direction.

✔ **Number of borrowers:** Fannie Mae allows up to three borrowers on the loan. This is pretty uncommon, but it can come in handy in certain situations. This is usually an adult child and his or her parents (for example, a 65-year-old woman and her 87-year-old parents), or a senior couple and a single (very senior) parent. As you can imagine, the lending limits would be much higher for the 87-year-olds, so Fannie Mae bases the loan limit on the ages of the youngest *two* borrowers. If, as in the example above, that's 65 and 87, the ages are considered in the same way they would be for a married couple of the same ages.

Although your loan limit goes down by listing adult children as borrowers, having adult children on the loan is often a good way to feel secure that the home will go to the proper heir (the adult children) if you don't want to create a trust. You also have the security of knowing that the loan is not repaid until the last surviving borrower dies or moves out. Keep in mind, however, that any adult child on the loan must use the home as his or her primary residence. They actually have to live in the house to be a borrower.

Factoring in interest rates

All Home Keeper loans are based on a monthly adjustable rate mortgage (ARM), a rate that changes every month for the life of the loan. The sections that follow discuss how the rate works and how it affects your loan.

Understanding the monthly ARM

Although the rate changes every month, Fannie Mae put rate caps in place for the monthly ARM to keep you from paying outrageously high interest rates in the future. Over the course of your loan, your interest rate can never (ever, no matter what) go up more than 12 percent higher than your original rate. If you got a Home Keeper loan today at a rate of 4.09 percent, and in three years the same loan is going for 20.3 percent (not likely, but let's just imagine), you will only be looking at an interest rate of 16.09 percent (4.09 plus 12) because you have that 12 percent rate cap in place.

Home Keeper rate caps don't put a limit on how much your interest rate can change month-to-month (as long as it's not more than 12 percent), so you may have a rate of 4.09 percent in May and 8.34 in June. While this seems like a big jump, don't worry too much about the rates. Monthly rates change so often that if you don't like where your rate is this month, chances are that you'll be happier with it next month.

Your interest rate has an effect on the total loan balance you're accumulating, but it doesn't have any effect on your monthly payments. Although a higher rate will grow your debt at a faster pace, you will keep receiving the same checks — no matter what.

Calculating interest rates

The Home Keeper factors in two things when calculating its interest rates:

> ✔ **The most current weekly average of secondary market interest rates on one-month CDs.**

You can see for yourself what the current one-month, secondary market CD rate is by going to www.federalreserve.gov/releases/h15/current. Scan a few rows down and you can see the CD secondary markets, and below that, the one-month row. Now look to the right and find the column with the heading closest to today's date. That's the one-month secondary market CD rate.

If you've ever invested in a certificate of deposit (CD) at your bank, you know that there are different term lengths for CD investments. Most are one-year or five-year terms with fixed rates, but certain accounts adjust more often than others. Usually, the longer the term, the higher the interest rate, which means a better return when you finally cash it out. Long-term CDs are good for investors, but the shortest-term CD, the one-month, is great for borrowers. Not only does it have the lowest rate, but it changes so often that even high rates don't stick around for long.

> ✔ **A margin.** A *margin* is the amount that originators can add to the index to create your rate. The maximum margin on a Home Keeper loan is 3.40 percent. For example, if the secondary market interest rate for one-month CDs is at 2.20 percent, your interest rate at that moment could only be a maximum of 5.60 percent (2.20 plus 3.40).

Every week is a new week for interest rates, so don't make yourself crazy trying to time the markets or choose your reverse mortgage product based on getting the lowest rates around. This week, the Home Keeper loans may be offering a lower rate, but next week, the Home Keeper loans could be offering the highest. So, when it comes down to it, it's better to find a loan you're comfortable with, get an originator you like and trust, and feel good about your decision, than to rush into a loan because you think the rates are going to rise. Besides, by the time you find an originator, start the paper work, and close the loan, rates will have already changed.

Evaluating the Costs

You can't get something for nothing in this world, and Home Keeper loans are no exception. 359,650Closing cost fees are usually less on a Home Keeper loan than they are on HECMs (see Chapter 5). Admittedly the difference isn't huge, but if every penny counts, this is a good time to start counting. Fannie Mae doesn't charge you the up-front mortgage insurance premium (MIP) that the FHA does for the HECM loan, which means lower fees for you (but not as much peace of mind).

We list some of the common fees associated with closing costs here:

- ✔ **$2,000–$6,674 for origination fees:** Home Keeper origination fees can't exceed $2,000 or 2 percent of the adjusted property value, whichever is greater. Generally speaking, if your adjusted property value is $100,000 or less, you will only pay up to $2,000, but if your home value is near the maximum, you will pay $7,193 (which is 2 percent of $359,650). But remember — these are maximums. Originators have the option to charge a lesser fee if they wish, so it can pay to shop around for lower fees. Think about it: If your home's adjusted value is at or near the maximum, you're going to be paying the maximum fees — any fee reduction may be worth it.

- ✔ **$20 for a credit report:** Originators use the information from your credit report to determine whether or not you have any outstanding federal tax liens (if, for instance, you didn't pay your taxes and the government has a claim on your home) or other judgments. You will most likely already know if you have outstanding debts, but a credit report keeps everything on the "up and up."

- ✔ **$20 for flood certification:** If you live on a federally designated flood plane, insurance and repair costs may affect your loan. If you live in an area like this, you would have had to have a similar certification on your previous loan.

- ✔ **$50 for a courier:** Just as it sounds, this is what the originator charges you to cover the costs of mailing things with regards to your loan. It's so costly because they send everything by overnight mail so your loan is processed quickly.

- ✔ **$50–$100 for recording:** Your county needs accurate information about all housing-related information, including Deeds of Trust and ᵤortgages. Every loan (also referred to here as a *mortgage lien*) must be recorded at your County Recorder's office, and this fee covers the charge to do so.

✔ **$75–$150 for document preparation:** This is really an arbitrary service fee, because it doesn't actually cost a specific dollar amount to fill out paperwork, and it isn't based on a per-page or per-hour system. Some originators outsource this work, and may charge you exactly what that firm charges them. Others rely on an in-house processor to do it, who gets a salary that has nothing to do with this fee. Either way, it's a relatively inexpensive service.

✔ **$100 for pest inspection:** Because your home has to be structurally sound in order to receive the loan, pest inspectors will be deployed to test your home for things like termites and other destructive bugs. If they find a problem, your home will be debugged and you may need a follow-up inspection. Some charge a secondary fee for the follow-up inspection, and some only charge you once.

✔ **$400–$600 for closing/settlement:** This fee covers the title search and any incidentals associated with the closing of the loan. The title search shows who is currently on the home's title (who legally owns the home) and whether there are any outstanding liens on it, like past mortgages you have yet to pay off.

✔ **$250 for the survey:** Six years ago, your neighbor built a fence that was two feet over on your side of the property line and you've been fighting about it ever since. Well, you'll finally get your justice. In some states, a surveyor will come to your home and establish the official boundaries for your property. Start practicing your "I told you so."

✔ **$300–$400 for an appraisal:** As with all FHA loans, your home must be in good condition before the loan can be approved. The appraiser will check for structural defects (leaky roof, cracked foundation, and water damage, among others), as well as make sure the property is up to code. If not, you'll need to make the changes (completed by a certified contractor) and submit to a re-exam. Don't worry if you can't afford to make the changes right away — the FHA thought of that, too. These costs can be bundled into your total loan, giving you up to one year to fix your home's glitches.

✔ **Varying fee for title insurance:** Your fees will include title insurance, which is designed to protect both you and the lender. The cost depends on the size of your loan (the higher the loan amount, the higher the title insurance premiums). Usually your originator will arrange this for you. All you have to do is sign on the dotted line.

✔ **At most, $30 per month for servicing fees:** A servicing fee helps pay for all the man-hours the lender puts in after your loan has closed. This can include processing monthly payments to you, sending you a monthly (or at least quarterly) statement of your account, providing draws on a line of credit, and monitoring on an annual basis that you have paid your property taxes and kept hazard insurance in force on your property. Servicing fees are a flat rate, which means that they will not fluctuate as your interest rate changes, or your loan balance grows.

Fannie Mae has set the servicing fee limits at a maximum of $30 a month, but the servicing fee charged can vary from lender to lender, so you'll want to show you're savvy and ask about it.

Getting the Check

Designed with your individual needs in mind, the Home Keeper loans offer three payment options: monthly payments, a line of credit, or a combination of these.

Fannie Mae also has a less-publicized lump sum option. Ask your originator or counselor to consider this choice if you need to access your entire payment in one fell swoop.

Payment decisions are made at closing, but don't feel pressured to make a choice that's set in stone. You have the right to change your mind at any time for a moderate fee (no more than $50), which can be financed as part of your loan. You can also have the fee taken out of your next payment, which is usually a good option if you have the money to spare and don't want interest charged on that small fee.

Simplifying with monthly payments

Home Keeper monthly payments are set up on a tenure plan, which means that they are evenly distributed throughout the life of the loan. Your tenure monthly payments never change, no matter what (as long as you uphold your end of the mortgage agreement: paying your taxes and homeowner's insurance, and keeping up with home repairs).

Consider these advantages to monthly tenure payments:

 ✔ **Feeling secure:** Because your monthly payments never change, tenure payments are a great way to ensure that you'll always have a steady income.

✓ **Saving extra cash:** You can deposit the money any way you wish. Build a savings account with any leftover funds, or open up a CD, which typically earns interest at a higher rate than the rate of inflation. You'll be ahead of the game, securing a nest egg for yourself.

✓ **Stopping payments temporarily:** You have the option of stopping and starting payments as necessary. Many borrowers choose to suspend payments to avoid losing certain benefits that may be affected by income. For example, borrowers who receive Supplemental Security Income (SSI) or Medicaid payments may want to let their funds accumulate, since they probably don't need the Home Keeper payments right away. If you are trying to get SSI and are afraid you'll appear to have too much money to qualify, suspending payments is a smart (and legal) alternative. Keep in mind, however, that interest and fees will keep building even though the checks have been temporarily stopped.

Don't forget to also consider these drawbacks:

✓ **Unchanging payments:** Payments don't adjust for inflation. While $500 per month sounds pretty good now, in 20 years it could only be worth half that in future dollars.

✓ **Needing to make a large purchase:** Consider what you plan to use your reverse mortgage payments for. If you want to make a large purchase and can't take the time to save up for it, a line of credit may be a better option because your monthly payments aren't likely to be enough to make large purchases.

If you fit into the following situations, monthly tenure payments may be the best choice for you:

✓ You're one of those undisciplined folks who may be in danger of spending all your money at once on a fancy new car, then have nothing left for the basics like food.

✓ You don't have a plan for your money beyond day-to-day living expenses and don't need a large sum.

Building a line of credit

With a Home Keeper line of credit you can take out any amount you wish — up to your total available amount — at any time. Use a little here to pay for your new computer, a little there to buy a new muffler for the car, then take out a larger sum to fund that dream Hawaiian holiday. When and how you get your cash is up to you.

Check out the benefits to the line of credit option:

✔ **Paying yourself back:** You can pay yourself back as you draw on your funds. You may hear this referred to as a *revolving* line of credit. You can take out $650 in March for that trip to Las Vegas, and pay yourself back $650 in June when you win it all back at your weekly canasta game. That money is then ready to be used again.

Accruing interest only on what you use: Interest is only accrued on the amount of money that you have actually taken out — not on the entire amount available. That's why it pays to only draw on what you need at one time.

If you know you'll need a certain amount of money for an upcoming expense, that's one thing, but if you're just estimating how much you think you'll need for groceries in the next month, a tenure payment (see "Simplifying with monthly payments," earlier in this chapter) may be a better choice for you.

✔ **Relieving a mortgage burden:** You can pay off significant portions of your loan, making this a great tool for people who want their heirs to inherit their homes, without inheriting a mortgage burden.

The only caveat is that if you pay the loan back in full, you end the loan. This can be a good thing (you don't have to worry about your family repaying the loan or having to sell the house) or a bad thing (you won't have access to any more loan money).

Consider the following drawbacks:

✔ **Making no money off of interest:** A big (and potentially costly) difference between the HECM (see Chapter 5) and the Home Keeper loans is that the available funds in your Fannie Mae line of credit do not accrue interest in your favor as time goes by. One of the benefits of the HECM line of credit is that your unused funds grow, creating a larger amount available to you (similar to a savings account earning interest). With the Home Keeper, you only get what you started with.

✔ **Running out of funds:** Some people get a bit overzealous at the prospect of such a large amount of money at their ready disposal and spend their money too quickly. Once you've used up your line of credit, you're tapped out — you won't have access to any more reverse mortgage funds. Be sure you budget carefully before you start to spend your line of credit.

If you fit into the following situations, monthly tenure payments may be the best choice for you:

✔ You have a large expense in mind, have another form of income or savings, or only plan to use the reverse mortgage funds every once in a while.

✔ You need money to spend but plan to pay off large portions of the loan so your heirs can inherit the house but not the mortgage burden.

The line of credit option isn't available in Texas — this isn't a Fannie Mae rule, it's Texas's. For those who live in the Lone Star State but need a lot of cash right away, the HECM lump sum may be a better choice for you (see Chapter 5).

Combining your options

Under the Home Keeper loan, you are allowed to combine your payment options into what Fannie Mae calls a *modified tenure* plan. With modified tenure, you get the best of both worlds: steady, predictable monthly payments plus a line of credit. The money is split however you like — for example, on a $94,000 loan, you could choose to take $6,000 in a line of credit and the remaining amount ($88,000) as monthly payments. Or you could reverse that. Or shift the percentages of each payment type up or down in whatever way works best for you. Your counselor or originator can help you split your money in a way you're comfortable with.

Consider some of the following advantages:

✔ **Gaining financial autonomy:** The modified tenure plan is a popular choice for Home Keeper borrowers because it gives you a backup fund (the line of credit) as well as a monthly income.

✔ **Retaining flexibility:** Those who prefer a higher monthly payment but want a small cushion of money can get their funds exactly the way they want them. Others who don't need as much per month can choose a higher line of credit.

✔ **Changing your mind:** You can always redistribute your money however you see fit. You may be charged that $50 "paperwork" fee, but many lenders may waive it just to stay in your good graces. It's worth asking for a discounted fee, since many won't advertise the fact that they often let it slide.

But check out the following drawbacks:

✔ **Lower monthly payouts:** If you use up your line of credit for a large expense and rely solely on your monthly checks, you may have to tighten your belt — your monthly payouts are decreased to account for the line of credit you've borrowed.

✔ **Keeping track of two accounts:** As if you didn't have enough on your mind! If you choose a combination, you'll have two bank books to balance, and two sources of income to account for. If you have any trouble managing your money, a simpler method is to choose a single payout option.

The modified tenure plan may be the right choice for you if:

✔ You know that you need a larger amount of money up-front (perhaps to remodel, travel, or start your own business) but don't need the entire principal at once.

✔ You think you may need access to a big chunk of money in the future (for medical bills or continuing education, for example) and need a great way to ensure that you'll have that money set aside.

You don't have to be a math whiz to work out your distributions. You can choose how much of your principal you want to set aside for your line of credit, and Fannie Mae will divide the rest into monthly payments (minus any monthly or financed fees). For example, if they've estimated that you will keep your $75,000 loan for 10 years and you choose to sock away $10,000, that leaves a $65,000 balance or $500 per month. This is where monthly budgeting can really come in handy — if you know how much you'll need per month, it's easier to guess how much to set aside.

It's up to you how much you want to allocate to each part of the loan. Just keep in mind that the more you stash in reserve, the lower your monthly payments.

Planning for the future

Try this experiment: a few months before you decide to meet with an originator or counselor about your reverse mortgage, estimate how much you will need per month. Write it down and tuck that hypothesis in your nightstand drawer. Then keep a detailed account of every penny that goes in or out of your home. Groceries, haircuts, veterinarian bills, car insurance, gifts — anything that affects your bottom line. Don't try to spend any differently than usual, because you want an accurate reflection of the way you really live. At the end of your experiment, take a hard look at how much you actually spent per month. Average the totals (add each month's total and then divide that dollar amount by the number of months in the experiment) and compare that to your guess. If you were close, good for you! If you guessed too low, you'll need to assess your finances to make sure that whatever you'll get from a monthly payment that's been reduced by the credit line is enough to live on comfortably. The best part is, you'll be fully prepared to explain your financial needs at your first counselor or originator meeting. You'll be ahead of the game and they'll be very impressed.

Chapter 7

Jumping into Jumbo Cash Accounts

*I*n many neighborhoods, housing prices have gotten so out of control, only a small percentage of residents can actually afford to purchase a home. When that's the case, you may not want to sink all your equity into a new home that could start to drop in price when the housing "bubble" bursts. Jumbo reverse mortgage loans allow you to keep your home, use the equity you've built, and never worry about a decrease in the value (inflated or not) of your home.

Still others live in neighborhoods that were always pricey and, presumably, always will be. In high-cost areas — like Southern California, parts of Colorado, and Manhattan — you'd be hardpressed to find a home below the Fannie Mae limit of $333,700 (see Chapter 5). A jumbo loan can help you stay where you are and give you the extra money you need. Use it to maintain your property, take a long holiday . . . anything you like.

In this chapter, we show you the nuances of the jumbo loan and its main proprietor, Financial Freedom.

Figuring Out Jumbo Cash Accounts

A system with loan limits and maximums doesn't work for everyone, especially those who own homes that are worth more than the Fannie Mae (see Chapter 5) and FHA (see Chapter 4) limits combined! If you fall into that category, have we got good news for you — Jumbo Cash Account reverse mortgages have virtually no limits.

Meeting Financial Freedom

Those enormous loans don't materialize out of thin air. That's a lot of money to lend, and someone has to foot the bill. Jumbo Cash Accounts are also often called *private lender* or *proprietary* loans because the companies who fund them are individual private corporations. They have no ties to the government (which has its benefits and challenges) and can essentially create their own interest rate basis, loan requirements, and eligibility.

The biggest and most prevalent financer of reverse mortgage Jumbo Cash Accounts is called Financial Freedom (you can find out more about Financial Freedom and get free supplemental information by calling 1-888-738-3773 or visiting www.financialfreedom.com). The company was founded in 1996 and is owned by IndyMac Bank, a nationwide mortgage lender. It's natural to be a little suspect of a company whose name you may not recognize and isn't backed by government programs, but rest assured that Financial Freedom is a deep-seeded corporation that's here to stay. They have a vested interest in reverse mortgage loans, are active in the National Reverse Mortgage Lenders Association, and pride themselves on being one of the largest reverse mortgage lenders in the country. There are other companies who offer these loans, but so far they only originate in a few of the larger states.

Financial Freedom actually has the capacity to fund all kinds of reverse mortgages, but the Jumbo Cash Account is their pride and joy. You'd have pride and joy too if you could afford to lend someone a couple million dollars.

The founders of Financial Freedom know that this is a big decision, and want to make sure that you feel absolutely confident in their practices. After all, they're asking you to put your financial future (via your home's equity) in their hands. They have created a six-step "consumer safeguard" system to ensure that every borrower is protected from what the industry calls *predatory lending* (originating loans that are not in the borrower's best interest for the purpose of making more money) and gets an objective, honest assessment of their financial situation. The program consists of:

1. Requiring originators to give every borrower a document (made by Financial Freedom) that clearly shows all of their reverse mortgage options.

2. Encouraging any of the borrower's personal advisors — whether friends, family, lawyers, or others — to attend meetings with the originator.

3. Using HUD-approved and other "specially trained" counselors to meet with the borrower before filling out any final applications.

4. Reviewing the loan program and product choice with a regional processing center before the application is sent to the underwriters.

5. Conducting a secondary review at the underwriting center.

6. Sending a customer-satisfaction survey to all borrowers to make certain that everything went as smoothly and easily as possible.

Once you and your counselor choose a Financial Freedom loan, you may consider going to a *correspondent lender,* an originator who is affiliated with the company. Their originators are trained in all aspects of reverse mortgage lending, but will be especially knowledgeable on the Cash Account options. They will have support from Financial Freedom's training and product literature sources and are held to the company's standards.

It's only fair to say, however, that most — if not all — approved reverse mortgage originators (and you should only ever go to an approved originator) have similar rigorous standards that they adhere to. Any member of the National Reverse Mortgage Lenders Association (NRMLA) will be held to strict codes of conduct.

Understanding Cash Accounts

Jumbo Cash Accounts figure your loan amount just like the other reverse mortgage products: by primarily considering the value of your home and your (and any other borrower's) age. And, like other reverse mortgages, the loan won't be due until you move out of the home permanently.

A Cash Account works like a line of credit: The total amount you will borrow (your *principal* amount) sits in an intangible "account" (literally the equity in your home), which you can access at any time like a bank account.

The Financial Freedom Cash Account is a jumbo loan, which means you're going to get a lot more out of the equity in your high-priced home. Jumbo loans start where traditional loans leave off. Generally speaking, homes worth more than $359,650 (the Fannie

Mae maximum; see Chapter 6) will get the best deal from these expanded loans, and the more your home is worth, the better you'll make out.

If you've done the math on the HECM (see Chapter 5) and Home Keeper loans (see Chapter 6) and discovered that you won't be able to borrow nearly what you imagined your could, take heart. With the Jumbo Cash Account, you'll be pleased to see what a huge difference this loan can make. For example, the principal loan amount for a Jumbo Cash Account for a 66-year-old borrower with a home valued at $1,500,000 and no outstanding mortgage debts would be $290,550, as compared to an HECM ($166,474) or Home Keeper loan ($62,956).

As you can see, Annie will get a lot more bang for her buck with a Jumbo Cash Account than she would with either of her other options — almost twice as much as the HECM offers, and nearly five times as much as with Fannie Mae's Home Keeper. If she waits a few years to get her loan, Annie will receive even more money since the older you are, the more money a reverse mortgage company lends you.

However, not all loans are created equal. Almost anyone can get a Cash Account, but people with moderately priced homes will probably get a better value out of HECM or Home Keeper loans (but more often HECM). Or you may find that you're better off with an alternative, such as selling your home or getting another forward mortgage (see Chapter 8 for more on alternative options). For example, the principal loan amount for a Jumbo Cash Account for a 66-year-old borrower who owns a $545,000 home and owes nothing on a previous mortgage would be $101,631, but it would be $162,942 with an HECM and just $62,956 with the Home Keeper, making the HECM the clear winner in this example.

Clearly this borrower would get a greater benefit from an HECM than the Jumbo Cash Account, even though his home is valued above the HECM lending limits ($290,319 in high-cost areas).

Unfortunately, there's no magic age or home value where it becomes obvious which loan option to take. It would be impossible to say that everyone over a certain age would get the most out of a Jumbo Cash Account, or that anyone under a certain home value would benefit more from an HECM. Your counselor will be able to show you what you can expect from each loan option and help you weigh the pros and cons of each.

For a side-by-side comparison of how a Financial Freedom loan looks for your individual situation, go to www.financialfreedom. com/calculator/input.asp and input your age, home value, and zip code (along with any outstanding debts). The calculator will give you an estimate of what you may be able to borrow from each loan type. These numbers won't be set in stone, but it's a good place to start.

Withdrawing your equity

Other reverse mortgages have payment options that let you choose your preferred cash vehicle: monthly checks, a lump sum, or a line of credit (see Chapters 4 and 5). Financial Freedom operates on a different payment system — it doesn't offer monthly payments, just a line of credit. Plus, most of its programs require that you take out a minimum of $500 per withdrawal. If you can set a schedule for yourself (for instance, on the first of every month you take out your minimum withdrawal), you can think of it as a $500 monthly payment. If you need more, you can add to that withdrawal, or take out another $500 as you need it.

In fact, there are several great features to the withdrawal system of Jumbo Cash Accounts. We describe those features in the following list:

- ✔ **Withdrawing flexibility:** For example, if in August you've decided that you only needed the minimum for daily living — groceries, paying the housekeeper, a few dinners out — you only withdraw $500. But in September you know you're going on a cruise and will need more for "fun money." You can take out as much as you think you'll need (don't forget to factor in presents for the grandkids) and save any leftovers in your personal bank account.

    What if you've already taken out a withdrawal this month and two weeks later your refrigerator breaks down? Simply take out another withdrawal. It's really that easy. You can even skip months if you don't need the money right away. With a line of credit you have complete freedom to get, spend, and enjoy your money whenever and however you like. It's all up to you.

    This, of course means that you have to exercise a certain degree of responsibility. It's very tempting to spend your money as soon as you get it, even for those accustomed to having access to seemingly endless supplies of money. Go ahead and take that trip, remodel your master bath, buy a deluxe mini-mansion for your dog, but make sure you'll have enough left over for the life of your loan (or however long you expect to need it). Following are some ways you can make sure you have money when you need it:

- **Create a budget for yourself.** Be honest about the standard of living you expect to keep in the next decade or so. Some borrowers don't actually need their Cash Account on a daily basis — they just want it for a sense of added security, or perhaps to help with a large expense that they expect in the future. If that describes you, this could be the perfect reverse mortgage for your lifestyle. If not, take a serious look at your finances over the past year and make sure that a Jumbo Cash Account will be able to meet your expectations.

- **Estimate how long you plan to keep the loan.** When Financial Freedom determines how much to lend you, they estimate how long you'll keep the loan — you need to do the same thing. If they lend you $400,000 on a seven-year loan and you spend $350,000 on a new 64-foot boat and matching sailor outfits the next day, you're only left with $50,000 for (approximately) the next seven years. If you break it down, that's only about $600 a month, which isn't going to go very far when you've got a new boat and all those dock parties to keep up with. Plus, if you end up spreading out the loan for longer than seven years, that monthly allotment is going to shrink by about $100 per month for every extra year you have the loan. Take a look at Chapter 2 for tips on creating a budget and determining how much you'll need from month to month.

✔ **Paying back with no prepayment penalty:** One of the most innovative features of the Financial Freedom withdrawal system is that you have the option to pay back your loan as you go with no prepayment penalty, which means that you can take out $1,000 one day and deposit $500 the next. You can then reborrow that money . . . it's like recycling! The only rules are that you can't pay back more than you've borrowed (and what would be the point?), and if you pay back the entire loan, your loan is usually considered over, which means you can't borrow any more money from your account.

It's in your best interest, however, to only withdraw as much as you'll need (after the minimum $500). In fact, it's literally in your best interest, because your cash account will grow by a rate of 5 percent per year — that's more than you'll earn on even the best CD or savings accounts. That 5 percent only grows on the amount left to borrow, so whatever you have in your hands isn't growing.

> The growth in your line of credit is *compounding,* which means it's similar to an interest-bearing savings account where you earn interest on your interest. If you have $200,000 available in your line of credit and you don't touch it, the first time it compounds it will increase by 5 percent ($10,000). If you don't touch any of that money, the next time it compounds the increase would be 5 percent of $210,000.

Qualifying for a Jumbo Cash Account

You'll find that loan qualifications for the Jumbo Cash Account are a little different than the other two loan products identified in Chapters 4 and 5. There are more restrictions in some senses, and more freedom in others. If your home didn't qualify for either of the other loans, the Jumbo Cash Account may be a pleasant surprise.

Loaning in the Lone Star State

Wealthy oil tycoons in Texas, you can stop reading this chapter right now. We're sorry to report that your state does not allow lines of credit, even for reverse mortgages. They do, however, allow monthly or lump-sum payments, so turn back to Chapters 4 and 5 and take a moment to reconsider the HECM or Home Keeper loan.

You also have several options available to you that don't involve reverse mortgages at all. If you absolutely must have more money than either of those plans can offer, you may want to consider selling your home and moving to a lower-cost area. You can also refinance or take out a Home Equity Line of Credit. For more on additional options, skip ahead to Chapter 8. You may find an alternative that makes you happier than an armadillo in a patch of Texas Bluebonnets.

Checking out eligibility

Now, for everyone in America's 49 other states (if you're from Texas, see the previous section, "Loaning in the Lone Star State"), most of the Financial Freedom eligibility requirements are just the same as the other reverse mortgage products. You must:

- ✔ Be at least 62 years old
- ✔ Be a homeowner with at least some equity in your home

> ✔ Live in your home full time
>
> ✔ Meet with an approved counselor

Eligible home types are much more lenient with the Financial Freedom products, so chances are that if you meet the above requirements, you'll be able to get a Financial Freedom loan. Borrowers must live in either:

> ✔ A single-family home (a detached property)
>
> ✔ Manufactured home (and own the property)
>
> ✔ Condominium
>
> ✔ Planned unit development (PUD)
>
> ✔ one- to four-unit rental property (as long as you are the owner of the entire property and live in one of the units)
>
> ✔ Co-op (only available in the state of New York)

Your home must also be valued at a minimum of $75,000. Financial Freedom states that there are "virtually" no upper limits, which is merely a protection against someone trying to take out a loan for $50 million on their central California castle. But they will fund just about any reasonable loan.

It's not uncommon to see a Jumbo Cash Account on a multimillion dollar home, but if you're still not convinced that your palace will qualify, give Financial Freedom a call at 1-888-REVERSE (888-738-3773) and ask them to tell you what the home value was on their largest ever loan to date. As long as you have them on the phone, ask them about their products and request an informational packet. They can also put you in touch with an originator in your area, or send you a list of Financial Freedom specialists.

Taking an Interest in London

You knew there had to be a downside, right? Here's the Jumbo Cash Account's greatest downfall: higher interest rates. The good news is that like all reverse mortgage products, you are only charged interest on the amount you've borrowed. Since it's up to you how much you take out, you control how much of your money is charged.

Financial Freedom uses the six-month London Inter Bank Offered Rate (LIBOR) as their *index* (the basis for their interest rate). The LIBOR is the rate at which banks lend money to each other in London, England. Despite being a British index, it's actually used quite commonly in American exchanges. One of its benefits is that the LIBOR usually only changes slightly from period to period. Since your rate will be charged on the six-month LIBOR, the index has six full months to go up or down before the monthly averages are pooled to affect your rate.

The LIBOR index can be found in the *Wall Street Journal,* along with most other interest rate indexes. Pick up a copy to see where rates are — if nothing else, just think how smart you'll look reading the *Wall Street Journal!*

Financial Freedom adds a *margin* (the maximum percentage that a originator can add) to the LIBOR index to create your interest rate. However, Financial Freedom offers a lower six-month introductory rate to new borrowers. For the first six months of your loan, your interest rate will be the LIBOR plus a margin of 4.50 percent. After that point, the margin jumps up to a full 5.00 percent.

If the LIBOR is at 2.10 percent, and we assume that it goes up by about 0.50 percent (to 2.60 percent) after six months, your introductory rate, which adds a 4.50-percent margin to the LIBOR, would be 6.60 percent (2.10 percent + 4.50 percent), and after six months, the interest rate would be 7.60 percent (2.60 percent + 5.00 percent).

Financial Freedom caps the interest rate at 6 percent over the original rate. If you got a Jumbo Cash Account loan today at a rate of 6.5 percent, the most it could ever be is 12.50 percent, no matter what the rest of the world is paying.

Because the LIBOR is a six-month term, your interest only adjusts every six months (semi-annually). This can be good news if markets are slowly changing, since you have six whole months to let the markets go down. This is bad news, however, if you're used to a rate of 7.20 percent and suddenly jump to 8.50 percent. But as we've said before, don't let interest rates bog you down too much. When you play the stock market you have to allow a few years to let it all settle so that you come out on top. In the same vein, interest rates are constantly up and down, so worry more about how you'll enjoy your money and less about interest.

Paying for Splendor

The Cash Account is considered one of the most expensive loans out there because of its origination fees. The upside is that you can usually borrow more with the Cash Account than with other loans, so you simply have to decide which is more important to you: more money to spend now or less money to spend later.

✔ **Varying origination fees:** Financial Freedom's standard fee is up to 2 percent of your home value for the first $500,000. Any part of the next $500,000 adds a 1.5 percent fee, and anything over $1,000,000 is an additional 1 percent.

For example, a $600,000 home would fetch $10,000 in fees for the first $500,000 and $1,500 for that remaining $100,000, giving the originator a grand total of $11,500 in fees. A $1,700,000 home would cost you $10,000 for the first $500,000; $7,500 for the next $500,000; and $7,000 for the last $700,000 of your home's value, for a total origination fee of $24,500.

✔ **$20 for a credit report:** Originators use the information from your credit report to determine whether or not you have any outstanding federal tax liens (if, for instance, you didn't pay your taxes and the government has a claim on your home) or other judgments. You will most likely already know if you have outstanding debts, but a credit report keeps everything on the "up and up."

✔ **$20 for flood certification:** If you live on a federally designated flood plane, insurance and repair costs may affect your loan. If you live in an area like this, you would have had to have a similar certification on your previous loan.

✔ **$50 for a courier:** Just as it sounds, this is what the originator charges you to cover the costs of mailing things with regards to your loan. It's so costly because they send everything by overnight mail so your loan is processed quickly.

✔ **$50–$100 for recording:** Your county needs accurate information about all housing-related information, including Deeds of Trust and mortgages. Every loan (also referred to here as a *mortgage lien*) must be recorded at your County Recorder's office, and this fee covers the charge to do so.

✔ **$75–$150 for document preparation:** This is really an arbitrary service fee, because it doesn't actually cost a specific dollar amount to fill out paperwork, and it isn't based on a per-page or per-hour system. Some originators outsource this work and may charge you exactly what that firm charges them. Others rely on an in-house processor to do it, who gets a salary that has nothing to do with this fee. Either way, it's a relatively inexpensive service.

✔ **$100 for pest inspection:** Because your home has to be structurally sound in order to receive the loan, pest inspectors will be deployed to test your home for things like termites and other destructive bugs. If they find a problem, your home will be debugged and you may need a follow-up inspection. Some charge a secondary fee for the follow-up inspection, and some only charge you once.

✔ **$400–$600 for closing/settlement:** This fee covers the title search and any incidentals associated with the closing of the loan. The title search shows who is currently on the home's title (who legally owns the home) and whether there are any outstanding liens on it, like past mortgages you have yet to pay off.

✔ **$250 for the survey:** Six years ago, your neighbor built a fence that was two feet over on your side of the property line and you've been fighting about it ever since. Well, you'll finally get your justice. In some states, a surveyor will come to your home and establish the official boundaries for your property. Start practicing your "I told you so."

✔ **$300–$400 for an appraisal:** As with all FHA loans, your home must be in good condition before the loan can be approved. The appraiser will check for structural defects (leaky roof, cracked foundation, and water damage, among others), as well as make sure the property is up to code. If not, you'll need to make the changes (completed by a certified contractor) and submit to a re-exam. Don't worry if you can't afford to make the changes right away — the FHA thought of that, too. These costs can be bundled into your total loan, giving you up to one year to fix your home's glitches.

✔ **Varying fee for title insurance:** Your fees will include title insurance, which is designed to protect both you and the lender. The cost depends on the size of your loan (the higher the loan amount, the higher the title insurance premiums). Usually your originator will arrange this for you. All you have to do is sign on the dotted line.

✔ **$20 per month for servicing fees:** The servicing fee is a monthly payment that covers everything the lender has to do after they've closed the loan. It's financed right into your loan, so you won't even have to think about it until the loan comes due. If you live in Illinois or Maryland, you've lucked out: Financial Freedom does not charge a servicing fee in your state.

Your originator will arrange most, if not all, of the third-party services for you, but you are responsible for each fee.

Choosing Loan Options

There are three loan configurations available to you with a Financial Freedom reverse mortgage. Each is similar, but one may have a feature that fits better into your financial goals. All Financial Freedom loans have these six things in common:

- ✔ Virtually no loan limit

- ✔ Six-month introductory interest rate of 4.50 percent above the LIBOR

- ✔ Lifetime interest rate cap of 5 percent above the LIBOR

- ✔ $20 servicing fee

- ✔ Eligible homes including single-family, condo, manufactured, PUD, one to four unit (if you live in one unit), and co-ops (in New York)

- ✔ Minimum home value of $75,000

But each of your options — the standard loan, Simply Zero, and Zero Point — has its own particular characteristics. Your originator and counselor will be able to advise you on these choices, but it helps to go in there knowing which option you think you'll prefer.

Selecting the standard Cash Account

The standard Cash Account offers great features for most qualified borrowers, but it also has its drawbacks — the standard loan is actually the only Financial Freedom loan that charges an origination fee. Why would you choose a loan with fees if you could skip them altogether? Because the standard loan has more flexibility and fewer restrictions, making it an excellent choice for those who want more control over their funds.

As we mention in "Withdrawing your equity" earlier in this chapter, you have the option to repay your loan over time and, in theory, reborrow that money again. This is what is called an *open-ended revolving line of credit,* and it definitely works to your advantage. You can truly take out as much money as you need (just shy of the total available) and replace it whenever you like. Using this tool, you can all but pay off your loan in the timeframe that works for you before it's even due, leaving little for your heirs to deal with if you move out, or upon your death.

Another benefit is that you can withdraw your money in any amount over $500 at any time. This means that if you didn't actually need your money right away, you wouldn't have to receive any payments until you were ready. Instead of being tempted with a pile of cash that you can't really think of a practical use for (unless you consider champagne fountains "practical"), you can leave your money where it is while it quietly grows by 5 percent each year.

The standard option is a good choice for those who want flexibility with their loan and aren't necessarily getting a reverse mortgage to pay for a large purchase in the very near future. Although you certainly could use this loan for that purpose, you'd be better off with one of the following loans to help pay for a looming high-ticket expense.

Selecting the Zero Point option

The Zero Point option is appealing to many seniors because it charges no up-front origination fees. When you consider how much you'll spend on fees with a standard loan, this is often a great alternative for those who are watching every penny.

Don't let that fool you: You still have closing costs to consider that are involved with the Zero Point loan. You will still pay for all of the regular closing services, but they are fortunately capped at $3,500. Since closing costs for homes of "jumbo" value usually come out to over $4,000, you're saving $500 right off the bat.

However, whatever you're saving in origination and closing costs will probably be eaten up by interest charged on your balance. No matter how much you're borrowing with your Jumbo Cash Account or how much you actually intend to spend, the Zero Point loan requires you to withdraw 75 percent of your total available funds at closing. For example, if you had a principal amount of $200,000, you would walk away with a cool $150,000 check. This can work out well for you if you have a large expense coming up, but it definitely works out well for Financial Freedom because they begin collecting interest on all of that money from day one. You will still earn a 5 percent annual growth rate on any leftover money, just like you would with a standard Financial Freedom loan, but it won't be as significant of an increase because it would be growing on a reduced scale. After the first big withdrawal, you must take out a minimum of $500 any time you need to draw on that account again.

It's also important to consider that the Zero Point option doesn't let you repay any of your balance for the first five years. Many people like the sense of security they get from paying off their loan as they go (especially with jumbo loans) because the more you repay now, the less you (or your heirs) will owe later. Repayment certainly isn't a requirement, however, so this is only a shortcoming if you feel strongly about "paying down" your balance.

The Zero Point option is best for people who need their reverse mortgage money for a specific purpose, or who feel comfortable handling their funds so that they will last for the next several years.

Checking out the Simply Zero option

The newest member of the Financial Freedom family is the Simply Zero option, unveiled in summer 2004. Since it became available, the Simply Zero loan has been a very popular choice for the jumbo loan borrower. When Financial Freedom says "Simply Zero," they mean simply zero. You will pay no origination fees (which saves you the equivalent of 2 percent of your home's value), nor will you pay any closing costs, which can easily top out around $4,000 depending on where you live. You will pay any state or local taxes of course, but as far as Financial Freedom is concerned, you don't owe them one red cent in fees or closing costs.

The concept of Simply Zero extends even further, requiring you to withdraw 100 percent of your loan (your principal) when it closes, which leaves you with simply zero dollars in your available funds. If you plan to get a reverse mortgage in order to pay for something immediately (like starting a small business or an upcoming medical procedure) then the idea of getting a check for a $100,000 or so makes perfect sense. Other investments can be a good choice, as long as you will earn at least 5 percent (the amount you'd earn with a standard loan on your unused funds). However, if you don't need the full amount right away, the standard loan is probably your best bet.

If you don't trust yourself to spread the money out for your remaining golden years, but you feel that Simply Zero is the best option for you, you may be able to have a friend, relative, or financial planner help you portion it out. A good resource for help with managing your finances (especially a huge chunk of change like this one) is *Personal Finance For Dummies*.

Simply Zero has the same "no prepayment for the first 5 years" rule that the Zero Point option has, so keep that fact in mind when choosing your loan.

Comparing options

Deciding whether or not you need a Jumbo Cash Account is some-times easier than deciding which of their three products works best for your individual needs. Table 7-1 below shows the loan options and their benefits, which may help you determine if one is right for you.

Table 7-1			Jumbo Loan Options		
Financial Freedom Product	Minimum Initial Withdrawal	Minimum Subsequent Withdrawal	Origination Fees	Closing Costs	Prepayment
Standard	$500	$500	Up to 2% of home value for first $500,000. Any part of the next $500,000 adds a 1.5 percent fee, and any-thing over $1,000,000 is an additional one percent.	Varies	Any amount up to the total, at any time
Zero Point	75% of total funds available	$500	$0	$3,500 or less	No prepay-ment for first 5 years
Simply Zero	100% of total funds available	$0 (there's nothing left!)	$0	$0	No prepay-ment for first 5 years

Part III
Taking the Plunge

The 5th Wave   By Rich Tennant

"Can you explain your reverse loan program
again, this time without using the phrase
'yada, yada, yada'?"

In this part . . .

*O*nce you've decided on a loan that may work for you (see the Chapters in Part II), Part III ushers you into the next steps. We include lots of great tips (if we do say so ourselves) to equip you so there are no surprises as you take each step of the reverse mortgage process on your own.

Chapter 8, the first step, gives you the scoop on arranging a meeting with a reverse mortgage counselor, what to expect during the visit, and what you can do to make the meeting go smoothly.

Chapter 9 covers the procedure of choosing an originator, applying for a loan, and the loan approval process.

Getting your home appraised may be a familiar experience, but Chapter 10 gives you some tips from reverse mortgage originators on how to make a good impression, and how to boost your home's value.

Last but not least, Chapter 11 gives an overview of the closing process. This is the part where you sign those last documents and get your first check, so we give you all the info you need to make it hassle-free.

Chapter 8

Taking the First Step: Seeing a Counselor

*M*any people hear the word "counselor" and instantly think of laying uncomfortably on a big leather couch while someone asks about your mother. In fact, the reverse mortgage counselor is nothing of the sort. You can think of them more like a school counselor: Instead of helping you pick your classes, they help you pick your loan. Plus, like a school counselor, their services are free. You don't have to pay one cent for your session.

Counselors are unbiased (they have absolutely no stake in whether or not you get a reverse mortgage), completely confidential, and are only looking out for your best interests. Everyone who wants a reverse mortgage is required (yes, this means you) to visit a counselor prior to getting their loan. We identify ways in this chapter to find a reverse mortgage counselor, things to look for when choosing one, and examples of some options they may give you in lieu of a reverse mortgage.

Finding a Counselor

The easiest way to find a counselor by far is to go online. There are a few counselor listings, but you can save yourself time by going straight to www.hud.gov/offices/hsg/sfh/hecm/hecmlist.cfm. If you're uncomfortable with computers, just ask a friend or family member to guide you, or use the computers at your local library (they're always willing to lend a hand). You can also call the Department of Housing and Urban Development (HUD) at 800-569-4287 for counselors near you.

Another easy way to find a counselor is to simply ask your originator (Chapter 9). They know who's out there and who can help. Until recently, originators were not allowed to recommend counselors. In 2005, regulations changed to allow originators to give you a list of five counseling agencies in your state.

Don't despair if you don't see a counselor in your area. While they certainly prefer to spend an hour with you in person, counselors will also conduct phone meetings. It may take a little longer — probably two or three calls — but it's worth the time if there aren't any counselors near you, or you are unable to get to their offices. If you live in a less-populous state or rural area, there may only be a handful of counselors around, so a phone meeting may be in your future.

Before you can go see a counselor, you must request counseling — they don't let just anyone take up their time! The application simply verifies that you are actually eligible for a reverse mortgage and that you understand the basics. They won't turn you away unless you are underage (when's the last time you were carded for anything?) or do not show sufficient comprehension. This is very rare, so don't worry. Anyone who is reading this sentence and is over 62 is likely to be eligible.

If you just want to speak to a counselor but aren't ready to set up an appointment, you may be able to get a counselor on the phone to answer a quick question or two. This is also a good opportunity to feel them out to see if you will be compatible.

Here are some great picks for finding counselors:

✓ **HUD counselors:** No matter which loan you think you want, we recommend visiting a HUD-approved counselor. Although it's HUD that offers one of the loan options (the Home Equity Conversion Mortgage, or HECM), their counselors have undergone extensive training and are virtually guaranteed to be the best in the business.

Most HUD counselors are paid through a government grant. They get a dollar amount based on how many counseling sessions they've held. That's why almost all HUD counselors are free — be sure to ask if they charge a fee before you visit. If they do, find a different counselor. Costs are usually around $75 — it's up to you whether or not it's worth it to spend that money, but it's usually unnecessary. You don't get a better counselor for a fee, and there's no reason for you to pay.

The best place to find a HUD counselor is at, you guessed it, the HUD Web site. Follow this string of letters to an easy-to-navigate site: `www.hud.gov/offices/hsg/sfh/hecm/ hecmlist.cfm`. Then just click on your state and you'll find a whole slew of information about the counselors in your state. Take some time to read through the list, visit their individual Web sites, and narrow it down to one or two. You can also call 800-569-4287 and ask for a reverse mortgage counselor in your area.

✔ **National Center for Home Equity Conversion's (NCHEC) "preferred" counselors:** These are counselors who work for non-profit or public agencies and have all the same detailed information and unbiased policies that HUD counselors have. You can find an NCHEC counselor by visiting `www.reverse. org`. Take your time and explore this site — they are a virtual "wealth" of information.

✔ **The AARP network:** If you want to go one step up from these very qualified professionals, the AARP Foundation (affiliated with AARP but not the main organization) created a counselor network with the best of the best HUD-approved counselors in the country. These counselors scored the highest on a test administered by AARP's Reverse Mortgage Project, and they must operate in keeping with the project's policies and standards. There are only about 90 in the whole country, but they're spread out, so you should be able to find one in your state.

Aside from scoring high on their AARP exam, network counselors are an actual network of counselors (it's not just a fancy title). Every week, all of the network counselors hold a conference call where they share recent experiences, help each other troubleshoot, and discuss ways to make the network's counseling sessions consistent from Washington to Florida and everywhere in between. They also keep up-to-date on any changes in the loan products, financial regulations, and eligibility requirements.

To find a certified AARP Project counselor, start at `www. hecmresources.org/requests.cfm`. On the left-hand side, click on "USA Map" and then click on your state. You'll see a brief explanation of services, and then a table of all the Reverse Mortgage Project "network" counselors listed by city. You can also call 800-209-8085 and ask for information about reverse mortgage counseling.

For those who know without a doubt that they will need a Jumbo Cash Account (your home is worth around a $1,000,000 or more) counseling is required as well. The counseling on the Cash Account program will be done during the time your application is being processed. Your originator requests that an independent third party counselor calls you to go over the program. This counselor may be HUD approved, but not always — it's worth it to check (you can always request a HUD counselor from your originator as well). The counselor will review the disclosure forms you were provided at the time of application to ensure that you understand all the aspects of the loan (have a look at Chapter 9 for more on application forms). If after the counseling session you feel you need more input, you may seek additional advice from a financial professional of your choice, such as a financial advisor, senior attorney, or a CPA.

Knowing What to Expect

The reverse mortgage counselor's job is to help you find the right loan or alternative for your individual situation. That's it. They don't originate, fund, or process the loan. Counselors just help you choose it.

As a matter of fact, counselors are supposed to:

✔ **Assist you in making a decision on your own.**

✔ **Keep their opinions to themselves when it comes to your personal decisions.** If they ask what you want to do with your reverse mortgage money and you reply, "I'm going to open a brothel," the counselor's next question should be, "Will you need a line of credit or a lump sum?" While they may not agree with your choices, their job isn't to impart judgment on you.

✔ **Keep your session confidential.** This means that if you don't want your family present and they call up the counselor demanding to know what went on, all he or she will ever say is, "sorry, that's confidential." The only time this may not be the case is if the counselor determines that you are not quite lucid, or if you have given your permission to tell certain people what you've decided.

✔ **Know the options inside and out and get enough information from you in your hour-long session.** Counselors are good, but they're not psychic; when you come, come prepared. You need to have a few things ready to discuss before you make your first appointment:

- Make sure that you are eligible (Chapter 3).

- Develop a basic idea of the loan options and how the reverse mortgage works (see Chapters 5, 6, and 7).

- Get a sense of your finances (how much you owe in monthly debts, how much you think you'll need per month, and so on; see Chapter 2).

- Know approximately what your home is worth (ask neighbors who recently sold their homes, or look in the newspaper for homes listed in your area).

Coming prepared makes the counselor's job easier and gets you out of there faster.

When you meet with your counselor, you may be surprised to find that some of the options suggested to you don't involve reverse mortgages at all. That's because counselors are required to weigh all of your options and make you aware of every viable, practical choice so you can take an active part in selecting your loan. They are experts on lots of senior services and programs, and may know of one that would cost you less, or get you more.

While all counselors operate a little differently, most will follow a basic four-part counseling session: making the appointment, discussing your motivations and needs, understanding the options, and getting your certificate. You'll find a discussion for all of those parts in the sections that follow.

Making the appointment

It may seem like a no-brainer, but there are some guidelines for making your counseling appointment. First, you need to determine whether you will do your session in person or over the phone. Most counselors prefer meeting in their office, but if a phone meeting is necessary due to distance or immobility, they will happily hold a phone session.

The person who needs the reverse mortgage is the only person who can make the appointment. That means that if you feel a little tired and would rather your daughter called for you, she'll have to do a darn good impression of you to set up your session. Counselors want to know ahead of time who they will be in contact with, and what sort of mental capacity you're in. If you can't make a phone call to schedule a meeting, chances are you aren't fit to take out a new mortgage. Of course, family members are encouraged to join in on the sessions, but only the borrower can make the appointment.

Discussing your needs

Some counselors do an initial phone "interview" with you and send you all the necessary handouts and packets before your session so you have a chance to look them over. Others prefer to go over everything in person so they can get a full sense of your situation, face to face. Both ways give them the information they need, so it comes down to what you and your counselor can agree on.

Once you're inside the counselor's office (or on the phone) your counselor explains his or her role to you and then asks you about your motivations for investigating a reverse mortgage. Questions (that you should have some ready answers to) may include:

- ✔ Why do you want a reverse mortgage?
- ✔ What do you plan to do with the money?
- ✔ How long do you expect to stay in your home?
- ✔ How much money do you actually need?
- ✔ Do you have any outstanding debts, and if so, how much?
- ✔ Does your home need repairs that you know of?
- ✔ How much (if any) of your estate do you want to leave to your heirs?

Start thinking about the answers to these questions now, and your counseling session can go a lot smoother (and faster).

If the questions sound invasive or make you feel defensive about your finances, take a deep breath and remember that the counselor has to know everything about your living situation to help you decide on the best loan for you. If you hold back information (or worse, lie about something) you may be sent down the wrong path . . . and that's not a place you want to be when you have your home on the line.

Your counselor will also try to assess your comprehension. It's not a test, and you don't need to start popping ginseng just to appear sharp in front of your counselor. Most seniors seeking reverse mortgages are of sound mind, but some face dementia, stroke, or Alzheimer's, which may require a durable power of attorney to be present. Still others may have a language barrier, making it difficult to explain complex lending terms (although many counseling agencies are jumping on the bilingual bandwagon). If you have hearing or eyesight problems, let your counselor know ahead of time. None of these issues are anything to be ashamed of, but it does help your counselor to be aware before you arrive.

Your counselor also won't expect you to be an expert on reverse mortgages. It helps if you know the gist of it, but counselors take the time to explain the whole kit and caboodle during their sessions.

At the end of your session, you will receive a HUD Certificate of HECM Counseling. The certificate essentially proves that you showed up at your counseling session, and that your counselor has disclosed all of the information required. It also shows how you held the sessions (by phone or in person) and how long, to the minute, you spent with your counselor. The HUD certificate (by far the most common, although non-HUD counselors may have variations) has six discussion items that your counselor should have gone over with you prior to you signing the certificate.

1. They must tell you about other options besides the HECM (HUD's loan), including other living arrangements, social services, health benefits, and financial options.

2. They must consider other loan programs and let you know that they're available. These may be other reverse mortgages, deferred payment loans, or property tax deferral.

3. They have to fully explain the monetary implications of getting a reverse mortgage.

4. They must disclose that reverse mortgages may affect your taxes, eligibility for assistance under government programs, or have an impact on your estate.

5. They must talk about whether you signed an agreement with an estate planning service or other firm that requires, or seems to require, that you pay a fee upon closing that may exceed legal amounts.

6. If you did sign an agreement like this, that you understand there are free resources available to you making that firm unnecessary.

If you still have any questions about any of these items, this is the time to ask — before you sign. Your signature (along with your counselor's) is required on the certificate. The counselor will probably ask you to sign three original (not photocopied) certificates. One is for the counselor, one is for you to keep, and one is for your originator. You'll need to bring the originator's copy with you to your first meeting with the originator. If your originator loses it (seriously, it happens), you can hand over the one you kept at home for just such an occasion, or ask your counselor for a new one.

You'll also see a note on the certificate that it's only good for 180 days. If you plan to speak to an originator, do it fairly soon so you don't have to go through the counseling process all over again.

Understanding your options

When he or she has a good assessment of your finances and expectations, your counselor will create computer printouts of all of your options, based on the information you've given. This boils down to a tangible summary of all your options with information on which may work best for you. This is often called a *Personal Reverse Mortgage Analysis,* and it's a great tool to take back to your family (if they didn't come along) to show them exactly what your choices are.

The counselor can tweak the printouts to reflect any number of different options and show you how an endless combination of loans will suit your needs. Hopefully, he or she will have such a good reading on you (because you will have been so open) that the first couple of choices will be options that you can agree on.

This is one reason why counselors prefer office sessions rather than speaking over the phone. In the office, they can keep printing out new choices as long as you keep changing your mind. Over the phone they'll have to help you agree on one to try, mail you the printout, call to go over each line, and then do it all over again if you want to see another option. In the office this can take minutes. Over the phone it could be days before you reached a satisfying loan option!

The printout will show what you can expect to receive — and give — with a particular option. It covers estimated loan costs, interest rates, maximum fees, and approximate home value and age, so what you see there should be close to what you'll see in the originator's office.

Take these printouts home and review them after your counselor has gone over them with you line by line. You don't have to make a decision in the office, and they encourage you to call them again if you have any follow-up questions. If you're completely lost or aren't satisfied with your options, schedule another session. Most people will only need to go once, but if you are utterly confused or don't see an option that would work for you, make another appointment. That's what counselors are there for.

Once you and your counselor have established that a reverse mortgage is right for you, he or she will most likely provide you with a list of all the originators in your area. Counselors are not allowed to favor or endorse any of them, and as tempting as it will be to ask for a recommendation, it would be unethical for them to give you one.

Bringing the Whole Gang

Counselors will almost always encourage you to bring people with you to the counseling session. Some seniors are hesitant to discuss their finances with their families. and although family, friends, or professionals aren't required to be at the session, their presence can have a lot of benefits.

Including family and friends

The people closest to you can be a great help during this big financial decision. Their moral support and outside perspective can make a huge difference in the way you perceive the whole loan process. Here are some benefits to having your friends and family accompany you:

- ✓ **Family and friends can help you feel more at ease during the counseling session and throughout the loan transaction.**

- ✓ **Family and friends can interpret confusing legal terms in a way that a counselor may not.**

- ✓ **Your family and friends know you better than your counselor ever could, and they may be able to see a glitch in a particular program that you and your counselor have missed.** Maybe you donate $5,000 to your favorite charity every year; this kind of spending will affect your bottom line once you get a reverse mortgage, because they won't have factored that into your estimated monthly budget.

- ✓ **Your family and friends can advise whether you've been entirely honest about your spending habits, which could make a big difference in which payment schedule will work for you.**

- ✓ **Your family can see how your financial decisions will affect them.** Family will be able to see how much of an inheritance they can bank on and whether or not they will realistically be able to keep your home. These days very few families feel the need to keep their parent's homes, since most seniors aren't living in the homes they raised their families in, but adult children are sometimes reluctant to liquidate their parents' home. Bringing family to the counseling session allows everyone to understand the most likely scenarios for your estate, based on different loan options.

Using professionals

It may also be a good idea to bring along the financial or legal professionals who oversee your accounts and/or your will. These may be financial planners, family lawyers, elder law specialists, estate planners, tax attorneys, or any other significant professional.

You may not be fully aware of where your money is or what your money has been up to since you handed over your investments to a financial planner. You may not realize what kind of tax benefits or ramifications a reverse mortgage will have for you (sometimes it's a great tax saver, sometimes you'll end up owing). You may learn that you need to move some assets around to make this loan work for you. Although your counselor knows the general rules and regulations related to these issues, your personal professionals probably know your financial history and goals better than a counselor can glean in one short session.

Knowing what you're doing with your home and your money will also effect how they manage your finances. They may need to change your investment portfolio drastically, or file your taxes in a whole new way, simply because you got a reverse mortgage.

At least two weeks in advance, let your financial professionals know that you'll be attending a counseling session and invite them to come along. Provide them with some information about reverse mortgages (you can even send them a copy of this book) so that they have an understanding of the loan ahead of time and won't use up your meeting peppering the counselor with questions. Ask them to come prepared with any financial documentation that may help in your loan decision, like tax returns, home evaluations, or investment records. By priming them for the session you can help everyone get the most out of their presence. Some professionals will charge you at their regular rate to attend your counseling session. If you can, try to help them see that this is like a free crash course in reverse mortgages for them. You or a family member may be able to talk them down to coming for half price or even for free. Use key terms like "business opportunity," "growing market segment," and "informational session" to get your point across.

Knowing What to Look For

When you settle on a couple of choices for your counselor, keep the following important points in mind:

✔ The counselor should be HUD-approved (see "Finding a Counselor," earlier in this chapter).

✔ The counselor must be objective and unbiased.

✔ The counselor must treat you with respect and keep all information confidential.

✔ The counselor should not charge a fee (it is completely legal for them to do so unless they are HUD-funded, but you can probably find another counselor who's free if that's the case).

You can find out whether the counselors on your list meet these requirements by simply giving them a call.

Exploring Other Options

Your counselor will give you many options based on your age, home value, future plans, and monthly expenses. Whether some or any of these will work for you can be discussed with your counselor.

Waiting it out

One of the most common reasons not to get a reverse mortgage is age. When they made the minimum age 62, the reverse mortgage bigwigs meant it in the truest sense of minimum. The very least allowed. It's a pretty standard retirement age — most people would consider someone who's 62 to be a senior. It doesn't mean that the day you turn 62 you need to run out and get a reverse mortgage.

The older you are, the more you'll get from any reverse mortgage product. A big part of your loan amount is based on how much longer the lenders think you'll be living in your home. They will have to pay a young person for a lot longer and handle a lot more paperwork than they would for an older borrower. That's why older borrowers get better loan amounts.

Your counselor may suggest that you wait a few more years to get the most money out of your loan. Of course, if you have an immediate need or have foreseen the future and know that you won't be around in a few years, you and your counselor can discuss the pros and cons to getting the loan early.

Thinking forward

Another option your counselor could have you consider is a forward mortgage. Remember, a forward mortgage is just another term for a regular old traditional loan where you pay the bank instead of the bank paying you. Why would you want to go back to paying off another loan? Counselors sometimes suggest forward mortgages for people who qualify for a reverse mortgage, but are on the younger side of the spectrum, or who want to retain more control of their income.

Home Equity Line of Credit

Many seniors who qualify for a reverse mortgage find themselves happily married to people who don't. The solution? Leave them and start a new life with oodles of money, courtesy of your reverse mortgage. Okay, if that sounds too drastic, your counselor may run the numbers for you on a Home Equity Line of Credit (HELOC), not to be confused with Home Equity Conversion Mortgage (HECM), the reverse product (see Chapter 5).

The HELOC is similar to a reverse mortgage in that you get to spend the equity in your home today, but it differs in several crucial ways. See Table 11-1 for a side-by-side comparison.

Table 11-1 Comparing HELOCs and Reverse Mortgages

	Closing costs	*Loan amount aAvailable*	*Payment to you*	*Loan repay-ment*
Home Equity Line of Credit	Usually very low ($500), if any at all	Depends on your home value and credit score: usually 80 percent of your home value.	Line of credit only. Money can be accessed with HELOC checks and credit cards.	Due monthly, as the money is withdrawn (usually with minimum monthly payments).
Reverse Mortgage	Can be expensive ($5,000), but is financed into your loan	Depends on your age, home value, and interest rate: usually around 50 percent to 70 percent of your home value.	Choose between monthly deposits, line of credit, lump sum, or a combination, depending on the loan.	Due when you sell your home, move out permanently, or die.

As you can see, the HELOC may be a less expensive route, but your options are limited and your repayment is immediate. Your counselor can show you how the numbers will add up for your individual circumstances.

ARMs

ARMs are adjustable rate mortgages, which means that the interest rate changes far more frequently than it would with a traditional forward mortgage. It also means that the loan terms are shorter. It's not uncommon to have a three, five, or seven year ARM. The best part about ARM loans is that the rates are much lower . . . often by a percentage point or two, which can add up fast. Most ARM loans change interest rates every 6 or 12 months, but there are some that do it every 3 months, or even once a month.

If you are old enough to qualify for a reverse mortgage but won't get as much money because you're on the younger end of the spectrum, or if you only expect to be in your home for a few years, your counselor will likely suggest that you refinance with an ARM.

Because it's a forward mortgage, you will still pay the lender (just as you would for a regular 30-year mortgage), but your payments will be much lower. The trouble with ARMs is that if rates go up, so do your payments. Your counselor won't try to predict the way interest rates are turning. They really aren't concerned with watching the indexes fluctuate. What they will do is help you assess the risks involved with this option and allow you to decide for yourself whether or not you are willing to assume the risk that your rates will go shooting up.

Sharing your home

Your financial situation may be such that you don't need a huge sum of money for any big vacation or fancy new bathroom. You just need money for the essentials to supplement your Social Security. Your counselor could bring up the idea of sharing a home with a friend or relative in a similar situation. Do you have a sibling or sewing club friend who is also in need of a little monthly help? Invite them to live in your spare bedroom, charge them a fair rent, and meet your monthly requirements.

In some cases, the best thing is for you to move in with an adult child or other friend or relative. This won't work in all families, but with a little compromise and a lot of love, it can be a good solution — maybe not ideal, but good. If you can afford it, you and your new roomies could get a lot out of a few sessions with a family counselor (no relation to the reverse mortgage counselor).

There you'll have the chance to identify everyone's needs, find out what each person expects from this living situation, and work out some of the kinks before you start feeling resentful that your kids treat you like a live-in babysitter.

Checking out government loans

Your local or state government may have their own version of a reverse mortgage available that is more in tune with your needs. There are two species of state loans that you need to know about. Your counselor will probably make you aware of these options if they are appropriate to you and available in your area.

Using your equity

The most common state loans are generally called *Deferred Payment Loans* (DPLs) but they may masquerade under other names depending on your area. Essentially, they are just like any other reverse mortgage — you will receive money based on the equity in your home, which isn't due until you permanently leave your home.

The state loans differ from the loan products featured in this book in three significant ways.

- The funds from DPLs can only be used for specific purposes, and the purpose depends on the loan. They are, however, almost always home-repair related. We're not talking a fancy new kitchen — these are necessary repairs or modifications, like fixing your wiring or installing a roll-in shower. All three loan products described in Chapters 5, 6, and 7 allow you to use your money for whatever you see fit, home repair or otherwise.

- Interest charged on a DPL is usually fixed, which means that the rate you get when you sign your loan documents is the rate you'll keep for the life of the loan. If you get your DPL when rates are very low, this can be a tremendous benefit. You may secure a 5.32 percent rate forever while others pay 8.97 a few years later. The downside is that if you lock in a higher rate, it can be difficult, if not impossible, to refinance and get a lower rate. The loans in the following chapters all follow adjustable rates, which may change every month, every six months, or annually.

- DPL funds are only available in a lump sum; you get all of your money in one very big check. This can be either a blessing or a burden, depending on how you manage your money, what you need the cash for, and what your interest rate is (since the more you owe back at any given time, the more interest you're charged). Other reverse mortgages offer you a range of choices for payment disbursement, which may or may not fit your lifestyle better.

State loans like DPLs are sometimes harder to get, since eligibility requirements tend to be more strict. In some areas they are limited to those with very low income; in other areas they are dictated by home value or the degree of your disability (if the loan is to be used for disability modifications).

It may sound like we're being harsh on DPL loans. In fact, they can be a great advantage for just the right borrower. They have a much lower cost in the end than the loans in this book and usually don't charge origination fees, closing costs, mortgage insurance premiums; they also have lower interest in most cases.

But we saved the best for last. In some areas, DPL loans are dubbed *forgivable* loans because if you live in your home for a certain period of time (it will vary by state) you may not have to pay back some or all of your loan. Your loan, or part of it, can be forgiven and you won't have to repay it. Ever. It probably sounds too good to be true, but many governments have set aside funds to aid seniors in keeping their homes. Next time you curse your taxes, think about the DPL. To find out if these loans are offered in your area, ask your counselor or call your city/county housing department. You may also find information with the area agency on aging or state financing agency. Their phone numbers are located in your phone book in the government pages.

Paying the taxman

When money is tight, you have to make choices: pay your property tax or keep your electricity running? Ok, your situation may not be that dire, but you may have slipped up on your property tax at some point, or it may be an obligation you suddenly can't entertain. This is a surprisingly common problem for seniors, so there's no need to feel ashamed if you fall into this category. For those who find themselves indebted to their tax collector, your counselor will probably suggest a *Property Tax Deferral* (PTD) loan.

Even good people get behind on their property tax. It won't win you any merit badges, but it's not the end of the world in some states. PTD loans will give you the money you need to pay off your property taxes. But that's all they do. You can't use them for any other purpose, period. You may have guessed from the name that this is another deferred loan — you won't have to pay off any of it until you leave your home for good.

About half of the states in the United States offer PTD loans, and each state has its own guidelines. You may find that two people with identical ages, home values, income, and tax debt get completely different loans from state to state, or even county to county. Two common requirements are that in most areas you need to be at least 65, and have a low to moderate income.

A big drawback to this loan is that it may not last as long as you do. Whereas most reverse loans pay out as long as you live in your home, the PTD can be capped in many programs. A major benefit is that, like the DPL, the cost of the loan is negligible. You won't usually pay for any part except the principal (the actual amount borrowed) and maybe a low closing cost.

One important note is that you can't have a PTD loan and a reverse mortgage at the same time. If you really only need the money to pay off your property tax then by all means, pursue a PTD. But if you think you'll need additional funds, consider a reverse mortgage. Your counselor can help you compare the benefits of each.

You can find out if PTD loans are an option for you by contacting the agency you pay your property tax to. If they don't offer the loan, ask if they offer an extension or lower-payment program.

Chapter 9

Working on Step Two: Your Originator

*Y*ou may have heard them called "loan officers," "lenders," "originators," or "mortgage planners," but you may never have known that these people are all one and the same. Despite the abundance of different titles — making it all the more confusing to look them up in the yellow pages — mortgage originators are the middlemen and women who shop for the best rates and service from lenders so you don't have to. But let's not oversimplify. Originators are also the people who organize your entire loan from start to finish and complete the necessary paperwork and various tasks to ensure that your loan is the best loan it can be for *you*. This chapter explores the details of the originator's job, how to find the best originator for your circumstances, and how to protect yourself from those few nefarious "predatory" lenders.

Meeting Your Originator

This is the moment you've been waiting for since you opened this book: meeting the person who can make all of your financial dreams come true (or at least point you in the right direction). You can choose to meet with an originator before or after meeting with the required reverse mortgage counselor (see Chapter 8). We recommend that you meet with your counselor first for these reasons:

✔ If you go to your originator first, they're just going to give you a list of approved counselors and tell you to come back once you've been through a counseling session.

✔ The counselor will give you a better idea of which loan is the right choice for you, and you can make your first originator meeting go much more smoothly and quickly if you already know what you want.

✔ Between the counselor and the information in this book, you are going to walk into that originator's office with confidence, knowledge, and reasonable expectations — the originator will be very impressed.

✔ You can also benefit by realizing what you can reasonably anticipate and require from the originator.

Throughout your loan process, you may hear the terms *lender* and *originator* used interchangeably. You'll see *servicing lenders* mentioned as well (also called *servicers*). It can get a bit confusing, we admit, so let's break it down into two kinds of lenders: originating lenders (we'll call them Ollies for short) and servicing lenders (or Sallies, just for fun).

Understanding originating lenders

The originating lender is the person that this chapter is devoted to. Ollies can be called an originator or a lender, but it essentially means the same thing: it's the person who "makes" your loan. It is not, however, the person who actually hands out the cash. The originating lender is the person you go to once you've decided to find more about how a reverse mortgage can work for you. The originating lender is the one whose office you sit in for hours on end, asking questions and signing papers.

Figuring out servicing lenders

On the other hand, you will never meet your servicing lender at all. Your originating lender is required to give you all the contact information you'd ever need in case you want to reach them, but chances are good that Sally is a silent partner.

You pay the servicing fees discussed in Chapters 5 through 7 to the — you guessed — servicing lender. For their fees, the servicing lender agrees to:

✔ Send your checks (either monthly or when you request them, depending on your loan type)

✔ Keep track of your loan balance and send you a statement regularly

✔ Handle the payment of your property taxes and homeowner's insurance straight from your account (if you want them to)

✔ Make sure you're satisfying your end of the deal (still living in the same home, maintaining the property, and paying taxes)

✔ Change your account information (such as how you want to receive payments) at your whim

You may hear an originator referred to as a lender, but the ones who write the checks are the real lenders — you're borrowing their money throughout the life of the loan.

Although you won't have much contact with theses companies, it's good to know whose body is attached to the hand that feeds you. Ask your originator for an example of what your statements from the servicer will look like, and make sure you leave there with the servicer's contact information.

Looking for the right stuff

Your originator is taking on a very serious role in your life: This person can secure your financial future and guide you in making a big life decision. Knowing what to look for before settling on an originator is important because the right originator can make the whole loan process much easier and stress-free. We give you a list of tips on finding a good originator below:

✔ **Look for an originator who is a member of the National Reverse Mortgage Lenders Association (NRMLA) and HUD approved.** You should always do this, without exception. Not only do these professionals have access to every scrap of information, ongoing training, conventions, regulation updates, and a network of their peers, NRMLA members must sign the Code of Conduct as part of their application for membership. A reverse mortgage originator doesn't have to be a member of NRMLA to get you a loan, but we strongly recommend that you go with one who is. While membership isn't a guaranty of ethics, your chances of being taken advantage of by a senior swindler are lower when you work with an NRMLA originator.

✔ **Look for a licensed originator.** Once you've run down the list of originators in your area and found the name of an NRMLA member that looks good to you, call and ask if he or she is a licensed originator. Originators do not need to be licensed in all states, but it's best if you can find one who is, regardless of state requirements. They tend to have a higher standard of ethics and will have undergone substantial training. Ask to see their certification — don't be shy, they'll be glad to show it off.

When you go in to meet your originator for the first time, and all throughout the process, keep the following points in mind:

✔ You need to be able to ask questions, sometimes the same one several times, without your originator getting frustrated or losing his patience.

✔ You need someone who takes the time to explain every last detail of the loan to you until you feel comfortable.

✔ You need to be treated with respect, dignity, and consideration. Don't work with anyone who condescends to you.

✔ If you feel you're being pushed in a certain direction or that the originator isn't taking your opinion into account, find a new originator. This person is probably more interested in selling you a loan than helping to plan your financial future.

✔ Ask for a comparison chart of all the loan products available. Every originator should have this handout ready.

✔ Find out how long the originator has been doing reverse mortgages. More experienced originators may be better prepared for any little "snags" that come up along the way.

✔ Use your best judgment; only you know what's best for you.

If your originator isn't living up to these standards, find a new originator. Your money and future are too important to put in the hands of someone you aren't comfortable with.

Originating the Loan

Originating a loan has three main parts:

✔ Taking the application and completing the paperwork

✔ Securing a loan from the lender

✔ Closing the loan

If the originator seems to be "passing" you along to an assistant or processor, this is very common — don't feel cast aside right away. However, if you begin to feel that you're not receiving the attention you so greatly deserve, speak up. The originator may not even be aware that you're feeling put off. If, after that, you still aren't getting the personalized service you're entitled to, it may be time to look for another originator.

Applying for your loan

Just as you had to apply for your forward mortgage, reverse mortgages require an application, albeit less exclusive. There are 15 separate documents totaling 41 pages altogether — we're not going to attempt to list them all here, partially because many are self-explanatory (such as the Borrower Notification, in which you acknowledge that you've seen all the necessary paperwork) but in the following list, you can find a brief description of the more complicated forms that will require you to take an active role:

- ✔ **The application:** You start with the Residential Loan Application for Reverse Mortgages (form 1009). While you can easily provide some of the information collected here (address, date of birth, marital status, and things of that nature), you also need to provide your residence type (primary, secondary, or investment property), which is actually a trick question — only primary residences, a home you live in as your main address, are eligible for reverse mortgages. Your originator will need documentation of your monthly income (if any), your real estate assets (the value of your home), and social security number, which you can provide at any time during the application process. The application also asks for all liens (debts) against your property, which could include outstanding mortgages, government liens, or other financial commitments on your home. This is not the place to list your credit card debt; that comes later.

Your signature on this application doesn't mean you're indebted to a loan . . . yet. Your signature asserts that you, the potential borrower, certifies that the information on the application is true and correct and that you do indeed understand the implications of (and still want) a reverse mortgage.

Below your signature is an optional section that describes your ethnicity and gender, intended to educate the lender as to who is getting reverse mortgages, and who is possibly being discriminated against. This information is collected only for the sake of your and future borrowers' protection. You can choose not to fill it out, but your originator will do it for you after you leave, so you may as well make sure they get it right.

There's also an addendum to the application that HUD created, which is necessary for anyone getting an HECM loan (see Chapter 5 for more on this loan type). The supplement is used for Mortgage Insurance Premiums and simply gets data like your name and address (yes, again), whether or not you're a first-time homebuyer (obviously not) and what the purpose of the loan is (you'll check "refinance"). It also, oddly enough, asks if you've received information about lead paint poisoning. Can you blame them for wanting to cover their bases?

✓ **Tax and Insurance Disclosure:** Okay, technically speaking, anyone could figure out this form, but this disclosure requires you to make a big decision so you should know all you can. Essentially, it allows you to choose whether you want to pay your property taxes and hazard insurance premiums yourself, or let the lender withhold part of your check to do it for you.

If you forget to pay your property taxes or insurance, your loan may be terminated, forcing you to pay up right away. Of course, they won't yank your loan out from under you if you're late on one payment, but if you consistently miss payments, they have the right to revoke your loan. Unless your originator advises you not to have tax and insurance paid by the lender, it can't hurt to take one more thing off your to-do list. It's vital that taxes and insurance are paid, and allowing your lender to do it ensures that you won't accidentally default on them.

If you choose this route, the lenders will take out a portion of your available loan funds either ahead of time, setting aside the amount they estimate you'd pay if you stayed in the home for as long as the loan was intended, or they'll pull it out as you go if you've chosen to receive a monthly payment. The form allows you to choose to let them withhold just the money for your taxes, just the money for your insurance, both, or neither.

✓ **Reverse Mortgage Comparison (RMC):** It's the crowning moment . . . when your originator tallies up your variables and tells you how much they think you can borrow. The Reverse Mortgage Comparison (RMC) is a chart that calculates how much money you can expect to get when you sign off on your loan. It is not (repeat, not) a guarantee. The nifty part is that it shows you how your loan would break down if you chose an HECM with the monthly or annual ARM (Chapter 5), or the Home Keeper (Chapter 6). The RMC doesn't typically include the Jumbo Cash Account, but you can request that your originator factor it in. Although this form is based on guesses and assumptions only, it helps your originator give you a pretty good idea of what your money will look like when you start your loan and helps you determine whether the expenses of a reverse mortgage justify the loan.

✔ **Good Faith Estimate (GFE):** This is the last element of the loan application and is the originator's hallmark — a listing of all your fees and seemingly random costs that you can expect to pay either at closing or afterward, financed into your loan. The GFE is a great planning tool and lets you see exactly how much you're paying to get your loan, and how it breaks down. Once you see your GFE, you can decide whether you want to pay your fees up-front or finance them into your loan.

Getting ready for closing

After the originator submits your file and all the forms to an underwriting department, where everything in your file will be checked to make sure that you received all the proper disclosures and that the documentation about your age is included. The underwriter reviews the appraiser's report and checks much, much, more just to be sure everything is as it should be. If everything is complete, the underwriter will issue the approval for the originator to prepare the loan documents for closing.

When the originator orders the loan documents to be prepared, the final calculation on how much you will get in funds from the reverse mortgage is determined. That calculation is based on what the index rates are as announced by the Federal Reserve on the Monday of the week your loan documents are prepared.

To find the index rates, go to www.bankrate.com. You can find listings of all the current index rates — just be sure you know which one you're looking for. Remember, the HECM is based on the one-year U.S. Treasury securities rate, Home Keeper is based on the one-month secondary market CD, and the Cash Account is based on the six-month LIBOR.

When the lender approves your loan, the originator draws up all necessary paperwork for closing. Once the loan is closed, the checks start rolling in. This is also the time when any closing costs will be due to the originator, unless you decide to finance them as part of your loan. Almost everyone finances the costs into their loan, but if you have the financial ability to pay them in cash, you may as well (you can read more about the closing process in Chapter 11).

Most, but not all originators turn every duty after this point over to the servicing lender. However, you should still feel free to call your originator at any time if you have questions or problems with your loan. Even if they're not responsible for the problem, you can be sure they will want to help you fix it. Originators rely largely on referrals from customers just like you — they know that if you're happy, you'll tell your friends and family about it . . . and that if you're unhappy you'll tell anyone who will listen. A good originator takes your satisfaction seriously, so don't be afraid to use them to their full extent. That's what they're there for.

Going Behind the Scenes: Processors and Underwriters

Different mortgage companies work in different ways: Some introduce you to all the members of the staff, while others pretend that all the work is done by one very talented originator. The truth is, no one can do it on their own — even if you don't meet these important players, remember to thank them in your big fat check acceptance speech.

Giving processors credit

It's easy to forget that someone has to actually put together your loan documents and submit them for approval. The little elves who manage all of this are called processors, and you may or may not ever know they're there.

The processor starts by collecting all the relevant loan information from you and verifies that all of this information is true and accurate. Since they can't chop you down and count your rings, processors need proof that you're really the age you claim to be. In most arenas we try to pass ourselves off as younger than we really are, but because you get more money from a reverse mortgage as you age, people often try to appear older than their birth date would suggest. Don't bother trying to pull anything over on a processor: They know every trick in the book. Processors usually confirm your age with a birth certificate or valid driver's license, but they can also use a state-issued photo I.D., a passport, a military I.D., a permanent or temporary resident card, and a whole host of others. Some states have rules about which cards are valid, but your processor will let you know what they can accept.

Processors also need to establish proof of residency because reverse mortgages are only for your primary residence. They can get proof of residency off of that same state I.D., billing statements, government documents, or other records, depending on how strict the underwriter is. For more on residency rules, check out Chapter 3.

Some processors are responsible for ordering the home appraisal, although many originators take that task upon themselves (see Chapter 10 for more on the appraisal). They may also make sure that you have homeowner's insurance, are up-to-date on your property taxes, and get any other loan requirements out of the way before the loan leaves their desk.

Next, the processor prepares all of your loan documents and submits your whole file to the underwriter. If the underwriter comes back with certain conditions that must be met prior to you getting your loan, the processor will share that with you (sometimes via the originator) and then make sure that you've done whatever was necessary to satisfy the underwriter. If you've made arrangements to have those conditions taken care of after the loan closes, the processor makes a note of it and creates fresh loan documents for you to sign.

Deciding your future: underwriters

Strangely enough, the person who approves your loan — the underwriter — will never meet you. Although underwriters are intimately involved in your loan, know everything about you, your finances, your home, your age, and your life expectancy, they don't know you. Some originators have in-house underwriters (in the same office or company) but most rely on outside help, either from individuals or from the lender. Their main job is to make sure your loan application and all the documents are complete and accurate. It's also their job to ensure that everyone receives the information to properly structure and finalize an incomplete loan package.

Once the underwriter has approved your loan, the documents are sent back to the processor and your loan is completed. It can take anywhere from four to eight weeks to get an answer from the underwriter (although in emergencies they can usually get it done sooner) so just relax and wait. Unless you've lied about your age, live in a refrigerator box under the freeway, or refuse to comply with the appraiser's repair requirements, you should have no problem getting approved for the loan you and your originator have been expecting.

Finding an Originator

Finding an originator is actually the easiest part of the process. It's finding a good one that can be hard. You may have already received several mailers from reverse mortgage originators in your area who are trying to get your business, or gotten a call from a telemarketer offering you a free assessment. How do you find a worthy originator? There are five main sources: national associations, friends and family, community centers, the Internet, and advertisements. Each has its pros and cons, so combining these techniques can be the best way to ferret out the best of the best. We describe each of these sources in the sections that follow.

Starting with national associations

When trying to find an originator check with these associations:

- **National Reverse Mortgage Lenders Association (NRMLA):** The obvious place to start is the NRMLA. A complete list of NRMLA members can be found at its Web site, www.reversemortgage.org or by calling 866-264-4466.

- **AARP:** You can also get a list of NRMLA originators from AARP at its Web site, www.aarp.org, or call 202-434-6042.

Although their members have signed a Code of Conduct, NRMLA does not (and will not) endorse any particular originator (nor will AARP or HUD). They may give you a list of 20 people in your city, but they can't tell you who has the nicest receptionist or who gets the best reviews. Fortunately, those originators who break the Code of Conduct and are reported will most likely be removed from the list.

- **Housing and Urban Development (HUD):** Another unbiased organization that can suggest reverse mortgage originators in your area is your local HUD office. Its Web site (www.hud.gov) offers information on the reverse mortgage and how to find a HUD-approved lender.

- **American Society on Aging:** A local chapter of this organization will probably have information on well-respected reverse mortgage originators. Contact them by calling 415-974-9600.

Asking friends and family

Your originator not only depends on you for referrals, but you, too, have a chance to be on the receiving end of that axiom of the mortgage business. Do you know anyone who has gotten a reverse mortgage? Chances are good that you do, even if you weren't aware of it. Ask around, and we bet you'll be surprised at who already has one. You can also ask if your friends or family know anyone who has one. Even if you have to talk to your sister's neighbor's hairdresser's mother, it can be worth getting an assessment of one originator's work.

Once you've identified a few of your friends or family members who have received reverse mortgages (and whose opinion you trust), ask some of these important questions:

- Did you feel comfortable with her?

- Did he answer all your questions?

- Did she ever offer to come to your house instead of making you go down to the office?

- When you call him, does he return your calls promptly?

- Was the staff friendly and helpful?

- Was the originator patient with you?

- Did she encourage your family to be a part of the transaction?

- Do you feel like he explained everything in clear, easy-to-understand terms?

- Has she followed up with you since you got the reverse mortgage?

- Were you happy with the originator as a whole?

Try to get some meaty answers to these (and any other) questions: A simple "yes" or "no" won't do. Asking "how" or asking for examples can help get you more complete answers.

You can also ask your financial advisor or other professional to suggest someone, but keep in mind that they may have a "you scratch my back, I'll scratch yours" arrangement with the originator. Often, industry professionals have a "preferred" list of people to refer customers to, and although they want to send you to someone who will do a great job for you, they may also be a little biased.

Checking with community centers

If you live in an age-restricted neighborhood with a community center, near a public library, or have a general community center in your area, check the activity roster for presentations by reverse mortgage originators.

Originators often give free talks with question and answer sessions in order to introduce themselves to prospective customers and teach you more about their services. Ask your community center or library if there is any such event planned, and if not, ask them to set one up.

During the presentation, the originator will explain what a reverse mortgage is, the basic qualifications, and how you can benefit. Some will actively plug their own businesses, but many simply leave business cards and pamphlets with their contact information fanned out on a nearby table next to the complimentary punch and cookies. If you feel a certain affinity for this person as an originator, go up and say hello afterward, or set up an appointment right then and there.

Community Center and library presentations are a great way to get to know an originator and get a feel for his or her demeanor and level of expertise. You may also feel more free to ask questions such as "How long have you been doing reverse mortgages" if you're not sitting face-to-face in a private office, but rather as one of many faces in an activity room. In the event that you don't like the presenter, or feel that he or she may not be the right originator for you, at least you'll get free punch and cookies out of it.

Surfing for originators

Not everyone is Internet savvy. Some seniors have never even sat in front of a computer up to this point in their lives. But the Internet is a terrific resource for finding reverse mortgage originators. If you don't own a computer but feel okay about operating one, you can use those at your local library, or ask a friend; if you think a computer mouse must be some kind of little robotic rodent, call your grandchildren or other family computer experts and ask them to sit down with you at their computer to get you started.

The easiest way to search for a reverse mortgage originator online is to go to a search engine like www.google.com (a Web site that works like a virtual Dewey decimal system of everything on the Internet). In the box that says "Search" you'll type in specific key words; try "reverse mortgage" in quotes, followed by a space and then your city. For example, if you live in Dallas, you'll type in:

```
"reverse mortgage" Dallas
```

If that gives you too many results, try to narrow it down by typing in:

```
"reverse mortgage" originator, Dallas
```
You can also try:

```
"reverse mortgage" lender, Dallas
```

The search engine will bring up lists of all the Web sites out there that have anything to do with reverse mortgages in Dallas. You may have to wade through them to determine which ones are actually useful (this is where a friend or family member who knows about searching online can really come in handy).

You can also use the Internet to find out more about the originators on your list from NRMLA or AARP. If there's a Web site listed by their names, you can often read about the people, their businesses, and their mission statements on their sites. In cases where a Web site isn't listed, you can search for that person the same way you did above. For example, if you wanted to get the scoop on John Lucas in Van Nuys, California, you'd type in:

```
"John Lucas" "reverse mortgage" "Van Nuys"
```

Find out as much as you can about any particular originator before going in to meet them in person — you'll feel more comfortable talking with someone you feel like you already know.

Paying attention to advertisements

You know all that junk mail you get every day and instantly throw away or even shred? You know those radio commercials that you ignore or change the station to avoid? Start paying attention.

Originators are smart marketers. They have access to public records that tell them the demographic information in any given neighborhood; they know where seniors frequent; and they know which radio stations and television shows you tune into. It can be a little unnerving when you think about it, but it's just part of their job: finding their target audience and advertising profusely.

Now that you've got your mind on reverse mortgages, keep your eyes and ears out for originators advertising their services. Listen for phrases like "retire on the house" or key words such as "seniors" and "home equity." Look for ads that feature seniors prominently.

You can also tell a lot about the originator by the style of their advertisement. Is it something they just threw together like a black and white photocopy? Or a nice full-color glossy flier? Is there a photo of the originator in the ad? Do the words they've used seem overly aggressive? While you can't always judge a book by its cover, you can get a pretty good idea of the kind of person you'll be dealing with by their ad. Use clues like these to choose an originator that seems right for you.

Once you've narrowed it down to two or three candidates, give them each a call (don't just drop in, since they may be busy with other appointments). Try to get a feeling for their demeanor and expertise. You need an originator who treats you with respect and kindness from the very first phone call. Then, if your instincts tell you to go ahead, make an appointment to meet and discuss your options.

Avoiding Predatory Lending

The reverse mortgage has been called the "antidote to predatory lending." Unfortunately, there are still some individuals who try to take advantage of borrowers — especially seniors. These people are called "predatory lenders" because they target certain groups (most often seniors, low-income families, and minorities) and exploit them for profit.

Outsmarting a predatory lender

We can't let a few bad apples spoil the whole barrel, but here are a few key points to be aware of when shopping for a reverse mortgage originator:

- ✔ Don't go through an "estate planning" service. They will charge you fees just to find you an originator, which is something you can do for free.

- ✔ Don't use anyone, for that matter, who offers to find you an originator for a fee.

- ✔ Don't pay anyone to give you information about reverse mortgages. Your originator and counselor will do that for free.

- ✔ Don't sign anything that requires you to pay a fee *before* you've closed your loan.

- ✔ Don't sign any document that has blanks that will be filled in later.

- ✔ Don't let anyone pressure you into working with them. Be wary of people who tell you they're your only chance at getting a loan.

- ✔ Don't get a loan without a Good Faith Estimate from your originator. This document should be a very close guess as to what you will owe upon closing, and you don't want any surprises.

- ✔ Don't be afraid to ask questions if you're suspicious of a charge. Know what your fees should be and look carefully at your statement.

Staying protected with RESPA

"RESPA . . ." it sounds like a fancy perfume or new kind of sports car. Actually, RESPA stand for the Real Estate Settlement Procedures Act, which is enforced by the department of Housing and Urban Development (HUD). RESPA is an enforceable law, and violators can face warnings, fines, or even jail time for especially heinous or repeat offences. Its main purposes are to protect home-owners and keep everything clean and fair in the real estate world. For the most part, RESPA has two areas that could apply to you:

- ✔ RESPA requires that originators give you estimates and disclo-sures of all costs associated with the loan, such as their own fees and closing costs. They also have to tell you if they are associated in any way with anyone they have referred you to (like a contractor).

- ✔ RESPA prohibits originators from giving you or anyone else involved in your loan a "kickback" or other "thing of value" in exchange for referrals.

Reverse mortgage originators are very rarely guilty of these prac-tices, since their HUD and NRMLA approval hinges on compliance with rules and regulations just like these. If you do come across an originator who tries to get you to sign off on a loan without telling you what you should expect to pay, or who offers you anything (even something small like coffee gift cards) as a reward for telling others about him, a red flag should go up in your mind, and you should call NRMLA, AARP, or your counselor to find out if their actions are legal.

To find out more about predatory lending and RESPA, visit the HUD Web site at www.hud.gov.

Knowing Your Role

Did you think you wouldn't have a job, too? This is your loan and you need to hold up your end of the proceedings as well. Don't worry, your part is actually quite simple.

Asking questions

From the very moment you decide on an originator, start carrying around a little notepad and a pen. Write down every question about reverse mortgages that pops into your head — even the tiny ones. If you tell someone that you're getting a reverse mortgage and they ask you a question about it that you can't answer, write it down. If your family has questions, have them write down their questions, too. If you're confused about any detail of your personal loan at all, write it down.

When you meet with your originator, run down the list with her. If you still have unanswered questions, don't be afraid to keep on asking. Many of us will pretend to understand something even though the concept is still just beyond our grasp because we feel embarrassed or shy. This is one time when asking questions makes you look smarter. Get involved in your loan and show your originator that you want to learn as much about this transaction as they can teach you.

Following up

Here's another place where you really get involved in the loan: If your originator asks you to bring in some kind of documentation or other paperwork (like proof of residency) you need to follow up and do it. Your originator may make an appointment for the appraiser who will need to come to your house for a visit before your loan closes, and you need to remember to be home to answer any questions they may have about your house. You also need to take charge of your destiny and make your wants and wishes known. Originators aren't mind readers, so let your opinion be heard.

Getting help

If any part of the loan process starts to seem overwhelming, confusing, scary, or just a little too frazzling, get help. Ask your adult children, grandchildren, nieces, nephews, friends, or professionals (like attorneys or financial planners) for their assistance. You can ask someone to stay with you while the appraiser is there or drive you to the originator's office (although your originator may be willing to come to you). You can also call on your reverse mortgage counselor to ask for additional advice.

We all get a little frightened when faced with the idea of signing papers with fine print, especially when it involves large sums of money and your home. Having a support system in place helps you get through it all with nary a hitch. Letting your friends and family help you is also a good way to initiate them into the reverse mortgage process and educate them as to what their individual roles may be later on in the loan.

Chapter 10

Going Forward with Step Three: Getting Appraised

*Y*ou may have some idea of your home's value . . . to yourself. You may love your home so much that you think it must be worth $600,000 even though other homes exactly like it are selling for $285,000 down the street. Of course *they* don't have your stunning hand-painted wallpaper, which surely brings the price up a few notches. Then there's the tree that your kids planted when they were small, which is worth more to you in sentimental dollars than anyone could imagine. And your kitchen is so well cared for it hasn't needed to be updated since 1972; that must count for something, right?

You may or may not be surprised to find out that not everyone has the same view of your beloved home. We're sure it's lovely, but it takes a professional to determine exactly what the fair market price would be if you were to sell it. That professional is the appraiser, whose job is crucial to the reverse mortgage process. One of the biggest determining factors in your reverse mortgage is your appraisal. Although you may find it amazing that such a huge aspect of the reverse mortgage process is based on the opinion of a stranger, you should understand how important it is to have an unbiased set of eyes appraising your home. In this chapter you get to know the appraiser's duties and see how an appraiser determines the value of your home.

Meeting Your Appraiser

When an appraiser visits your house, the whole idea is to come up with a *market value* for the home. Market value is the closest indication of what your home would sell for in a competitive market, based on how much similar homes are selling for in your area and what sort of condition your house is in. Essentially, if you put your home up for sale today, the market value is an estimate of what you could probably expect to get for it.

The role of the reverse mortgage appraisal is to help the lender, who isn't anywhere near your home, decide how much your home is worth so that they can figure out how much to lend you. All of this takes place long before you actually sign off on the loan. All you'll have done so far is visited the counselor and filled out the application with your originator — you're not locked in, and you can still change your mind about getting the loan.

Securing an appraiser

In Chapter 9 we show you how important it is to choose the right originator — it takes time, effort, asking lots of questions, and finding someone you really trust. But finding an appraiser is nothing like that — it's just the opposite. In fact, you won't need to find an appraiser at all. When you decide to start the application process for a reverse mortgage, your originator contacts the appraiser for you. The appraiser or originator then contacts you to set up the appointment based on both of your schedules.

Appraisers are busy folks and often only have specific windows of time available. They need to get a feeling for your schedule, but flexibility is important. Try to be as accommodating with your time as possible when you make the appointment, and be sure to schedule it with enough time before you plan to close your loan. You can't expect them to arrive the next day — appointments are usually made for three to seven days in advance. Once the appointment is set, all you have to do is be sure that you're home.

Technically, you aren't required to be at the appraisal, but we highly recommend it. You need to be around to produce permits and repair or construction records, answer questions about the home, and explain any oddities. This is not, however, your chance to follow the appraiser around showing off every little detail about your home. If the appraiser needs you, the appraiser will come get you.

Of course, the appraiser isn't just some schlub off the street. Every state requires that appraisers be licensed or certified by the Office of Real Estate Appraisers in order to appraise homes for federally regulated loans. Licensing and certification boards hold their members to a code of ethics, and they are required to meet very strict standards. Since the vast majority of reverse mortgages are regulated through the Federal Housing Administration (it has the word "federal" right in its name), you can rest assured that you'll have a competent evaluator.

Most originators have a trusted collection of appraisers that they use on a regular basis. These originators know that these professionals will give an honest and fair assessment of your home and will be pleasant to work with. If the originators get complaints about appraisers, the appraisers are usually off the list — after all, originators stake their reputations on the associates they pair with you. To be fair, however, appraisers don't have to be your friend. They are simply there to do an evaluation of your property. Still, it's better to have a nice stranger traipsing through your home and peeking behind your oven than a grumpy one. If the appraiser has your originator's seal of approval, you can bet you're in good hands.

Understanding your role

It's the appraiser's job to be completely impartial and objective when he or she goes through your home. And because most appraisers realize they're an intrusion in your home, they make an effort to be affable, wipe their feet on the way in, and show patience if you want to ask questions (just don't go overboard). Appraisers only ask two things of you:

- ✔ **Leave them alone.** It's very distracting to have someone, even a nice and helpful someone like you, talking to them about your new tile flooring and offering to hold one end of the measuring tape. Let the appraiser do his or her job, and he or she will be less inclined to rush the evaluation and can spend more time taking note of your beautiful home.

- ✔ **Be available if they need you.** Appraisers will always have questions for you: when was this kitchen redone? Have you ever noticed this leak? When was your last exterior paint job? Who built this patio cover? Get ready for questions like these, but let your appraiser ask before you give him or her extra information.

Preparing for the Visit

You know how your friends claim that they don't mind if you clean up before they come over? Well the appraiser does mind. You don't need to hire professional cleaners, but if you've been letting a few chores go unattended for a while, you'll want to take care of them. The pride of ownership that is apparent by the tidiness of your home will probably translate to how well your property has been maintained. The nicer your home looks, the more impressed the appraiser will be. Before your appraiser comes, run down this easy spruce-up checklist to make a good impression:

- **Tidy up around the house.** Take a weekend to get organized. Put away your seasonal items that aren't in use, make some sense of your junk room, and try to keep things neat. It's a lot easier for the appraiser to get a good idea of your home's value if they don't have to wade through 13 years of old newspapers.

- **Clean the exterior.** Hire a neighbor kid to come clean your rain gutters for a few bucks, trim up the hedges, and clear out anything that makes your yard look like a garage sale. This is what they call "curb appeal," and it can make a big difference in market price.

- **Replace the broken stuff . . .** but only if you can afford it. Some people aren't in a position to start fixing things (that's why they need a reverse mortgage), but if you can, it may increase your lending limit. Think of it as an investment.

- **Give your home the once-over.** Try to go around your house with the eye of an appraiser. If you can attend to a problem right now then by all means, do it. Get your plumber nephew to fix your running toilet, ask your daughter-in-law to help you clear a path to the attic — you want your home to be just a few degrees shy of the way you'd want it to look if you were going to try to sell it.

At the same time, there are definitely things that you don't need to worry about. Major renovations that are for aesthetic purposes will never reap the full value of your investment. If you spend $50,000 to upgrade your bathroom, there's no guarantee that your home will be worth $50,000 more when the appraiser comes a-knockin'. Unless you plan to install $100 bills as your wallpaper, an appraiser can only judge the improvements subjectively — despite your receipts, what a brand new bathroom is really worth is all up to perception. Since your appraisal value is based on recent market values in your area and the safe-and-soundness of your home, a big upgrade is quite a gamble if housing prices in your neighborhood won't support it. Three major renovations that they suggest you only do if it's for your own pleasure (and not to increase your home value) are:

- ✔ **Tear out your kitchen or bathroom just to increase your home's value.** If you want to do it for your own enjoyment, that's great, but it won't return an equal dollar amount on your investment.

- ✔ **Put in a pool or spa, unless you think you'll get your money's worth strictly from your own use.** Pools are nice, but the cost and hassle aren't worth it if your only goal is to amp up your value.

- ✔ **Build a new patio or deck, unless you love to sit outside, since you'll only get a fraction back of what you spend to erect it.** Anyone can build an outdoor area, and it won't add enough to your home value to make it worth your while.

There are some areas where, if you can afford to do it, investing in your home now can help increase the appraised value of your home. For instance, a house can be lovely and charming on the outside, but inside it can be wall-to-wall avocado-colored shag carpeting (you know who you are). If the appliances in the kitchen are 30 years old, that brings your value down, too. In the 1960s, matching upholstery and wallpaper were the height of home décor; now it just makes a house look dated. Remember, there's a difference between outdated and vintage.

Retro style

How do you know if the features that you've loved since your home was built 50 years ago are fashionable and desirable or just plain old? One easy way to see how hip your house rates is to check out the home décor and antique magazines on your newsstand. No one's home really looks like those glossy pages, but you can get a good idea of the style that's popular today. Home decorating shows on television can also help you assess what's "hot" and what's not. If you haven't redecorated in over 10 years, there's a good chance your décor could use some freshening up. The biggest point to remember is: You only need to worry about things that won't leave the house if you moved out. Will you be taking your furniture? Of course. Your carpet? No way.

At the same time, there are certain elements that are definitely desirable, and considered "vintage." That translates roughly into "something old that we'll pay a lot for." Some good things to keep as long as they are in excellent condition may be:

* An oven from the 1940s

* Original ceramic or porcelain tiles in your kitchen or bath

(continued)

(continued)

* Original crown molding

* Claw-foot or cast-iron bathtubs

* Pedestal sinks in the bathroom

* Built-in features in the dining room (like display shelves or a sideboard)

* A laundry chute

* Hardwood floors

* A unique fireplace mantel

* Elegant lighting fixtures

Getting Your Home Evaluated

The appraiser projects the value of your home in three main ways:

✔ Is your property safe?

✔ Is your property in good condition?

✔ How does it compare to others in your neighborhood?

The appraiser attempts to answer those questions by investigating the visible components of your home and property, by taking photos, and by reviewing the home's records. Try not to take any of the appraisal personally; it's not a judgment of you, just the home.

The appraiser takes note of things that the lender needs to know to make sure it's not investing its money in a dud of a house. First the appraiser measures all around the home and creates a pretty accurate floor plan. Square footage is noted, as well as what type of garage, windows, foundation, flooring, appliances, and air conditioning you have. The appraiser also jots down what condition each of these elements is in and whether or not they will need to be repaired or replaced. If your water supply comes from a well or other private source, the appraiser will put in an order to test the water, and trust us, he or she will let you know if that needs fixing, too.

The appraiser also checks your site and property condition. The appraiser typically considers whether you get a lot of noise from the street or live near a highway; whether there any sink holes on your property; whether you're near anything that may suddenly explode, like a gas tank; and whether your home is located close enough to a high-voltage tower that if it fell over it would squish your house.

Of course, the appraiser checks for things such as termite damage, inaccessible roads, cracked floor supports, unventilated attics, leaking roofs, poor plumbing and several other considerations, none of which will automatically disqualify you from getting a reverse mortgage — but they may lower your property value.

Taking snapshots

One of the most effective ways for the appraiser to evaluate your home is by taking pictures all over the place. This serves three main purposes:

✔ **It jogs the memory.** Your appraiser may hit four or more houses every day. That's a lot of properties to keep straight. Photos help the appraiser keep track of what was seen and also helps the appraiser look in greater detail and take more time examining a photo than he or she may have at your home.

✔ **It protects the appraiser, and it protects you.** Call it evidence, call it good measure — the point is, photos offer proof of the condition of your home. If the appraiser comes back with an estimated value for your home that you feel is incredibly low, they can whip out their photos and show you exactly why they made the assessment that they did. This can also work to your advantage if they cite "severe foundation damage" but the photos reveal only a tiny sliver of a crack. In that case, you may be able to get a new appraisal.

✔ **It helps the lender understand the valuation.** When your lender (the organization lending you money) sees your appraiser's report, it has to take the appraiser's word that your home is worth what the appraiser has established. The photos of comparable properties will also show you and the lender that the appraiser was indeed comparing your home to homes similar to yours.

All appraisers take photos of the front and back of the home, the sides, the view from the street, and the "street scene," or what you may see if you were to stand in the driveway and look around. But here's the weird part: They also take pictures of similar homes in your area. This is for comparison's sake. You may hear them refer to this other house as a *comp* or *comparable*. Getting photos of your neighbors' homes helps the appraiser get a better idea of what a house in your area *should* look like. Appraisal isn't an exact science, so it helps to have as many variables as possible.

Checking safety

One of the most important aspects of the appraisal — if not the most important — is whether your home is safe for you to live in. The appraiser can see what condition your home is in, and determine whether it's livable, fixable, sellable, or just plain demolishable. Of course, the appraiser's first concern is your safety. If there are too many necessary repairs that must be completed in order to meet FHA standards, you may not be able to get a loan.

Nearly every "yes" or "no" box that they check off on the appraisal forms dictates how safe your house is. This is partly for resale purposes (let's be real here) but it's mostly to ensure that the home you're staying in is fit for living. If your toilet doesn't work, that's a problem. If your heater doesn't work and you live in Maine, that's a problem. If a broken window is letting birds into your attic, that's a problem. Luckily, problems like these all have simple solutions. Just fix them. Not so simple problems may be more in the sinking foundation range, where the cost to repair the issue isn't worth the value of the home. If the costs to make your home safe are more than 15 percent of your home's estimated value, you're probably better off moving. In fact, Fannie Mae rules (see Chapter 6 for more on Fannie Mae loans) state that any home with more than 15 percent repairs is ineligible for a reverse mortgage. On a $300,000 home, that's $45,000 worth of restoration — unless you need a whole new roof or would have to gut your kitchen and start over, you probably won't need such extensive repairs.

Checking out the safety controversy

We recently read an article written by a professor of geology that stated that reverse mortgages are dangerous to seniors because they force our nation's "most vulnerable residents" to live in unsafe housing. The author's reasoning is that seniors often live in older houses, ergo their homes are unfit for human habitation. It follows logically, argues this professor, people who get reverse mortgages stay in their treasured, yet dilapidated homes because they are too weak and afraid to have necessary repairs made.

Now, if that doesn't offend you maybe this will: He also argues that the best thing is for these frail seniors to move to assisted living or other senior developments and sell their homes to younger people so that they can make the necessary improvements, thereby revitalizing the community. You didn't know you were such a hazard to the neighborhood, did you?

This is actually a very common misconception, but a misconception nonetheless. Not only do all reverse mortgages require a detailed and accurate appraisal, but anything that comes back questionable *must* be repaired or tested and reexamined. No ifs, ands, or buts about it. In fact, if the lender asks you to make the repairs and you can't afford it at the time, they'll set aside some money from your reverse mortgage to make darn sure you have the funds you'll need to make your home safe. If that's the case, you'll be required to sign a repair addendum, in which you solemnly swear to make the repairs within a certain timeframe.

Our aim is not to sell you on reverse mortgages, but rather to give you all the facts you need to make an informed decision for your own future. If someone tries to convince you that you should move over and let the younger people take over for the sake of your own safety, we want you to be able to educate them, too.

Keeping up with the Joneses

Your home is compared to others in your neighborhood to see how your house stacks up. This neighbor's house is, for obvious reasons, called a *comparable*. Comparables are used in real estate all the time, both for loan appraisals and purchase appraisals. The appraiser looks at about three additional properties and does a sales comparison analysis for each. If your property has an anomaly on it, like a barn or a pool in a neighborhood without many pools, they have to make sure to get a comp house with similar features.

You've heard the phrase "there goes the neighborhood." You may have even said it yourself once. The kind of house and property your neighbors have reflects directly on the value of your home. Whether it's upgrades or noisy teenagers, living conditions of those around you will impact your home's ability to be appraised at a fair market value.

You probably already have a good idea of how your home compares to others on your street. Is yours the only one with two stories? Does everyone have a two-car garage but you? Is your yard particularly well landscaped? These things make a difference. Unfortunately, they're largely out of your control. It's hard to keep up with the Joneses, especially if you get caught peeking through their windows to see how many fireplaces they have as compared to you. Don't stress over your appraisal — just do your best to make the property represent your love of your home and you'll be fine.

Chapter 11

Sealing the Deal with Step Four: Closing

In This Chapter

▶ Finalizing your loan

▶ Deciding whether to change your mind

▶ Getting paid

▶ Following up

*W*hew! It may take a lot of time, meetings, and decision-making to get to this point, but you can get here — closing your loan. This is a big process from the originator and other staff's standpoint, but for you it's a piece of cake. Just like your last forward mortgage, a reverse mortgage wraps up, signaling the beginning of payments . . . except this time you're the one getting the checks. Unlike your last mortgage, you don't need to dread going to the mailbox to find your mortgage bill. Now you can run down to meet the mail carrier at the curb — arms outstretched — to get your money, or delight in the magic of direct deposits. But before any of that can happen, use this chapter to check out the things you and your originator need to finalize first.

Making Your Loan Final

Your loan process, from meeting your counselor (see Chapter 8) to closing the deal, can take anywhere from two weeks to several months, depending on how determined you are to get a reverse mortgage. By the time you're ready to talk about closing, you may be anxious to get this whole ordeal over with — even if everything has gone smoothly, it's nice to have mortgages off your mind. The loan closing will definitely be an exciting day for you, just as it was when you bought your home. After all, this will be the day you get yourself one step closer to financial security.

Getting an overview of closing

At closing, your originator meets with you for one last meeting to go over your closing costs, Total Annual Loan Cost (TALC), and any last-minute details. This is also your originator's last chance to impress you enough to make you refer a friend, so get the most out of your time together. Make your originator earn the referrals — here are some ideas how:

- ✔ Find out about other senior resources.
- ✔ Ask for the name of a good contractor for your remodel.
- ✔ See if your originator knows of any deals you can get for future financial services.
- ✔ Use this opportunity to ask questions and settle every little lingering concern.

In addition to you and the originator, there will also be a few extra people present at your closing: there will most likely be additional staff from the originator's office (an assistant or junior originator, for instance), and the escrow or title company's agent.

Don't be alarmed by the words "title" or "escrow." The title company simply handles the recording of your mortgage in the county records, and the escrow agent covers any legal documentation. You should know by now that when you get a reverse mortgage you keep the title on your home. Even so, like any mortgage, the reverse mortgage is recorded as a lien against your property. This exact same thing occurred when you took out a mortgage on your home last time.

Your appointment may take at least an hour, but most of that time is spent going over things you already know: which loan you chose, how you'll receive your payments, and what your responsibilities are as a homeowner.

After the initial pleasantries and congratulations, you and your originator can get down to business, which includes determining your actual loan cost, getting your signature on lots of documents, and (the best part) getting your payments ready. You can happily sit back and start dreaming of all the wonderful things you can do with your new-found money.

Finding out more about repair addendums

During closing, the originator wants to ensure that anything that could hamper your loan process has been taken care of. Were you supposed to get your plumbing fixed or other repairs completed? Was there an unsafe tree in your yard that needed to be felled? Make sure you've settled all of this before the closing.

If you've made arrangements to make repairs or other changes *after* your loan has been signed and sealed, one of the documents you have to sign at closing is the repair addendum. Review this carefully to make sure you understand the details of the agreement. If the lender requires you to make a repair by a certain date and you choose not to do it, your lender has the right to terminate your loan. Don't ignore these conditions.

Of course, anyone who owns a home knows that there are thousands of little things that can go wrong. So repair addendums are common, especially in older homes that may not have had any improvements or updates in the past few years. Your appraiser will note anything that needs to be repaired on the appraisal forms and hands these recommendations over to the originator. He or she includes all this with your application for a reverse mortgage, and the lender reviews it to see if there are repairs that must be completed in order for the loan to be processed, or if your home simply needs too many repairs and is ineligible for the loan.

The repair addendum simply forces you to stop putting off those home improvements and to make your house a safer place to live. If any of the required repairs are considered to be either "health and safety" items or structural in nature, they may be required to be completed prior to closing. Your originator can advise you whether it's likely you'll have immediate repairs, or whether you can expect to receive a repair addendum from the lender after you get your appraiser's report.

Examples of some frequent causes for repair addendums include:

- ✔ A leaky roof
- ✔ Termite infestation
- ✔ Poor plumbing or roots growing into your pipes
- ✔ A damaged foundation
- ✔ Unsafe structures (maybe a staircase that's on its last breath, or a homemade gazebo)

✔ Mold problems (not just the stuff in your bathroom grout)

✔ Hazardous appliances

✔ Bad wiring

✔ Excessive brush (in wildfire areas)

Finalizing calculations

The originator can't make the final calculations until two things happen:

✔ The lender formally approves the loan.

✔ The originator orders the closing documents to be prepared.

Unfortunately, you don't have any control over either of these things. On the upside, these events usually happen fairly quickly once the loan starts rolling along — your originator wants you to get your money almost as much as you want to see it sitting safely in your bank.

The interest rate is set based on the week that your closing documents are prepared. Then the originator plugs all your information (age, home value, and interest rate) into a program and presto — your loan amount is finally totaled!

At closing you get your Total Annual Loan Cost (TALC), or the true cost of the loan over time. Note that the *cost* of the loan is different than the *value* of the loan. Cost refers to what you will pay to take out the loan (the principal loan amount, plus interest, fees, and other costs) while value refers only to the principal amount. The TALC's aim is to give you an idea of what this loan will cost you. (See Chapter 4 for more on this topic.)

The TALC isn't always as straightforward as it seems. No one knows how long you'll really stay in your house, or what will happen to your home's value, so even this "true" TALC is another guess by your originator. For more information about the TALC, see Chapter 4. You can also find out more on TALC by visiting www.aarp.org/revmort.

Up until closing, the total amount you can expect to borrow is really only an estimate, based on your age, home value, and interest rates. Which of these factors do you think could affect your loan amount by fluctuating in the span of a few weeks? Not your age, because everyone knows how old you'll be, and not your home value, because an appraiser has already signed off on exactly how much your home is worth. Your interest rate, however, changes every week.

Unlike a forward mortgage, you can't lock in a rate when you start talking about your loan. Many forward mortgage originators use rate locks as marketing tactics, and incentives for people to hurry, locking their rates in right that second. Then all the borrowers have to do is sign off on the loan within a certain timeframe. Reverse mortgage originators don't have that luxury. Instead, the lender and originator use the current rate in effect at the time you make your initial loan application to give you an estimate of the amount of funds you may receive at closing. That rate is called the *expected rate*.

To get the expected rate, your originator simply takes the latest index for your loan product and adds a margin to it (see Chapters 5, 6, and 7 for more specifics on how your reverse mortgage's interest rate specifically calculated). We give you some examples for each loan product here:

✔ If this week's index for an **HECM** is 4.04, the originator would add a margin of 1.5 to that index for a monthly adjusted loan, for a total expected rate of 5.54 percent.

✔ If this week's index for the **Home Keeper** is 2.20, the originator would add a margin of 3.40 for a total of 5.60 percent.

✔ If this week's index for the **Jumbo Cash Account** is 2.60 and the originator adds a margin of 5.00, your total expected rate would be 7.60 percent.

Interest rates and loan amounts are inverse proportions: the higher the expected rate, the lower your estimated amount borrowed and vice versa. You may have your loan amount estimated at $75,000 with a 6.72 percent expected rate, but by the time your loan is actually ready to close, rates are down to 5.03 percent, which may bring your available loan amount up to $80,000. It can also work in the opposite direction, which can be more than a little disappointing.

Gambling on your rate

Expected rates are pretty close to the actual rate that will determine your loan amount, but only if you act in a timely manner. Let's say you go talk to your counselor, get all fired up about your prospective mortgage, and see your originator the next week. After talking about your options and figuring out an estimated loan amount, based on the three magic factors (age, home value, and expected rate), your

(continued)

(continued)

originator gives you that total to build your dreams on. If you decide to move forward with the loan within in next few weeks, there's a good chance that the actual amount you can borrow will be similar to the estimated total, because rates will probably not have shifted too much in that timeframe. However, if you aren't quite sure about the loan, or you've started to feel scared that the loan is too big of a step, every week that you put it off is another week that the rates can change. Never rush into a loan, but try to stay realistic about your concerns as well. Your concerns that make you wait a few months before going forward with your loan could mean you get a lot less (or maybe a lot more) money than you had hoped.

Executing the loan: Your signature

Painful as the loan process can sometimes be, executing a loan does not involve a firing squad. *Execution* simply refers to your signature. Warm up your wrist and bring your lucky pen, because you have to sign and initial pages and pages of documents. Even so, the execution process is actually very straightforward.

By the time you're ready to close, your originator has already gone over all of the documents with you, explaining the fine print, helping you wade through all the technical jargon, and giving you ample time to have a family member or professional look them over, if you wish. You should find no surprises when you signing your closing documents.

If something looks foreign or you've forgotten what something means, just ask. You need to fully understand what you're autographing.

Some documents must be signed in the presence of a notary public. Your originator should provide a notary public for you (often it will be the escrow or title agent) to make this as hassle-free as possible. If a document needs a notary verification, don't sign it by yourself — notaries are there to verify that your signature came from your hand. If the document is executed without a notary present, your originator has to throw out that form and start all over. This is solely for your protection: If a fraudulent person (or even a well-meaning family member) has gotten away with posing as you up to now, this is where that person is stopped.

After your originator sets up a particular time and day for your loan closing, make sure you show up on time. Besides having gathered all the necessary people to close your loan at precise moment, it causes problems for the originator if you skip your own closing because closing documents are prepared and dated for a certain day. You must sign the documents on that day, or they need to be redrawn (prepared again).

Changing Your Mind: Your Right of Rescission

You've signed the documents. You get home. You feel like you've just made a terrible mistake. Now what? All reverse mortgage products have a three-day *right of rescission,* which means that within the first three days after signing your loan, you're allowed to change your mind and cancel the whole thing.

The right of rescission is designed to protect you in case something changes in your household, you feel you've been bamboozled, or you just plain aren't comfortable with the mortgage. It shouldn't be taken lightly, however. You, your counselor, and your originator put in a lot of hours choosing just the right loan for you: This isn't the sort of thing to throw away willy-nilly.

Knowing when to rescind

Life can change in a heartbeat — there are over 300,000 heartbeats in three days, which leaves a lot of room for change. Unfortunately (or fortunately, depending on how you look at it), the chances that things will change drastically in the three days after you sign your documents are slim — rescissions are pretty rare. But life happens, and that's why you get this time to call a "do over."

If you must rescind due to leaving your home, you may be able to start the loan process over with a Home Keeper for Purchase (see Chapter 7), which would enable you to move out and buy a new home. Remember, don't take the three-day rescission lightly. Some situations that constitute a good reason to rescind your loan include the following:

- ✔ Your home is damaged or altered making it in some way unsuitable for you to live in.

- ✔ You suddenly become seriously ill and may not realistically live long enough to make your loan worthwhile.

- ✔ Your children or grandchildren need to come live with you, forcing you to move into a larger home.

- ✔ You unexpectedly inherit a large sum of money and choose to hold off on the loan until you're a bit older.

✔ You or your spouse needs immediate care that cannot be tended to in your home (in other words, you need to move into assisted living).

✔ Your home inexplicably shoots up in value and you want to switch to a jumbo loan (see Chapter 7).

✔ Your home inexplicably declines in value and you want to switch to a Home Equity Conversion Mortgage (HECM; see Chapter 5).

✔ Your family invites you to move in with them (which you've secretly been hoping for all along).

✔ You decide you'd rather sell the house and relocate.

Essentially, you should only cancel your loan if, for whatever reason, you could no longer live in your home, or project that you need to leave it very soon. Again, the chances of this information coming to you in the three days following your closing are very slight, but the right is there, just in case.

Understanding when not to rescind

You've embarked on a significant financial responsibility, just when you thought you were free and clear. Now you're having second thoughts. Don't call up your originator and rescind your loan. Who hasn't had buyer's remorse? It feels great to get a new outfit or fishing lure or furniture, but when the euphoria of the purchase wears off you start to wonder whether you can afford it. If nothing has changed and you've been working with a competent originator and counselor who have assessed your financial situation, then the answer is yes, you can afford it.

Some people are chronic "returners," taking back half of what they buy. But this is a serious endeavor, and "taking it back" isn't just a matter of bringing in your receipt. Don't exercise your three-day right of rescission if:

✔ You're just nervous. Don't worry, this loan was tailored to you.

✔ Your family is uneducated about reverse mortgages and wants you to cancel the loan.

✔ You giggle every time you say "Fannie."

✔ You or another borrower becomes moderately ill — remember, reverse mortgages can help pay for medical expenses.

✔ You find that you need day-to-day help — instead of rescinding the loan to go into assisted living, consider hiring in-home care.

✔ Someone offers you the same loan at a lower interest rate (even if they could, who knows what the rates would be by the time your loan closed?).

✔ You think you will get another reverse mortgage within the next year.

If you start to have doubts, talk to your family, call your originator, and contact your counselor. These individuals can help you determine whether or not your situation warrants a rescission. The decision is ultimately up to you — no one can force you to keep the loan within that three days — but weigh your options carefully. And remember, you don't get paid until the three days are up, so you can't buy a golf cart the same day your loan closes and then change your mind about the loan.

Starting Off Your New Loan

The three days are over (see the section earlier in this chapter "Changing Your Mind: Your Right of Recession,"), you've signed a pile of documents — now's your chance to sit back and enjoy your new cash flow . . . almost. We let you know, in this section, about some things that need to be taken care of before you officially begin taking full advantage of your loan.

Paying off debts

When your loan was created, you probably "financed" a lot of items with it: your closing costs, origination fees, servicing fees, mortgage insurance premium (if you chose a HECM; see Chapter 5), future repairs, your current mortgage balance (if your home wasn't paid off), and other outstanding debts. Some of these are spread out throughout your loan, but others, like compensating contractors who are working on your house and paying off your previous mortgage balance, need to be paid right away.

We list some items below that need to be paid before you can begin enjoying your loan:

✔ **The appraisal fee:** The appraiser is one piece of the puzzle that can't wait to be paid. Although some allow the fee to be incorporated in the closing cost financing, most want their money, and they want it now. Although that payment (usually about $350) is collected at the time of your loan application, it can be returned to you at closing by having it financed with the other closing costs.

✔ **Home repair costs:** For home repairs (especially those required by an appraiser/inspector), a lump sum from your total loan amount is set aside to pay for these services. You'd think they could trust you to pay for your own repairs, but too many lenders have seen borrowers promise to have work done and then spend all their money and claim they can't afford to hire workers. Other times, people just put it off until the last possible second. By withholding a portion of your loan, the lenders ensure that you have the funds available to get the work done — and you also have an incentive to get the work done because you can't touch that earmarked money.

✔ **Mortgage debt:** Any outstanding mortgage incurred before you ever heard of reverse mortgages will also need to be repaid before you can start receiving your checks. All of this will have been figured into your total available funds, so it shouldn't come as a surprise to you. For example, if your available loan totals $140,000 and you still owe $20,000 on your home, your total available funds reduce to $120,000.

Getting your first check

If you've given up your right of rescission (see the section "Changing Your Mind: Your Right of Rescission," earlier in this chapter) and paid off any outstanding debts (see the previous section, "Paying off your debts".), you're ready for your first check. How you get it depends on how you chose to receive your payments (see Chapters 5, 6, and 7 for more on payment options for each specific loan type). You should have already discussed the payment method prior to the loan closing, both with your counselor and your originator. Now is not the time to start changing your mind, unless there has been a change in your financial situation since you last talked about it. If you do need to change your payouts, just call your servicer (the phone number will be on your monthly statements) and tell them what your needs are, or give your originator a call. There is usually a nominal fee (around $50), but it's well worth it if a change will make a difference to your financial comfort. For a refresher on payout types, see Chapters 5, 6, and 7. Some examples of changes that might require you to change your payout options may be:

✔ You are receiving monthly tenured payments and suddenly have a large unexpected expense, such as a medical procedure, or car repairs.

✔ You have a line of credit and find yourself spending the money too quickly. In this case, a monthly payment (either tenured or term) can help control your urge to splurge.

> ✔ You chose term distributions and realize you'll need to receive money longer than your term allows. Switching to a tenure payment will prolong your payouts.

Check out the following sections to see how getting your money works with each payment option.

Requesting a line of credit

Probably the most popular choice in payments is the line of credit, because you usually have more flexibility and can choose to take out as much as you need when you need it. Your money can earn interest depending on which loan you choose (the HECM earns a certain percentage based on your mortgage's interest rate — see Chapter 5), making this a very cool option.

The Financial Freedom Cash Account loans require you to take out at least $500 each time you withdraw from your line of credit (see Chapter 7). If you have concerns about staying within certain public assistance income levels, the Financial Freedom line of credit may not be your best choice. An alternative would be either the HECM or Home Keeper lines of credit (see Chapters 5 and 6, respectively), which allow for more autonomy in withdrawals.

Getting your payments from a line of credit isn't always as simple as it is with a monthly payment. In fact, you don't even have to think about monthly payments: They just appear as if by magic in your checking account once a month (unless, of course, you decide to have them mailed to you). You may have seen people with home equity "credit cards" that automatically allow instant access to their money — the reverse mortgage line of credit doesn't make it nearly that simple, and instead requires you to request your money in writing. The silver lining is, it's not all that difficult to get your money out. It's just one more thing to add to your "to do" list.

To get your first payment (and any subsequent withdrawals), you fill out a request form and either mail or fax it to the lender, letting it know how much you want to withdraw (your originator then provides you with all the contact information you need). You then have the option of getting a live check or authorizing the lender to deposit the money in your bank account. You can also choose to get a chunk of your money right away (after the three-day rescission period) and save the rest for future withdrawals. After that, it's up to you when you get another payment. You will be provided with more request forms that you can use at any time (if you need more, just ask) and you control the cash flow.

Keep the request forms and contact information in a convenient place so you don't have to hunt for them every time you need more money. One easy solution is to put up a corkboard or other message center by your phone or in your kitchen — someplace you're sure to see it easily. Then tack up your lender's phone number, mailing address, and fax number, along with several request forms. You can even fill out the forms in advance (just leave the amount and date until the last minute). Then when you need to send one out, you're ready to go.

Depositing monthly checks

When you choose a monthly payment, your funds can be automatically deposited into your bank account. If you receive social security payments, they probably arrive in the same way: Your bank's routing number tells the organization (social security, lender, or otherwise) where to send your money, which effortlessly materializes in your account. We all get distracted in our day-to-day life, and getting your payments this way means going to the bank is just one less thing to have on your mind. Electronic direct deposits are safe, easy, and ensure that your money makes it into the bank, no matter how busy you are. It's also a great tool for people who are sometimes forgetful (there's a reason momentary memory lapses are called "senior moments") because all you have to remember to do is spend your money.

Some people are still uncomfortable with the idea of electronic direct deposits because they like to feel the crisp reality of a check in their hands. That's why you also have the option to have the checks mailed to you (a "live" check), but unless you plan to stuff them under your mattress, there's no reason not to have them electronically deposited. It's safer and easier than getting live checks, and they end up in the same place.

The first check will come to you in the mail because it takes some time to set up the electronic transfer. You'd think the lenders and banks would have it all figured out in this technological age, but some things still get tangled in red tape. From then on, your monthly payments will continue to magically appear in your bank account for as long as you keep the loan (or as long as the term you selected). Check your balance each month to be sure your payment made it on time. If you have any questions, don't hesitate to call the lender.

Pocketing a lump sum

Getting a lump sum, although not always the best payment option, definitely gives you the biggest feeling of satisfaction when you leave the closing. When's the last time you had tens of thousands of dollars sitting in your bank account? The lump sum is given to you after all the forms are signed and everyone is happy with the transaction (it has closed and been recorded in the county records). The escrow company or title company will prepare a check for the full amount of your loan, and you can either have your check mailed to you (convenient and simple) or arrange to pick it up (but why bother?).

Once you've received the check, it's your responsibility to deposit it. Take it straight to the bank and put it in whatever variety of accounts you've decided on. If you don't know what to do with that money, and you don't trust yourself to ration it, talk to a bank member or financial advisor about setting up different bank accounts to organize your funds. Your first check is your last, and it really has to stretch.

You may also wish to have a family member you trust unconditionally dole the money out to you. This can get tricky if your beloved nephew starts using your money to gamble or buy his friends new clothes without your knowledge. If someone already has durable power of attorney over your finances, this is a much easier transaction.

Staying in Contact with Your Originator

Your originator is your last point of contact, but that doesn't mean the closing is the last time you'll see her. Find out what other services your originator offers now if you haven't already. Many can become allies in financial planning well after your closing, and some are deeply involved in the senior community. They know of special senior benefits and senior organizations you can take advantage of, so don't leave your closing without finding out all you can about additional services your originator provides.

If your originator holds events for past clients or knows of events or classes for seniors in your area, be sure to sign up for your originator's mailing list. We all despise junk mail, but the originator can be a key source of community information. You may even ask him to keep you abreast of any senior happenings in town. Staying in contact with your originator after the closing can also be a benefit when you have questions about your loan in process. You should be on familiar terms with your originator by the time the loan is complete, making it easier to come back with questions later.

Now that your money is flowing, take a moment and assess your finances again (you should have created a detailed budget before even speaking with your counselor). Look at how much money is coming in, and how much you're spending. Have you elevated your lifestyle too much? Are you holding back out of fear of not having quite enough money? If after a few months your payments aren't meeting your budget, talk to your originator about changing your payment type. Maybe a sudden extra cost has come up and you need to switch from monthly payments to a line of credit, or a term plan. Your originator is there to help, so if after the closing things aren't going as planned, call him right away to talk about your options.

Part IV
Giving Advice for Adult Children

The 5th Wave · By Rich Tennant

"I know you don't need that much money, Dad, but I don't think you can get a reverse mortgage on just the porch and 3rd floor attic."

In this part . . .

We dedicate this part to all of the caring, loving children out there who are helping their senior parents get a reverse mortgage. This part covers helping your parents both hands-on and hands-off, setting your mind at ease, resources for outside help, and what role you play in all of this.

Chapter 12 gives adult children and other loved ones ideas for helping your parents during the loan process and afterward. We list a lot of great Web sites and support groups that deal specifically with assisting your parents at every level.

Chapter 13 deals with the question on every adult child's mind: the inheritance. How does a reverse mortgage affect your future bounty? Find out here.

For those who need to take an even more proactive stance in their parents' finances, Chapter 14 explains how to assist your parent through a durable power of attorney. We've included symptoms that indicate you need to step in, the best ways to secure your parents' financial future, and additional options.

Chapter 12

Supporting Your Parents

- -

In This Chapter

▶ Knowing how and when to support your parents' decision

▶ Getting guidance

▶ Understanding the deed

▶ Setting your mind at ease

- -

*A*lthough much of this book is geared toward seniors who are looking into reverse mortgages for themselves, there is a significant population of adult children who are faced with the prospect of helping to arrange a reverse mortgage for a parent or other elderly loved one. Maybe you need to find out more before you discuss the idea with your parent. Maybe your parents came to you with the notion of reverse mortgages and you want to make sure these loans aren't a scam against seniors, who are so often the targets of financial wrongdoings. Or maybe you just want to find out what you can do to be there for your parents as they travel down the reverse mortgage highway at full speed. If you're reading up on reverse mortgages for someone besides a parent, you can mentally replace "parent" with that person's name as you go along. Either way, this chapter is for you. In the following pages you can find tips to make this process as hassle-free for you and your parents as possible and get some great resources for additional senior help. You can also find out the truth about reverse mortgages, as we put to rest some common fears that adult children have about reverse mortgages for their parents.

Many reverse mortgage borrowers are perfectly capable of getting this loan on their own. Don't assume that just because someone is classified in our society as a "senior" they are automatically feeble and confused. You know your parents better than anyone, so keep in mind both their strengths and limitations before you step in to help. If your parents can successfully secure their own reverse mortgage without your meddling, step back and let them be.

Supporting Your Loved Ones

There may have come a time in your life when you suddenly turned around and found that your role in life has changed. One day you're walking down the street, minding your own business, and — boom! — your parents need you more than you need them. Okay, maybe it's a bit more gradual than that, but it can hit you rather unexpectedly just as you're sighing with the relief that your own children have left the nest.

As your parents decide to go through the major financial transaction of a reverse mortgage, they may need your support more than they may have ever needed it before. In fact, this may be the first time that you realize they need you at all. Just remember, if you need help, ask for it. The reverse mortgage originator and counselor are more than happy to talk to you one-on-one about the loan (although they may not be able to divulge private financial information without your parent's consent).

Knowing when to stay out of it

The names on the deed to your parents' house are your parents' signatures, not yours. It can be very tempting to step in and take over the finances for your parents — sometimes impossible to resist because your parents are people that you care very much about and you tell yourself that you're only butting in for their own good. The key words here, of course, are "butting in." Remember when you were a youngster and your parents would stick their noses into everything you did? Remember how deflating it felt to know that they didn't think you were capable of doing something on your own? Well, the tables have turned and your parents may feel the same way if you step in without their solicitation.

Allowing your parents to make their own decisions at this critical juncture in their lives not only empowers them in a world that is so eager to make seniors out to be crazy old coots, it ensures that they get what *they* want . . . not what *you* want. All children, adult or otherwise, feel a sense of entitlement when it comes to their parents. In this case, you believe, as they once believed of themselves for you, that you know what's best for them. And maybe you do. Since seniors run the gamut of 62 to 102-plus, their degrees of comprehension and ability will vary greatly. Generally speaking, a 65-year-old is going to be much more aware and able than a 95-year-old. Of course, there are always exceptions (that's why we're speaking generally) so you have to be able to truly look at your parents objectively (see the checklists later in this section).

We would never tell you to stay out of the reverse mortgage process entirely unless your parents expressly wish it and are of sound enough mind to complete a financial transaction on their own. Instead, we encourage your participation on as grand a level as you and your parents can tolerate. Just make sure that whatever limits your parents set, you respect. After all, these are adults. Your biggest role may simply be to hand them this book and say, "Call me if you want to talk about this."

You may also feel a twinge of guilt about suggesting a reverse mortgage for your parents in the first place; if the windfall will benefit you, you won't have to worry about them financially (or at least not to such a great extent), nor will you be forced to inherit their home since the majority of people sell it to pay off the loan. On the other hand, you may feel selfish because you're trying to convince them not to get a reverse mortgage, since you're afraid it will affect your inheritance. These are both perfectly normal, common reactions. And as long as you keep your parents' needs and wishes in the forefront of your mind and your needs and wants way in the back, you should all come out on top. Try not to sway their decision too much, especially if your reasons are based on your own agenda. Of course, we know *you* would never confuse your motives.

Have you ever heard the saying, "prescription without diagnosis is malpractice"? It means that giving someone a solution before knowing what their problem is can only lead to bad results. Reverse mortgages are a wonderful way for some seniors to live out their lives in their homes, but it is not a panacea miracle pill. If you haven't yet, check out Chapter 2 and run down the list of when a reverse mortgage isn't the best option, as well as the pre-reverse-mortgage checklist. You may discover that a reverse mortgage doesn't fit your parents as well as you thought.

You also need to know your parents well enough to feel secure in letting them go off and get a reverse mortgage alone. Some seniors are just as sharp about finances as they were in their youth, and some were never sharp with finances and can't be expected to suddenly understand interest rates and falling equity. If you are looking into reverse mortgages for a single parent, try to remember back to who handled the finances as you were growing up. Was it this parent? If not, is this one completely in the dark, or does he or she have a pretty good grasp of his or her financial portfolio? It may seem like we're feeding into a stereotype, but many senior women were never in charge of the money and have been left without the tools to manage their own finances.

Take a moment to evaluate your parents by asking yourself the following yes-or-no questions. The more yes answers you have, the better equipped your parents are to handle a reverse mortgage without your constant (loving) help. If you don't know an answer, skip it but try to find out after speaking with your parents (with theses questions in mind), and then come back and evaluate them again. The following checklists give you a great way to objectively evaluate your parents:

✔ **Financial Capability:**

- Do your parents currently pay their own bills?

- Do they keep a balanced checkbook?

- Are they able to remember where their money is (for example, savings accounts, investments, different banks, and so on)?

- Do you feel that your parents could be trusted with a very large sum of money?

- Are your parents able to keep track of their cash or does it seem to "disappear?

- Are your parents savvy about senior con artists?

✔ **Reverse Mortgage Understanding:**

- Do your parents understand the basics of a reverse mortgage?

- Was it easy to explain the rudiments of a reverse mortgage to them?

- Do they seem comfortable with the idea of reverse mortgages (not suspicious, scared, and so on)?

- Do they understand the cost of a reverse mortgage?

- Have they done a comparison of how much they need per month versus how much they can get with a reverse mortgage?

✔ **Emotional and Mental Capabilities:**

- Do your parents cope well with stress?

- Would you classify your parents as independent?

- Are your parents rational and free from (serious) mental lapses?

- Are they able to live on their own today?

- Will they be able to live in their home for the next few years (even with help)?

Discovering financial needs

There are as many reasons for getting a reverse mortgage as there are seniors who need them. Some common motivations are:

- ✔ Daily living expenses

- ✔ A little extra cash to improve quality of life

- ✔ Medical needs, like prescriptions or hospital bills

- ✔ Renovating the home for safety or accessibility

- ✔ Remodeling for purely aesthetic reasons

- ✔ A dream vacation

- ✔ Purchasing a new home (with the Home Keeper for Purchase loan; see Chapter 6)

- ✔ College tuition (often for a grandchild)

- ✔ A cushion to avoid draining a savings account

When you and your parents first discuss reverse mortgages, find out what their plans are for the money and try to determine whether or not these plans are realistic. Chapter 2 gives examples of a daily living budget, and how practical a reverse mortgage is for a senior's goals. Flip back there and take a look at the sample breakdowns of a monthly budget and a "wants" list. Then try the exercise with your parent. It may take more than one visit to complete, but it's worth it once you and your parents can clearly see what your parents' wants are versus their monetary needs.

Once you find out why they need the money, brainstorm some other options that may keep a reverse mortgage at bay for the time being. If their needs are medical, make sure they're receiving the maximum benefits from Medicare, Medicaid, or other health plans. If they need money to make ends meet, do some research to ensure that your parents are getting the most out of social security, Supplementary Security Income (SSI), and/or veteran benefits. AARP is an excellent resource for all things elder, and can point you in the right direction, depending on your parents' individual circumstances. You can find them online at www.aarp.org. You may also want to enlist the help of a financial advisor who specializes specifically in senior needs. Your reverse mortgage originator will no doubt have contacts in that field. If your parents' reason for seeking out a reverse mortgage is need-based, look to senior financial professionals to help you pad your parents' pockets.

You may also be surprised to discover that your parents' monetary plans involve you. Maybe they want to help you buy a home by using their money to put a down payment on your dream house. Maybe they want to help pay for your wedding or your child's education. There are also a group of seniors who strongly believe that they need to have something to leave their family and want to put the money away for you. This can be a treacherous area to get into. Sure, most people would be hard-pressed to turn down the wonderful gift of cash. But take a step back and consider what the financial implication of this selfless act will mean for your parents (and for you) down the road.

Reverse mortgages are not free money. This is a loan and not only does it have to be paid back in full when the senior dies or moves out permanently, it has to be paid with interest, closing costs, and additional fees as well. Interest and fees will most likely add up to tens of thousands of dollars over the course of the loan. For example, a $38,000 loan can accrue upwards of $20,000 extra in interest, closing costs, and fees over eight years depending on the loan program and interest rates. That's pretty darn expensive. Ask yourself if that price is worth the benefit of the loan. Do you really need their help financially? If so, and they're willing to give it, then congratulations on your score. But if you don't have to accept their generous offer in order to achieve your goals, then support their financial future by insisting that they use the money on themselves (or look for other ways of helping you out).

On the other hand, you may find yourself in precisely the opposite situation, whereby your parents need your help to make ends meet. Think about the cost of a reverse mortgage for a moment and consider whether you can find another way to assist your parents. Can you spare a few hundred dollars a month? Would you consider inviting them to live with your family? Is there anything you can do to make their lives a little easier that would negate the need for a reverse mortgage? Talk to your parents and your trusted financial advisor to see if there is an alternative solution that can allow you to partially or completely support your parents financially.

Chapter 5 details the process of paying back the loan; read up on the conditions of repayment and make sure you understand your part in it as well. Remember, if your parent passes away and terminates the loan, you will most likely be responsible for making sure it gets repaid. No one is going to come break your legs or repossess your house on account of your parents' reverse mortgage debt, but they will expect you to get the appropriate affairs in order in a timely manner. You and your parents need a financial plan when the time comes. It's not pleasant to talk about their impending death, but you may be surprised to find that it bothers you more than it bothers them.

Meeting emotional needs

Do you find that your parents call you more often than they used to? Do they rely on you to sort out their day-to-day situations? It can be hard to grasp, but you may have reached a point in the circle of life where your parents start to count on you as their translator for the world.

This is one of the biggest reasons that it is so important for you or someone you and your parents trust to be present during all of the reverse mortgage dealings. If you live out of the area, most reverse mortgage counselors and originators will let you call in and sit there on speakerphone while the meeting takes place (with your parent's permission, of course). If you can, however, try to send at least one delegate from your family (you, your spouse, your cousin, your own adult child) to all of the mortgage proceedings. There will probably only be three meetings to attend:

✔ **The counselor's meeting:** At this meeting, you find out about the different loan options available in your parent's state, receive a clear printout of the estimated loan amounts and costs associated with each option, and see which alternatives exist that may better serve your parents. This is the first stage in the reverse mortgage education process (aside from this book of course), so it's important that you get in on the ground floor and start out with the best understanding possible of the particular loan your parents may be applying. This is also a good chance to gauge how well your parent is retaining the information they're getting from the counselor. Forming a relationship with the counselor on your part now will also help you down the line of you have questions after the meeting. (See Chapter 8 for more about the counselor's meeting.)

✔ **The originator's meeting:** By the time of this meeting, you probably have a pretty good idea of which loan option your parents want to pursue. The originator runs the numbers again (rates will have changed by this point) and explains again the finer details of what this loan will means for your parents, specifically. If your parents decide to go ahead with the loan at this point, an application is filled out and signed, and the appraisal is ordered (you may or may not want to be present for the appraisal — see Chapter 10 for more on the appraisal process). If your parent decides to wait and think about it, you may be in for an additional originator's meeting. (See Chapter 9 for more about the originator's meeting.)

✔ **The closing:** This is the last stop on the reverse mortgage train. At this meeting your parents sign off on all of their documents, officially marking the beginning of the loan. Their closing costs are due at this point along with any additional originator fees (unless they were financed as part of the loan). This is usually the time when people realize the gravity of a new loan, and want to back out. Your presence can make your parents feel more secure in their decision, but, obviously, you shouldn't force them into anything they're not ready for. (See Chapter 11 for more on closing.)

When you think about it, three visits really isn't so bad, especially since they will probably be weeks apart. Depending on how much of a procrastinator your parents are, you may find yourself waiting a couple of months between the counselor's visit and the decision to go see the originator. Unless they specifically don't want you there (and that's their right) you should make every effort to be around, even just your presence can be a reassurance.

Of course, we don't mean to imply even for a second that all seniors are in need of hand-holding. There are plenty of independent, vivacious seniors out there who will have no problem understanding every element of the reverse mortgage process. Even so, be aware of parents who can fully comprehend their new loan, and those who are putting on a brave face and refusing help. Resist the urge to smother them with help, and instead of demanding that they let you be part of their mortgage proceedings, give them some space and offer up your ear if they want to bounce any ideas off you. If you truly feel that your parents are entering into a loan without a complete understanding of the implications, by all means step in and speak to the originator about your concerns. For more about stepping in and taking the reins, see Chapter 14.

It's easier than you think to be emotionally supportive of your parents during the reverse mortgage process. Below we give you five easy ways to be there for your parents as they embark on what can be a scary transaction — try to do as many of the following as you can (and more):

- ✔ **Talk to your parents *before* they decide to speak with a reverse mortgage counselor so there aren't any surprises in the meeting.** You don't want to find out then that your mother wants to use the money to get a face lift and chest, uh, expansion. Talking to your parents beforehand also gives you an opportunity to see how well your parents grasp the idea of the reverse mortgage. Make sure you're familiar with the different loan programs beforehand so you can help them weigh their options.

- ✔ **Go to the counselor session with your parent.** If you can't be there in person then arrange for a phone teleconference. You can help ensure that your parent is being honest with the counselor about his financial needs, help explain difficult concepts, and get an idea of where this transaction is heading. At the same time, remember to respect your parent's dignity as adults. They may not be fast anymore, but they're not toddlers.

✔ **Go along to the originator's meetings.** (Bet you saw that one coming). You need to know for your own peace of mind that this person can be trusted to advise your parents appropriately, and that they are taking your parents' individual needs into consideration. Try not to give in to a knee-jerk reaction, but do go with your gut feeling. Try to be present for the closing as well to look over the last-minute documents.

✔ **Follow up with your parent after the loan closes.** If they will accept your help, go over their finances to make sure the loan is providing enough money to meet your parent's needs. Don't be the wallet police, but do also make sure that their lump sum isn't being spent faster than planned. This is also a good time to talk about con artists and how to avoid being taken in by a senior predator.

✔ **Offer to arrange a meeting with a senior financial planner who can help them manage their new-found funds.** Your parents need a plan of attack to make their money stretch, and a professional may be able to offer up some suggestions for investments, budgeting, and saving. We don't have to tell you this, but you ought to be there for that meeting, too.

Finding guidance

It may seem like a huge burden has fallen suddenly on your shoulders, but you're not alone. There are countless resources out there that can help you with everything from finding an originator to considering alternatives, to arranging aid for your parent. You can take advantage of as many of these organizations as possible . . . that's what they're there for. And remember, their job is to assist you and your parents with their lifetime goals and day-to-day living. They've heard it all and no question is a dumb question. If one group can't help you, they will almost always be able to steer you toward the right path.

Ask your loved ones to help you out with doing the research. They may not even realize that you need help — sometimes a few loud sighs will do the trick, but you'll usually have to come right out and ask.

Checking out financial and quality-of-life assistance

Before applying for a reverse mortgage, you and your parents should make sure that there aren't other programs that would better meet their needs. Why pay thousands of dollars in fees and interest when the government may give them extra money for a lower cost (or even free!)? We give some places to start looking in the list below:

- ✔ www.benefitscheckup.com: At this site, you and your parents can fill out a confidential online questionnaire that assesses which state and federal assistance programs your parents are eligible for. These can range from extra monthly income to food vouchers to health care. You can also apply for the programs right from the Web site and get additional information on each one. It's definitely worth the Web visit.

- ✔ www.govbenefits.gov: Just to make sure you've covered all your bases, check out this site. Although it's the same idea as benefitscheckup.com (see bullet above), it may produce varying results. It's a good idea to try both systems, since one may connect you with a program that the other one didn't.

- ✔ **Social security:** Most seniors are already receiving social security, but if you have questions about the program go to www.ssa.gov. If your parents need to apply for their benefits, start at www.ssa.gov/applytoretire or call 800-772-1213.

- ✔ Your parent may also be eligible for Supplemental Security Income, which also comes from the government but is separate from social security. This is designed for seniors with practically nothing in their wallets and very little to their names. To see if your parent qualifies, call the social security office at 800-772-1213.

Finding alternatives to a reverse mortgage

In Chapters 2 and 8 we discuss some of the other loan programs available to seniors that may be a better choice than a reverse mortgage if their need is based on home repairs or certain taxes. You can find more information in the aforementioned chapters, but we've given you a peek at their basics in the list below:

- ✔ **Deferred Payment Loan (DPL):** The DPL is a state loan that works a lot like a reverse mortgage — your parents borrow money against their equity and pay it back upon leaving their home permanently. The downside to this loan is that the DPL can usually only be used to repair something dangerous or unlivable in your parents' home. Your state housing finance agency can tell you whether or not these loans are available in your area. To find your state's housing finance agency, go to the National Council of State Housing Agencies Web site at www.ncsha.org/section.cfm/4/39. Remember that these loans sometimes go by different names, but they should know what you're talking about once you describe the basics.

✔ **Property tax deferral:** Another state deferred loan is a property tax deferral. If your parents owe back property taxes or aren't able to pay upcoming taxes, this loan may be their best bet. One of the best features is that they often will only have to pay back a portion of the loan, depending on your state. To find out if this option exists in your parent's area, call the local agency that they send their property taxes to. They can give you all the details on how the program works in that state and go over qualifications.

✔ **Traditional mortgage:** Forward mortgages (traditional versions where you pay the lender instead of receiving payments) can be a good solution for some seniors. Popular options are the Home Equity Line of Credit — which works similarly to the reverse mortgage but with a very different payment schedule — or refinancing with an interest-only ARM (adjustable rate mortgage) which can lower payments in the short term. However, because these loans require monthly payments, they may not be the best for people who are already struggling to make ends meet.

Seeking out reverse mortgage resources

Throughout this book we mention several ways you can find out more about reverse mortgages and the people who provide them. A few of the best resources are:

✔ **National Reverse Mortgage Lenders Association (NRMLA):** NRMLA has listings of all the reverse mortgage originators in every state who are members of the association. You won't find recommendations or endorsements for any particular person or company, but it's a great place to start. You can also get informational packets, get an estimate of what your parents could borrow with the reverse mortgage calculator, and find links to other helpful sites. It's all at www.reversemortgage.org.

✔ **AARP:** AARP is always an excellent source of information for seniors, whether for reverse mortgages or any other senior issue. Their Web site is easy to use and covers everything from finding a job to finding adequate healthcare. For reverse mortgage links, go to www.aarp.org/revmort. There's a reverse mortgage calculator, lists of approved counselors, and much, much more. You can also be assured that they never endorse any reverse mortgage product or lender, so you can always get straight information.

While you're there, check out www.aarp.org/money/lowincomehelp/ for amazingly great tips on saving money, senior discounts, government assistance, and more. It's not all reverse mortgage related, but it gives you some easy and effective saving ideas for your parents.

✔ **Lender's Web site:** Once you've decided on a loan product, check out the lender's Web site for more information about the company and its loan. You can also find contact information for future reference, just in case you need to reach them with a concern.

✔ **Loan product Web sites:** To get specific information on a particular loan product, you can visit Chapters 5, 6, and 7 of this book as well as the following Web sites:

- For **Home Equity Conversion Mortgages,** visit `www.hud.gov/buying/rvrsmort.cfm`.

- For **Home Keeper** loans, go to `www.fanniemae.com`, click on "find a mortgage" and then click on "reverse mortgage."

- For the **Jumbo Cash Account,** visit `www.financialfreedom.com`.

✔ **Counselors and originators:** Once you and your parents settle on a counselor and originator, they can be flowing springs of information and guidance. Come prepared to the meetings with questions, and take lots of notes. Don't be afraid to call and ask questions afterward either. They want you to guide your parents to make the best, most well-informed decision they can. The originator and counselor also have lots of additional information about alternative or supplementary assistance programs. Use their great wealth of knowledge — don't waste a single opportunity to satisfy your concerns. Besides, if they're getting paid, they ought to earn that fee!

Aging resources

Another outstanding Internet locale is the Administration on Aging Web site (`www.aoa.dhhs.gov`). You can call them at 800-677-1116, but we highly recommend a peek at the site. It's not only clear and simple to use, but it is a gold mine of information on everything senior. It also has several language options, which is a big help if you or your parent is more comfortable in another language. If you're new to caring for (or even about) an elder person, this site has everything you need to know.

Knowing the Name on the Deed

People tend to get a little suspicious when they hear anything about the deed to their or their parents' home. You may conjure up images of a black and white movie in which a nice, hard-working family loses the deed to the bank or to the town's nefarious money grubber. In fact, a reverse mortgage has nothing to do with that kind of deed. There are three types of home deeds:

- ✔ **Grant deed:** This transfers property from one person or party to another. The grant deed is the document that essentially gives ownership to a property. In a sense it's similar to the title on your car. Remember in the '50s when greasers would race for pink slips? A grant deed is like the pink slip to your home.

- ✔ **Quit claim deed:** This removes someone's name from title or ownership of a property. For instance, if a child's name had been added on title to their parents' home, the child needs to sign a quit claim deed to remove his or her name so the parents could obtain the reverse mortgage.

- ✔ **Deed of trust:** The deed of trust is the one that is recorded with the county to secure a loan. This is the only one that can affect a reverse mortgage and the only one you need to worry about for our purposes.

A deed of trust does not transfer the property's title. Your parents still own their home. The deed of trust also won't transfer to you, the heir, upon their death. That's because, again, a deed of trust doesn't transfer anything. Its sole purpose in life is to make note of your parent's loan. If a deed of trust climbed a mountain in Tibet to ask a great and wise Dali Lama-type what the meaning of life was, the sage would reply, "For you? Your purpose is just to record loans my child."

A common misconception about reverse mortgages is that once your parents sign the loan papers, the home belongs to the bank. This couldn't be further from the truth. Your parents keep the title to their home until they choose to sell it, whenever that may be.

This is a good place to mention that if you buy your parent's home from them, the reverse mortgage comes due, even if your parent is still living in the home. To qualify for a reverse mortgage your parent must own the home, live in the home, and maintain the home. As we note in Chapter 2, some families choose to buy their parent's home and then allow the parent to continue living in it rent free (or for a nominal fee). This solves a lot of the senior's problems, but unfortunately disqualifies them for a reverse mortgage. Your parent must be the homeowner.

If your parents qualify for a reverse mortgage, it stands to reason that as of this moment, they own their home. Your parents' signatures on the deed of trust sustain this fact. Here's where people start to freak out: The lender's or servicer's name is also on the deed of trust. The lender or servicer's name on the deed of trust does not, not, not mean that the lender or servicer owns the home, nor does it mean the lender or servicer has any rights to the home. The lender or servicer's name on the deed of trust simply signifies that your parents have agreed to pay the lender or servicer back on a loan. That's it. The deed of trust has all the terms of the loan embedded in the text and is signed by your parents (the borrowers), the lender or servicer, and a notary public. Without your parents' signatures, the deed of trust means nothing, since your parents are the homeowners and the only ones who can set the loan in motion.

We can't stress enough the fact that at no time can your parents' home be taken away. This has been the biggest misconception swirling around reverse mortgages since they resurfaced 20 years ago, and unfortunately, that misconception is spread around more often than the truth. You can start a new (and true) rumor: The seniors own their homes in a reverse mortgage, not the lender. They can't take your parents' home away. Pass it on.

Resting Easily

We all worry about the ones we love. That's just part of being a family. Reverse mortgages are all but worry-free, since they were carefully crafted by lenders and government agencies to consider all the little things that could go wrong and nip them in the bud before they can sprout. There are several myths and concerns that many adult children have for their parents when considering a reverse mortgage. We spoke to several adult children whose parents were considering reverse mortgages or who were looking into the loans for their parents, and asked them to share their biggest concerns. We're going to attempt to set your mind at ease here, with the most common fears answered in the following list:

- ✔ **Your parents won't be forced to live in an unsafe home.** The idea of your parents living in some sort of condemned structure actually couldn't be further from the truth. Because of Federal Housing Administration (FHA) laws, your parents' home must be safe and sound. During the appraisal, your parents find out everything that may potentially be wrong with their home. Every reverse mortgage requires an appraisal, so there's no way to skip this step. What's more, Fannie Mae won't even lend to people whose home needs more than 15 percent of repairs. In any reverse mortgage, all repairs have to be made prior to the loan closing, or the lender withholds a reasonable amount of the loan total so that your parents have that money in reserve to make repairs after loan closing. No lender wants to invest in an unsafe house; your parent will not be left in a dilapidated shack. You can help by making sure that your parents complete the mandated repairs within a year of closing the loan.

✔ **The bank will never take your parents' home.** Throughout this book we repeat one of the most important facets of the reverse mortgage: The bank/lender has no authority to take your parents' home away. None. Nada. Zilch. Zip. The home is your parents' and no one else's. This myth stems from the fact that many people choose to sell their homes in order to pay back the loan when they move out (or their heirs sell it when parents die). Lenders can demand loan payment in full if your parents fail to hold up their end of the bargain (paying their property taxes and keeping up home maintenance), but this happens so rarely, it's almost not worth mentioning. Even so, they still can't seize the home. Your parents are secure in their home, which remains theirs until they want to sell.

✔ **The money won't run out.** If your parents choose a monthly tenured payment — one which continues at the same sum each month for the life of the loan — their lender must continue to keep paying them indefinitely. If they hold the loan for 3 years, 7 years, or 20 years, your parents are entitled to receive payments until they move or upon their death. However, if your parents choose a term loan, line of credit, or a lump sum and use it all up, that will be the end of the line. They need to consider carefully how long they plan to stay in their home and how much money they need. You can help with this by offering to go over their current budget and/or bank transactions to see how their money is being spent, and whether or not a reverse mortgage could feasibly cover their expenses. See Chapter 2 for even more information on assessing your parents' budget as well as their needs and wants.

✔ **They won't have to make up the difference if their home depreciates in value or the loan value exceeds the value of the home.** One of the greatest benefits of this loan is that your parents never ever owe more than their home is worth. If the loan balance comes to $180,000 at the end of a 17-year loan and their home is only worth $150,000, $150,000 is how much they owe. It's a wonderful system, ensuring no out-of-pocket expenses and no fear that they may have to sell any of their treasured items or live in a refrigerator box under the freeway because the loan tapped them out.

✔ **The lenders can't touch your inheritance.** As we say in the above bullet, your parents only owe as much as their home is worth. That means that unless your parents spend it before it gets to you, your liquid inheritance is safe. They may sell the home to pay off the loan, or they may choose to leave you the home and use other savings and investments to settle loan costs. Either way, you won't be left empty-handed through any fault of the lenders. If your parents blow it all on little porcelain figurines, well, that's another story.

✓ **Your parents won't be cheated out of a fair loan value if lending limits rise after their loan closes.** In Chapters 5, 6, and 7 we discuss the limits of each loan product — amounts that the loans simply will not exceed, no matter the actual value of the home. For example, in 2004, the upper limit for a Fannie Mae loan was $333,700. In 2005 that figure changed to $359,650. It's likely that these limits will continue to increase as the years go by. Seniors who have obtained a reverse mortgage may be able to refinance it in the future and obtain additional funds as a result of those increased lending limits.

✓ **They will be protected if their home is destroyed.** In 2004, Florida saw devastation in the wake of hurricane after hurricane. Because parts of Florida are considered a sort of Mecca for seniors, home destruction is a very common concern. Reverse mortgages require you to keep up homeowner's insurance; if the destructive force is covered under insurance, the home will be rebuilt and your parent can continue to live there and receive reverse mortgage payments as per usual. If the home was ruined by a force not covered by insurance, disaster relief funds (such as those from the Federal Emergency Management Agency) will often help to repair or rebuild the home. If all else fails and there is no way to save the home, lenders will consider the loan due, since the senior is no longer living in the home. But! While there may not be a home to sell to pay off the debt, there is property to cash in on. In many areas, the greatest value is in the land, not the home itself. If selling the land is not enough to pay off the reverse mortgage, it becomes the lender's problem, not your parents'. Again, your parents can have no liability beyond the value of their property. If their loan total comes to $89,000 and what's left of their home is only worth $5,000 then that's all they'd have to repay. Such circumstances are rare, but the provisions are there just in case.

✓ **No one will enter a mentally unfit senior into a loan.** Many adult children worry that their parents may run off and get a reverse mortgage, when they know that their parents are simply not capable of making such a huge financial decision, whether from Alzheimer's, dementia, or plain senioritis. In almost all cases, the counselor is able to determine that your parents don't quite have the wherewithal to fully understand a reverse mortgage. If your parents were somehow sly enough to fool these highly trained professionals (or just having an

"on" day), the originator has another crack at making sure
your parent can handle the loan. They're testing (not literally)
for understanding of reverse mortgages, as well as general
cognizance and orientation. An originator faced with a senior
who, in their opinion, can't be held responsible for this loan
would likely ask them if they have any family or financial advisors who may like to sit in on their meeting. This would
enable the originator to talk to the family and get a feeling for
how well the senior functions. It's a basic tenet of any good
originator or counselor to know their client well enough to
assess their mental faculties.

Keep these reassurances nearby so that when a friend or family
member brings up any of these common concerns, you will be at
the ready. They can also guide you and your parents through some
fears you may have had. Chances are good that your parents have
thought of most of these potential issues as well.

Chapter 13

Knowing the Impact of a Reverse Mortgage on Your Inheritance

In This Chapter

▶ Paying off the loan

▶ Getting everyone involved in the planning

*A*lthough most people don't want to appear selfish about their expected inheritance, most children want to understand how a reverse mortgage affects their parents' finances as well as their own future inheritance. Of course, you don't want to come off looking like an entitled brat or materialistic prima donna when discussing your parents' future and, eventually, their death. As a matter of fact, it sounds utterly inappropriate. However, while we don't recommend you start rifling through your mother's jewelry box, you should have a firm grasp on your parents' holdings, including any debts (say, for instance, a reverse mortgage) as a healthy, necessary, and crucial part of planning for your parents' financial future.

Of course, many seniors aren't ready to talk about these issues, or will flat-out refuse to participate in any such discussions (whether because they aren't comfortable with the thought of their own mortality or because they don't think it's any of your business). To ease any tension surrounding the will, remember to respect your parents' privacy just as you would expect them to respect yours. You can certainly suggest that they make out a will and ask that they give some serious thought to their future finances, but ultimately the reverse mortgage is your parents' loan. Unless your parents are at a point where they need considerable help with their loan (see Chapter 14), allow them to transition into this discussion slowly and delicately.

Remember that it isn't the size of the inheritance that counts — you may be surprised by what your parents have that you didn't even know about. Even if your inheritance consists of a toaster and a pack of gum, you need to be prepared to take care of their reverse mortgage debt before your parents are laid to rest. In this chapter, we show you how to keep your inheritance and still pay off a reverse mortgage that your parents left behind.

Repaying the Loan

There are three ways a loan can become payable: if the senior moves out, fails to maintain the home sufficiently, or dies. Unless you have durable power of attorney over your parents (more on that in Chapter 14) the only time you need to worry about your parents' debt is upon their death. And here's the good news: You really have nothing to worry about. Reverse mortgages are designed to make borrowing as easy as repaying so that anyone involved — your parents, you, and any other family members — can rest easy.

Generally speaking, when a reverse mortgage holder dies (as in any mortgage) the heirs are responsible for paying off the remaining debt. Heirs can be anyone named in the will and aren't exclusive to family members. If you're an heir, congratulations: You've just inherited a reverse mortgage debt. How in the world are you going to find tens of thousands — even hundreds of thousands — of dollars to repay your parents' loan? After all, the loan is due ASAP, and the lender doesn't take easy-pay installments. Don't fret; paying off the loan is simple, straightforward, and we guarantee you can afford it. No matter how much you have in the bank.

The biggest point in your favor is that golden rule of reverse mortgages: You can never owe more than the home's fair market value. No matter how enormous of a loan your parents amassed, their loan will never cost you more than the value of their home. And don't forget that if the loan is worth less than the home (for example, your parent's debt is $50,000 but their home is worth $425,000) you keep the difference. That equity is yours (or else it belongs to whomever it was stipulated to go to in the will).

Here are the ways in which you can pay off your parents' reverse mortgage (we discuss these options in more detail later in this section):

   ✔ Sell the home.

   ✔ Keep the home by:

       • Paying the debt out of your own savings.

       • Selling your house and moving right into your parents' house.

       • Taking out a new loan on your parents' home.

Of course, you may have some other way to pay off the loan (lottery, other inheritance, play the lender in a high-stakes game of poker, and so on), but these are some of the more typical methods. Whatever you choose just remember: plan, plan, plan. Get your game plan in place ahead of time to save yourself added aggravation later. Do it during the loan application process so you can involve the counselor or originator as well.

Selling the house

The most common way to pay off your parent's home is to sell the house because the home pays off the loan. You can never owe more than the home is worth, so even if your parents have accumulated $350,000 in loan debt, if the house sells for $235,000 that's all the lenders can ask of you. Of course you may actually get more than you bargained for, too — if your parent has only accumulated

---

Keeping the estate

An "estate" in legal terms doesn't mean the house: It means everything your parents own. Their estate can include everything from cash, stocks, brokerage accounts and IRAs to their furniture, heirloom rose bushes, and collection of teas from around the world. Your parents own a home, so it stands to reason that they own a few other things. No matter how much it turns out to be, anything that's left after you pay off the reverse mortgage and any other debts they had is your parents' estate. So, just because you may choose to sell the home doesn't mean you're actually selling the entire estate — just the house.

We can't emphasize enough that one of the most important things you can do for you and your parents is to make sure that they have a will, which is especially crucial if you have siblings. Even families who otherwise get along like saints find that the gloves come out when the topic turns to inheritance. A reverse mortgage is usually the responsibility of the adult children to take care of when a parent dies, but if your parents leave the house to someone else, that person is responsible for repaying the loan. You can imagine what a big help it is if everyone knows (or at least the parent has written down) who gets what.

$59,000 in loan debt and the home sells for $375,000 you're looking at a hefty chunk of equity, which is part of your parents' estate that goes right into your pocket. We give some ideas in this section of not only how to choose whether the house should be sold, but also, some tips on making the most of the sale.

Deciding whether to sell the home

The thought of selling your parents' home elicits different feelings in every family. Consider the points below to help assess whether you're ready to sell your parents' home. Not every statement begs a "sell" or "don't sell" conclusion, but it may put you in a more focused frame of mind.

You may want to sell if:

- **There will be equity in the home that you and your family could put to good use.** This is especially pertinent if there isn't much else in the estate. It's also a good solution when there are two or more siblings who want to keep the house, since not everyone can live in the home at once. You may be able to sell the house and split the equity, making everyone happy.

- **The value of the home is less than the value of the loan.** In almost all cases, it just wouldn't make financial sense to keep a home with a depreciating value, which is often the situation when the loan exceeds the home's value. Besides, you won't have to pay the difference if the home is valued less than the cost of the loan — the loan gets paid and no heirs will have to pay out of pocket.

- **The home is worth a lot more than the loan balance.** Here's where equity comes into play again. If the loan is $89,000, why keep a $675,000 home that no one in your family wants to live in, pay taxes on, or maintain, when you could sell it and reap the rewards of a low loan balance?

- **You have no sentimental feelings toward the property.** This is especially true if your parent lives in a senior community or recently bought a new home. If you never lived in the house and it's not particularly meaningful to you, there's probably no reason to keep it.

- **No one in your family wants to move into the house.** Remember that if you keep the house, you have to do something with it. If nobody wants it, why not sell it to someone who does? This is quite common since most adult children are settled in their own homes and don't need to move.

- **You just don't like the house.** Enough said. You don't like it? Get rid of it.

You may not want sell if:

- ✔ **You grew up in this home.** These are the steps you had your first kiss on, that's the tree you used to camp under on warm summer nights, this is the kitchen where you first learned how to make paella with your grandmother — this is a special house. They aren't just walls, they're memories. If this is how you feel, keep the home if you can pay off the loan reasonably (that is, don't sell your kidneys on the black market to pay off the loan).

- ✔ **The home holds a special significance to you.** Along the same lines, this house may be meaningful, even if you never lived there. It may be a historic home, or your parents may have made enough renovations on it to make it truly unique. If you love it, don't let it go.

- ✔ **Your parents have specific wishes regarding the home.** Don't discount your parents' ideas about their own house. If they want it to go to a charity and it says so in their will, don't sell it to someone else. Or if they wish for the house to stay in the family, try to make it work. Of course, this is where a will would be a handy thing to have, and another great reason to discuss all this reverse mortgage stuff well before the loan is even executed. You don't want to find out that your mother's last wish was for you to have the home, but her second-to-last wish was to blow all her money at the casino, leaving you to come up with the cash on your own.

- ✔ **You or another family member could live in the house.** In many families there's a young newlywed couple who need a starter home or an aunt who wants to be closer to the rest of the clan, and your parents' home is perfect for them. If this is the case, you or whoever plans to move in needs to start planning for that now. Start saving to pay off the loan, and make sure you (or whomever) can qualify for a loan to pay off the rest when it comes time.

- ✔ **The home has a low loan balance and is in an area with rising home prices.** Your parents may not know it, but they could be sitting on a goldmine. We know a woman in Pennsylvania who bought a beautiful home in 1967 for $35,000, and didn't know until she had her home appraised for a reverse mortgage that the value had gone up over 25 times its original price. Home prices were still rising when she closed her loan, and six years later, when she moved to a warmer climate, that was still the case. Her loan was a good-sized $180,000, but her family knew that the home would soon be worth over a million dollars. Her three children paid off the loan as a group, and a few years later they each walked away with over $300,000 in equity. If the home is a solid investment, don't sell yet.

✔ **You can rent it out for a good price.** Some areas of the country have rental prices at or above typical mortgage payments. You may be able to take out a new loan to pay off the reverse mortgage, and then rent the house at or above your monthly mortgage payment, making it all but free as long as you have a tenant.

✔ **You can afford to pay off the debt some other way.** Are you a saver? Do you have a nest egg that you've been hoarding over the years? You may be able to pay off the loan with your own money, or with other inheritance. Consider carefully whether it's worth your stash to "purchase" your parents' home. Just because you can doesn't mean you should.

Before anyone buys your parents' house, they usually want to get a more recent appraisal. Depending on the condition of the house, you may want to invest in a re-appraisal yourself so you know what you're dealing with before your best buyer prospect figures out that the roof leaks as of last autumn. This gives you a chance to get in there and fix anything that can be fixed before trying to pawn the home off on someone else. If you don't live near your parents or don't visit as often as they would like, you may not be aware of the state their home is in. Although the house may have been in tip-top shape when the loan began, ten or so years of wear and tear can do a number on a home.

Making payments for your parents before the loan is due

You can help lower that repayable amount (which increases the potential equity you may receive) by helping your parents pay off their loan as they go, as long as it's allowed in their particular loan. Broach the subject of offering help gingerly, as some parents dislike (or even resent) the notion that their children feel they need to

---

Protecting your investment

Paying off part of your parents' loan is not only a weight off their shoulders, it will be a weight off yours. However, you still need to protect yourself. Do you have other siblings who expect an equal share of mom and dad's equity? If you help pay off the loan, make sure you get your money back when the home sells. No one likes to mix family and money, and there's a very good reason: It's like mixing baking soda and vinegar — explosive.

In a very nonthreatening and congenial way, get it in writing that when the house sells, you are entitled to a return on your investment. You can ask your parents to draw it up in the will or other legal document, and it's best if your siblings or other heirs are aware of the arrangement. You don't want them all mad at you years from now when they find out you're getting a bigger piece of the pie.

Also remember that if your parents move out of the house for whatever reason, the loan becomes payable. If you're helping your parents pay off their reverse mortgage as they go and you expect repayment when they sell the house to move to Boca, be sure to work that into any documentation. On the other hand, you may consider it a gift and simply write it off in your head as a nice thing to do for your parents.

help them. Other seniors may think it's a great idea and pass the collections hat. Once you make a commitment, don't go back on it. You may skip a payment around the holidays when you need the extra money, but the more you put in now, the less you have to pony up later. You're almost paying yourself.

If you decide to help your parents pay off the loan and they accept your offer, we list a few ways to go about it. Neither is right or wrong — it's just a matter of what you and your family feel comfortable with. Also, keep in mind that any dollar amount helps. If you can only help out with a few dollars a month, it may at least cover the mounting interest. Take a look at the easy pay-as-you-go ideas here, and then talk to your parents and other family members to determine the best fit for your folks:

- ✔ **Agree to pay a certain dollar amount each month to the lender for as long as your parents keep borrowing.** Send the check directly to the lender or servicer (whichever is in charge of your parents' loan) so there's no confusion if your parents lose the money or can't remember if it was ever sent off. Ask your parents' originator for the lender or servicer's contact information.

- ✔ **Pay off a lump sum, not necessarily the lump sum your parents borrowed (although if you have the money, knock your socks off) but some large figure all at once.** You may decide to pay off an amount equal to that year's interest accrual, a few months of payments, or any random favorite dollar amount.

- ✔ **Choose an arbitrary dollar amount and work out a payment schedule.** You may get nauseated just thinking of handing over $9,000 to help your parents pay off their reverse mortgage. But over 15 years, that's only $50 per month. If your parent lives longer, you've held up your end of the bargain and can either step back or offer to keep up the payments. If they die or move out of their home earlier than expected, you've still put a dent in the loan.

✓ **Convince other family members to pitch in and help as well.** They may do it out of the kindness of their hearts, or you may have to explain it as an investment opportunity. Either way, two households giving $50 a month adds up twice as quickly. Or if you're cash-strapped, take turns paying off little bits of the loan. The more siblings and other contributors you have, the bigger the impact on the loan repayment.

It doesn't do you any good to pay off any part of the loan if your parents spend that money all over again. Let's take a line of credit option for example. Your parents will have a set dollar amount to draw from and only get charged interest on what they've used so far. If they've borrowed $100,000 and you pay off $5,000 over time, your parents should only owe the lender $95,000 (plus interest, which is lower than the interest would have been in $100,000). But if your parents respend that money, not only do they get charged interest on the aforementioned $5,000, but they owe $100,000 all over again. You may as well have given them the $5,000 to put in their pockets.

Keeping the house

A very common fear among heirs of reverse mortgage borrowers is that the lender can somehow swoop in and usurp your additional inheritance to pay off the loan when your parents are gone. However, even if the loan value is larger than the home value, if you sell the house all the lender can ever require of you is the selling price of the home. We can't stress this enough: The lender can't come after your inheritance or any of your personal funds for repayment. You, however, may decide that the best way to pay off the loan is to dip into your other inheritance, if any.

You don't have to be the heir to a dynasty to have money coming your way. Although there are certainly seniors out there without a penny to spare, many others (and the numbers are increasing) have saved up a little nest egg for retirement, emergencies, or perhaps to have something to leave you. Many people who lived through the depression or remember their parents talking about leaner times in their lives became almost chronic savers. Growing up without the privilege of low-interest credit cards and without the inherent need to shop online, seniors are often very good at keeping their money safe and sound in the bank.

For those of you who have your hopes set on retaining ownership of the house but don't have any other inheritance money coming in, using your own money may be your best option. If that's the case, you have a few options that make keeping the house possible: repaying the loan out of your own pocket, selling your own home, or refinancing.

Repaying out of pocket

You may be able to repay the debt and keep the house if you have enough money in the bank (or under your mattress) to repay the lenders. Obviously this option doesn't work for everyone — there isn't a huge percentage of people out there who can afford to plop down a few "thou" willy-nilly. For those non-millionaires reading this book, we list four situations below that usually allow you to pay off the loan and retain the home for yourself:

- ✔ **The loan balance is quite low.** Your parents may have been paying back the loan little by little as they received the money from their reverse mortgage, or they could have simply had a very small or very short-term loan. If your parents only held their reverse mortgage for a year, you may only be looking at $15,000 or so. Granted, it's still a lot of money, but compared to $100,000 it suddenly seems pretty manageable.

- ✔ **You and your parents planned for this very occurrence and you've been preparing to purchase the home for several years.** If you know your parents are getting a reverse mortgage and that you definitely want their home when they've moved or passed away, you can start investing and saving your money so that when the time comes, you and your checkbook are ready.

- ✔ **An additional inheritance covers the cost of the loan or brings you very close to being able to pay it off in one fell swoop.** If it isn't quite enough, you may have enough to supplement it in your own savings or can take out a small loan to make up the difference. This is another reason it's a good idea to know what's coming to you, so you can be prepared to fork over your monetary inheritance to pay the debt you've inherited as well.

Paying off the loan yourself is usually something that must be planned for and carefully orchestrated so that you feel comfortable with the transaction. It takes all the fun out of becoming the owner of your parents' home when you have to sacrifice everything unexpectedly to keep it. You don't want to be forced to sell the home you live in just to keep the home your parent lived in, or at least, not until you're ready.

Selling your own home

If you know you want your parents' home, you can sell your own house to pay off the loan, essentially buying your parents' home. This is common when adult children are looking to downsize into a more realistic house for one or two people after the kids have all moved out and have stopped coming home quite so often. You can sell your home, use that equity (which in many cases is more than your parents' home is worth) and pay off the loan. This circumstance is doubly good for you since it means no more mortgage payments!

Refinancing

Another very common solution to paying off the debt is to refinance, the same as you'd do with any other home. In effect, you're buying the house from yourself and taking out a new loan to do it. When your parents got their reverse mortgage, they met with an originator who showed them all of their options and laid out their financial situation in black and white. An originator can do the same for you: Let you know how large of a loan you qualify for, which loan product is the best choice for you, and what your options are within that product.

You can refinance with almost any type of loan, depending on how much equity is in the home and how much you can afford. There are countless loan products out there — more than we have room to list. Since this is a book on reverse mortgages we won't get into the nitty-gritty details of every loan option (check out *Mortgages For Dummies* for more details), but here are a few basics of the more popular refinance loans:

- ✔ **5/1 ARM:** This loan keeps the same relatively low interest rate for five years and then adjusts once per year thereafter. It can be a good choice if you only plan to keep the home for five years, or if we're in a period of particularly low interest rates. A warning: These rates can spike after your five years are up, so keep an eye on the financial sheets.

- ✔ **Interest-only:** With an interest-only loan, you do just as it says: You pay the interest only, for a certain amount of time. These have become popular because they allow people buying new homes to get "more house for their money" but they carry a risk. Your payments go up quite a bit when you start paying off the principal (the actual amount of the loan), so you have to be prepared.

- ✔ **Home Equity Line of Credit (HELOC):** Like a reverse mortgage, this loan allows you to borrow against the equity in the home; unlike a reverse mortgage, you have monthly payments (just like any other loan). This loan can work well for people who are disciplined with their money, but is sometimes not the best choice if you plan to use the money for other things in addition to paying off the reverse mortgage. Take a look at Chapter 8 for more on the HELOC.

✔ **15-year fixed rate:** This loan is just like it sounds — you pay the same interest rate for 15 years. This loan is a great choice if you are more comfortable with a steady interest rate, but don't want a 30-year basic loan. You pay more per month with a 15-year than a 30-year loan on the same house (simple math can tell you that), but you can also have the house paid off faster, which can make you very happy when you're living in it mortgage-free.

If you choose to keep the home by refinancing, you may be faced with two mortgage payments at once: the one for your own home and the new one for your parents'. Consider carefully whether that kind of monthly check writing fits into the rest of your financial goals.

Making Sure Everyone's on the Same Page

It's never easy to sit down with a loved one and say, "So, when you die, have you thought about what you're leaving me?" It sounds selfish and disrespectful to say the least. You may not be at ease with the idea of your parent's mortality, but chances are, they're just fine with it. No, they aren't looking forward to that big bingo hall in the sky, but it is a fact that they deal with every day.

The best way to plan for repayment is to plan ahead with everyone involved (your parents and other heirs), and to plan *way* ahead — as in, before the loan has to be repaid. This can be an uncomfortable topic for some, including yourself, but we give you some ideas in this section to get everyone comfortable and agreeable to a specific repayment plan before the loan needs to be repaid.

Getting comfortable with "the talk"

If you are involved in the reverse mortgage process (and you already know we recommend your participation highly) there comes a time when you have to have a conversation with your parents about what you should do if they die before the loan is repaid. Below we give you some tips for opening up that dialogue *before* they get a reverse mortgage:

✔ **Before you even say a word, do your homework.** Talk to their counselor or originator about the rules of repayment and prepayment. You want to know the facts before you start giving out misinformation (however innocent), and then have to go back and correct yourself later.

✔ **Create a comfortable setting.** If your parents are wary about finance and need a lot of information, you may want to conduct this conversation with the originator or counselor present. Or if your parents are largely independent, have it at their home, over coffee, or at your house. Avoid talking about this over the phone — it's too impersonal.

✔ **Start by asking your parents' opinion about how they think the loan is going to be repaid.** You may be surprised to find out that they're already planning to repay as they go; or planning to sell and move to assisted living within a few years; or they may have the mistaken notion that once they're gone the loan just goes away.

✔ **Discuss repayment options.** Depending on how much they understand, you can either start explaining, in a non-patronizing way, how the loan repayment works, or listen as they tell you how they think you should pay off the loan upon their death.

✔ **Approach the idea of selling their house gently if it is a family treasure.** When a home isn't practical for any other family members, it often doesn't make sense to keep it for memory's sake, but your parents may be resistant to the idea. Try to be open to their ideas if they've come up with scenarios that allow you to keep the home and pay off the loan easily.

✔ **Call in reinforcements.** Your siblings, cousins, and children — anyone who has a stake in the home — should take part in this conversation, which takes some of the burden off you (see "Keeping all the heirs in the loop," later in this chapter, for more information on making sure everyone stays involved).

✔ **If your parent isn't willing to discuss the matter, back off and wait a few days before trying again.** The important thing is to get it out in the open before you're left wondering how to repay a loan your parents left behind.

Keeping all the heirs in the loop

Family dynamics can be tested when presented with such big decisions, especially when there is more than one heir apparent (for example, you and your siblings, your own children, or other rela-tives). Reaching a common conclusion can be time consuming, frustrating, and very emotional. Here are some tips for keeping the peace as you figure out the best way to repay the loan:

- ✔ **Include all heirs in every conversation.** Leaving people out makes them feel hurt that they didn't get their say. Modern technology makes it easy for several people to talk all at once, even from remote locations. Don't forget to include younger relatives as well. Basically, if they have a stake in the home, they need to be part of the decision.

- ✔ **Make sure your parents are present.** This is their home and their money you're talking about, and they should be there to at least hear what your ideas are. Ask their opinion, and find out (if you can) what kind of additional inheritance you can expect. A sizeable amount may be the solution to keeping the home and paying off the loan. Talking openly like this can help your parent plan ahead as well. This is also a good time to mention their will and whether or not it is up-to-date (includ-ing any new grandchildren, excluding anyone who has died since the last revision).

- ✔ **Check your ego at the door.** You may be the oldest, or the favorite, or the one with the most business sense, but your family has a right to have their voices heard, too — even your hippie sister and video-game-playing brother. You or someone else in the family may want to play "moderator," but no one should have a dictatorship.

- ✔ **Keep an open mind.** Everyone comes into a meeting like this one with some idea of how they think the loan should be repaid. Try to stay open to their ideas and come to a compro-mise if possible. Bring some notes (as well as this book!) on your different options and be ready to offer up some informa-tion that could help educate others, but be ready to hear others' viewpoints as well.

- ✔ **Don't give up if things aren't going well.** Deciding how to pay off a loan, whether to keep the home, and how to dispense with equity is stressful to say the least. If the conversation is at a standstill, take a break. Go out for coffee, take a walk, play a game, anything to get your mind off of reverse mortgages for an hour. Then come back and try again. Talking about loan repayment may not be a barrel of laughs, but working the plan out before the time comes to implement the pay-back plan is worth it.

Taking advantage of renters' "insurance"

One of your options when the responsibility of the reverse mortgage falls to you is to refinance the home with a traditional forward mortgage and rent out your parents' home. A mortgage originator can let you know what your refinance options are, but the popular mortgages these days are interest only (where you only pay the interest on the payment for a specified amount of time) or adjustable rate mortgages (also called ARMs, which have a lower interest rate that changes more frequently).

Once you've repaid the reverse mortgage, the house is yours to do with what you wish. Renting out the house can be a good choice, especially if you want to keep the home in the family but no one is ready to move into it quite yet. Whatever you charge in rent should equal or surpass your new mortgage payment, so it's kind of like getting the house for free. There are certain tax and legal implications when you rent out a property, so make sure you know all the facts before you take on the title of "landlord."

Chapter 14

Getting Durable Power of Attorney

For adult children who are concerned that their parents' mental state may keep them from being eligible to take advantage of a reverse mortgage, you may not be aware that there are options out there that can help you help your parents. Parents who have Alzheimer's, dementia, or other mental incapabilities may be physically able to stay in their homes, and wish to remain where they are. In fact, many seniors with mental dysfunctions would be unnecessarily agitated by being moved. A reverse mortgage can help your parents enjoy life in the home they love, even if they aren't quite lucent.

One of the most common ways to do this is with a durable power of attorney. When you (an adult child) get durable power of attorney over your parents, you are entitled to make large-scale financial decisions on their behalf unless the written durable power of attorney says otherwise. This way, you can help your parent receive the benefits of a reverse mortgage without tearing your hair out trying to make them understand the concepts. In this chapter, we give you tips for recognizing mental incapacity, what your durable power of attorney allows, and how to get the help you and your parents need.

Understanding Power of Attorney

One of the unofficial requirements for a reverse mortgage is that borrowers must understand the basic principles of the loan and all of the implications that go along with it. In short, the borrowers have to know what they're getting into. The loophole that allows you to give your parents the comfortable life they deserve is a durable power of attorney. By definition, a *power of attorney* is written permission for someone else to act on another's behalf.

Almost every state in the country requires that a power of attorney is *durable,* which means that it goes into effect when the papers are signed (or on a date specified in the official paperwork) and that it stays in effect if your parent becomes incapacitated. The only way it is revoked is if your parents revoke it or if the paperwork specifies a date on which the powers are revoked. Your parents can specify what powers the durable power of attorney actually covers.

Whenever we talk about power of attorney in this book, we use the term *durable power of attorney,* since it's not only required by most states, but is the safest and smartest way to go. We're also assuming that you're looking for durable power of attorney for a parent, but the same rules apply no matter whose affairs you're looking to manage.

When dealing with durable power of attorney proceedings, you may also hear the term *springing power of attorney.* This is actually another kind of durable power of attorney, but with one key difference: The springing power of attorney doesn't go into effect *until* your parent is incapacitated. This can be good for seniors who want to retain independence until their last synapse pulls in at the station, and at the same time takes some of the pressure off you because you have time to get used to the idea before jumping in with both feet. But take heed; we don't recommend a springing power of attorney in many situations, particularly because it's not always clear that a senior is, in fact, unable to take care of his or herself. Because of this, it can be difficult to find institutions that accept the power of attorney without additional documentation, which just means a headache for you. In addition, unless your parent becomes suddenly or completely unquestionably incapacitated, a springing power of attorney could land you in a battle with other family members who disagree that mom or dad is unable to care for him or herself anymore.

You can see for yourself the benefits of a durable power of attorney versus a couple of alternative power of attorney forms in Table 14-1 below.

Table 14-1	Comparing Power of Attorney			
	Durable power of attorney	*Standard power of attorney*	*Springing power of attorney*	*Limited power of attorney*
Goes into effect . . .	As soon as the docu- ments are signed, or on a speci- fied date	As soon as the docu- ments are signed, or on a speci- fied date	Your parent becomes incapaci- tated	Usually upon a specified date
Terminates when . . .	Your parent revokes it, or on a speci- fied date	Your parent becomes incapaci- tated	Your parent dies	Usually upon your parent's death, or on a specified date
Covers . . .	Most powers, or as desig- nated in the documents	Most powers, or as desig- nated in the documents	Usually full powers	Very specific powers, to be deter- mined in the document

Assessing what your power may cover

When you hold durable power of attorney, you often have more control of your parents' lives than you ever thought you would (or ever wanted). Any major decisions your parents otherwise made on their own you are now allowed to do. If you're getting durable power of attorney expressly to apply for a reverse mortgage, con- sider whether or not you want this power to be exclusive to the loan, or across the board for all financial and real estate matters (not to mention medical decisions). A durable power of attorney that covers all aspects of finances gives you the power to:

✔ Apply for a reverse mortgage.

✔ Oversee and sign tax forms and returns.

✔ Open a bank account.

✔ Make donations.

✔ Pay yourself.

✔ Manage existing accounts, pensions, insurance, and health care.

In many cases, you or your parent is uncomfortable with all that power. After all, you're pretty much taking over another person's life. That's why you also have the option to do a limited durable power of attorney, which would either specifically include or exclude certain privileges.

Without a limitation clause, the durable power of attorney pretty much allows you to do whatever you like. The laws are very broad and far-reaching in most states. Because of this, whether you choose a general or limited durable power of attorney, be as specific as possible in the wording. An elder law attorney (see "Finding an Elder Law Attorney," later in this chapter) can guide you through spelling out your and your parents' wishes.

Knowing your responsibility

We would never accuse you of being selfish. After all, if you're reading this you obviously care about the well-being of your parents. But you may be wondering what your role is in the durable power of attorney and how your parents' loan affects you if you are the one who initiates and executes it.

First and foremost, you can't be held personally responsible for your parents' debts, even though you are the one with durable power of attorney, because you are signing on behalf of their estate. When you sign anything for your parent, including the reverse mortgage documents, you sign Chelsea Child as "an agent" for Susie Senior or Susie Senior, as Chelsea Child, "attorney in fact."

There are a few variations on the signature format, but the idea is the same; as long as your reverse mortgage originator accepts the signature, you're good to go. This "dual" signature absolves you of the responsibilities incurred on your parent's name, but it does not give license to sign off on things for yourself all over town, using your parent's name . . . okay, technically it may leave you open to that sort of debauchery, but don't do it. You'll land yourself in a heapin' helpin' of legal trouble.

Bigger than the signatures, of course, is the knowledge that you have a tremendous level of power over your parents. If the thought of this makes you rub your hands together like an evil villain, you are not the person for the job. You need to have the patience, time, morals, basic legal understanding, and mental stamina to take responsibility for your parents'. You may be the one who signs off on the loan documents, manages their budget, keeps an eye on any investments, staves off senior scam artists, doles out birthday money, in short, everything you do for yourself times two.

If all else fails and you decide that you are really not cut out to hold a durable power of attorney, your wingman can take your place. Most durable power of attorneys name an agent (you) as well as a "just in case" successor. This covers you if you want to step out of the equation, or become incapacitated in some way yourself, which just may happen if you let all these reverse mortgage transactions drive you crazy.

Determining Necessity

It can be heartbreaking to look honestly and candidly at the person who raised you — who kissed your scraped knee, helped you with your homework, and embarrassed you in front of your friends — and know deep down that they are no longer able to take care of themselves. It's hard, it's sad, it's scary, and it's easy to settle into denial about the whole thing. Not facing the facts doesn't help anyone and can make things worse for a parent who needs some extra care.

If your parent has gone to a reverse mortgage counselor who felt that mom or dad was unable to understand the basics, or you already know that there's no way you could explain declining equity to them, your durable power of attorney may be the ticket to their financial security. By using the money from a loan, they may be able to afford in-home care or a paid companion who can just hang out and make sure no one leaves the stove on overnight.

Going through a behavior checklist

We all have odd moments where we realize we've just put the milk in the cupboard and the cereal in the fridge. Everyone loses their keys and discovers them someplace completely random, and everyone has spent 45 minutes looking for their eyeglasses, only to find them sitting conveniently on their own head. These aren't signs of incapacitation, that's just life. But there are some clues that you can't ignore. Look at the list of common mental incapacity traits below with an open mind; not every point is an indicator of diminished mentality, but add a few together and you need to seek professional guidance.

 As you go down the list, try not to make excuses like "she's always been that way" or "he doesn't do it that often." Being honest with yourself about your parent is the best way to help them on the road to getting a reverse mortgage.

Review these indicators:

✔ Poor memory that just keeps getting worse

✔ Asking the same questions over and over

✔ Initiating the same conversation over and over

✔ Making bad decisions that could be harmful, such as walking five miles to the grocery store in the rain at night

✔ Having a sudden change in personality, good or bad

✔ Misplacing money

✔ Buying the same thing several times (before it's needed again)

✔ Being unable to make a decision, or having a blasé attitude about things

✔ Being often confused about place and/or time

✔ Being unable to plan for the future, even a day or a few hours in advance

✔ Forgetting basic personal hygiene and/or not taking interest in their own appearance

If your parent is exhibiting a few of these signs, that should be your trigger to get help; schedule a doctor's appointment, then if necessary, take the next step and get durable power of attorney. With the income from a reverse mortgage and you at the helm, you can ensure a safe and comfortable life for your parent, even if they don't seem to realize it.

Understanding that patience is a virtue

A senior with mental incapacities (full or partial) can be trying. It's hard enough to come to grips with an aging parent, but when their behavior starts to send you over the edge try to remember that they're still your parents. Seniors with dementia or other mental illness may not always know exactly what's going on, but they do know when things are going well, or something's not quite right. They still have feelings and emotions. They are not trying to aggravate you on purpose. When they ask two dozen times where you got your sweater, it's not to be annoying and it's not to get attention.

Most importantly, it's not their fault. No one asks to lose their mental faculties. It can be just as scary for them to experience as it is for you to watch. Summon all your kindness, patience, and composure and try your hardest to listen, smile (or whatever the appropriate expression is), and help them feel at ease. Remember not to lash out at your parents — this only knocks down their trust in you and could ignite an undesirable reaction from them. Just keep saying to yourself, "It's not their fault."

Taking the first steps

Once you've determined that your parents need a little (or a lot of) help, your first move should be to get an elder law attorney and sit down with your parents and the lawyer to discuss what level of durable power of attorney you need. Talk to your parents ahead of time so that they aren't taken off guard. Many seniors are less than receptive to the idea of you taking over their lives, but honesty really is the best policy here. If they are extremely resistant, go alone and get all the information you can without them present, and then explain it all in a more secure setting (like their own living room). It's not ideal, but if you're not getting anywhere with firm yet gentle insistence and don't want to pick them up and carry them there, making the first visit alone is a good alternative. For heaven's sake, don't tell your parents that you're taking them to the ice cream parlor and then pull up in the attorney's parking lot. It's not just a mean trick, but it also starts to destroy trust — which is one thing you need plenty of if you're going to convince your parents that you need to have durable power of attorney.

Never explain that you're going to "take care" of your parent or that you "know what's best" for them. Your parents probably won't take kindly to being treated like a child, and may (ironically) rebel, just like a child would. Instead, use words like "help manage your loan," "give you a hand with your checkbook," and "protect your money." These are much less threatening phrases that may be received more positively.

Afterward, contact a reverse mortgage counselor (Chapter 8 can tell you where to find a good one) and set up an appointment to meet. Explain on the phone that you have durable power of attorney, although they will probably still want to speak to your parent on the phone before making the appointment. If you have durable power of attorney you must be present for the counselor meeting.

If you look over at your parent during the meeting and they seem to be staring out the window, try to focus their attention back to the topic at hand. Do this three times, and if they can't seem to pay attention or aren't grasping the concepts enough to take interest, just let them be. Don't try to oversimplify the ideas of a reverse mortgage, because it may come off scarier than it actually is. If you have full durable power of attorney, your parent can flip through a magazine for the whole session and it wouldn't make any difference. However, if your parent seems to be trying to understand the reverse mortgage concepts, your counselor will be able to break down the ideas into easy, mentally digestible pieces. We don't have to tell you that if your parents seem to understand the basics of a reverse mortgage and are ardently against it, don't proceed. Your counselor can also help you assess your parent's reaction and direct you on how to go from there.

Remember that as the durable power of attorney agent, you'll need to be present at all meetings so you know what's going on at all times. If you could send your parent alone, you probably wouldn't need to have durable power of attorney.

Finding an Elder Law Attorney

Although law doesn't require you to have an elder law attorney prepare your durable power of attorney documents and preparing one on your own can save some cash in the very short term, lacking the legal knowledge to create a durable power of attorney for property management can cost you thousands, if not more, because of common mistakes or loopholes. A durable power of attorney needs to be tailored to your specific circumstances in order to be the most effective document possible. We don't recommend that you draft your own durable power of attorney, and we hope that you consider carefully the potential problems with do-it-yourself forms and kits.

Most lawyers don't specialize in serving a particular type of person. Criminal lawyers may have a knack for people with similar hobbies, say, knocking over liquor stores, but they don't focus on a precise segment of the population like an elder law attorney does. You may be tempted to use your own lawyer to oversee the durable power of attorney. This is common, but usually not the best choice. Here's why:

- ✔ General practice attorneys may buy into the myths that go along with old age. They may patronize a perfectly aware senior, talk loudly for no reason, or ignore them all together.

- ✔ Elder law attorneys have connections in the world of senior citizens, from in-home assisted living providers to gerontologists (senior doctors), senior-care psychologists, government program information, and more.

- ✔ General practice attorneys may not be familiar with all of the subtle aspects of a durable power of attorney, especially in relation to a reverse mortgage.

Your general family lawyer will probably be able to refer you to a good elder law attorney, however, so don't scratch them out of your phone book quite yet.

Knowing what to look for

Part of what makes finding a good elder law attorney somewhat difficult (besides the fact that there may not be one in your area if you live in a small town) is that there are so many fields of elder law. Different elder law attorneys specialize in all sorts of areas: medical claims, social security issues, estate planning, elder abuse, age discrimination, nursing home problems, and elder fraud, just to name a few. When you call around, be sure to explain up-front that you're looking for someone with experience in creating durable power of attorney authorizations, who is also knowledgeable about reverse mortgages.

And speaking of that first call, this is a good time to ask some preliminary questions. You may be speaking with a receptionist or assistant, but it's okay — that person should be able to spout off the answers without missing a beat.

Some good first questions to ask include:

✔ How long has the attorney practiced elder law?

✔ What associations is he or she a member of?

✔ What should I bring with me when I come in?

✔ What is the fee structure? Does that include the first consultation?

In fact, ask anything you want; just remember that the person answering the phone probably isn't a lawyer, so it's best to save detailed questions for the attorney. Once you're in and have explained your reason for coming, lay on the more difficult questions. Start with, "Have you ever done a durable power of attorney for a reverse mortgage before?" Don't be shy — if you don't understand something the first time, just keep asking until you do. You're on the clock, but it's worth it to get a satisfactory answer.

Some sample questions to take with you may be:

✔ What are the downsides to getting durable power of attorney in our particular situation?

✔ What provisions do you recommend to the written durable power of attorney?

✔ Judging by our conversation, do you think there are any better alternatives to getting durable power of attorney we haven't thought of?

✔ After seeing my parent in person, do you feel that a durable power of attorney is appropriate?

✔ How long does it take before the durable power of attorney goes into effect? (This may depend on who draws up the paperwork and the office's turnaround time.)

✔ How often should we revisit the durable power of attorney documents?

Since the answers to these questions can vary from family to family, we can't give you definitive answers here; that's why it's so important to discuss these issues (and any others you can think of) thoroughly with an elder law attorney.

In addition, your elder law attorney must possess the same qualities that a good reverse mortgage counselor or originator has: patience, respect for seniors, and superb communication skills. Just like you would with an originator, you and your parents need to feel that you can ask questions, get results within the promised timeframe, and receive personal attention that shows they care about you beyond your checkbook.

Elder law attorneys (like any other lawyers) usually charge by the hour or part thereof, plus whatever expenses they incur on your behalf (like making copies or mailing something). Fees will vary from office to office, but can run as low as $50 an hour at very generous offices with senior finances in mind, to as high as a few hundred dollars an hour. Discuss your financial situation with your attorney right off the bat. If you can't afford their high fees, many elder law attorneys may very kindly lower their rates or reduce the billable hours. After they tell you their rate and give you an estimate of how much the total cost will be, level with them — tell them how much you can spend, and ask nicely if they think they can help you stay within your budget. Most will, but many won't assume you even have a budget unless you say something.

You can make the experience of creating a durable power of attorney a positive one by being sure to bring all of the documents, statements, or other items that the elder law attorney requests of you. If your parents have already gotten their reverse mortgage, bring all the loan documents, including the Loan Agreement, which lays out all of the terms of repayment. You can also ask the reverse mortgage originator you're working with (or plan to work with) for sample copies to take with you so the elder law attorney knows all the details of the loan.

Finding a good elder law attorney

Beyond flipping through pages of "Call for a free estimate" ads that make your legal issues sound like a broken-down car, there are countless resources available to you that can help you find a highly regarded elder law attorney in your area. Remember, you don't have to go with the first attorney you talk to, and you don't have to worry about hurting their feelings if you choose someone else. At upwards of $250 an hour, they can use their wads of cash to dry their tears.

Some great places to start searching include:

- ✔ **National Association of Elder Law Attorneys (NAELA):** It may come as no surprise that the NAELA Web site is a great place to start when you're looking for an elder law attorney. Its "Locate an Elder Law Attorney" database has listings of NAELA members all over the country, some with information such as law specialties and links to their own Web sites where you can find out more about each attorney. Visit the site at www.naela.com or call 520-881-4005.

- ✔ **American Bar Association (ABA):** The "Senior Lawyers Division" of the ABA provides a directory of state and city senior lawyer groups in the U.S. The ABA Web site also has an option to search for lawyers by specialty. Find the ABA's senior groups at www.abanet.org/srlawyers/.

- ✔ **Alzheimer's Association:** Not only will you find incredible and up-to-date information about Alzheimer's tips and recent research on its Web site, you can also contact your local chapter, which can most likely give you a referral to a competent elder law attorney. Visit www.alz.org or call 800-272-3900.

- ✔ **AARP:** AARP is an excellent resource for all facets of aging, and here you can find that AARP really shines. Log on to www.aarp.org/money/legalissues/ to discover a "Find a Lawyer" link, plus an option to receive 30 minutes of free legal advice from one of AARP's network attorneys. If your parents are members, they can receive additional reduced-fee services. While you're on their site, check out the reverse mortgage links.

- ✔ **Children of Aging Parents (CAPs):** This non-profit organization has resources for many aspects of managing your parent's affairs. Its chapters are only in about 15 states, but this organization may be able to help you contact a similar group in your own area. Call them at 800-227-7294 for support and suggestions.

Knowing Who Gets the Check

And now the moment you've all been waiting for . . . the money.
Depending on which loan you and your parents have chosen and
which payment method works best in your family's individual situation, that reverse mortgage could come in the form of tenured
monthly payments (for the life of the loan), term monthly payments (for a specific amount of time), a line of credit, a lump sum,
or any combination of these. In this section we cover where that
money goes when you have durable power of attorney as well as
who gets that check.

Lining your parents' pockets

Although you're the agent for the durable power of attorney and
you sign the checks in your parents' names, the reverse mortgage
is in your parents' names. So any funds come in your parents'
names, even if you signed as your parents' agent. If they're receiving mailed checks, the payments come to your parents' house. If
they chose to have direct deposit, the funds must (no bending on
this rule) go into an account with the parent or parents' name(s)
on it.

Having the payments from a reverse mortgage deposited electronically into your parents' bank account is easy and a real time saver
(see Chapter 4 for more information). Your parents don't have to
run to the bank or worry about checks getting lost in the mail.
Another advantage to electronic automatic deposits is that you
won't have to worry about your parents accidentally throwing the
checks away with the day's junk mail, or losing it in a stack of mis-
cellaneous papers. The money always goes directly where it
belongs: in the bank.

Your powers may not come into play for quite a while if your parents are still cognizant enough to spend those reverse mortgage
payments on their own. If you're fortunate enough to be in this situation, use this time to watch your parents' spending carefully.
This financial voyeurism has two significant benefits:

- ✔ You can see how your parents spend their money and use the
  patterns to model your spending when it comes time to take
  the reigns.

- ✔ You can monitor their accounts for abnormal spending, which
  may be a warning sign that things "upstairs" are getting
  worse.

Use this chance to monitor your parents' spending habits and get a better understanding of what they buy, how well they keep their accounts balanced, and what their usual budget is. It can be a tremendous help when you're trying to manage it later on.

Spending the money that you've been appointed a durable power of attorney agent for is a serious responsibility. Depending on the state of incapacitation your parent is in, you may have to decide what they would want done with that cash on a larger scale than just paying bills. That's why it's crucial to talk about these sorts of things before the fact and write them into the durable power of attorney. For example, your parents may have made an annual donation to the Sierra Club before you took over. If it's written into the durable power of attorney that this is to continue, you need to carry on the tradition. Or your parents may wish to make investments with their reverse mortgage. Would you know where to put that money? Would you feel responsible if the market tanked and your parent's investments were lost? If you need help managing your parent's money, ask a well-respected family member, friend, or (ideally) a financial planner who is familiar with durable power of attorney and senior finances.

Putting the money into the bank

Of course, in order to fulfill the duties set forth in the durable power of attorney, you need access to your parents' accounts. How can you be expected to manage their money if you don't have any way to get to it? The answer is a joint account. You have probably had a joint account in the past, either with a business partner, spouse, child, or maybe even your own parent when you were young. When the funds from a reverse mortgage go into a joint account, whoever is on the account (the fewer people the better) is able to access it just like any other bank account; you can write checks, pay bills online, and make deposits among other things.

Depending on the type of account and the provisions made in the durable power of attorney, you may need your parents' signatures on some transactions. For instance, it may be written into the durable power of attorney that for any amount withdrawn over $500, your parent needs to sign off on it, too. Some families elect a third person to be named on the accounts and stipulate that for any big purchases, both the agent (you) and the third person have to approve it. There are endless combinations of account managers that can help make sure your parents' money is safe, sound, and being spent on what it was intended for: them.

If you see dollar signs dancing before your eyes, stop right there. One of the ways the banks and other fiduciary organizations have developed to protect your parents' money is to prohibit you from combining your bank account with theirs. This is actually a fairly common mistake (which doesn't make it okay). Many durable power of attorney agents think they're making a smart move by blending their bank account with their parents'. Although most banks won't throw you in jail for a seemingly innocent offense, you may be looking at fines or other punishments, depending on the severity of the account misuse.

Unfortunately, there's no foolproof way to safeguard your parents' money against, well, you. People in the reverse mortgage industry are always concerned about their customers' wealth being used prudently by the adult child who executed the loan. There are cases of inappropriate use that certainly don't apply to the population at large, but it does happen. Your parents' reverse mortgage originator and counselor's first priority is to their customers: your parents. That's why they often request a note from your parents' physician that explains the terms of the durable power of attorney in addition to the documents themselves.

Don't be surprised if your parents' originator, counselor, and even the title company look over the durable power of attorney meticulously. It's not a judgment on you or your intentions — they all have to be sure that the wording in the documents states that you are, in fact, legally allowed to take out a loan on someone else's house. You'd want them to check that out if someone were trying to put a lien on your house, wouldn't you?

Whether the originator remembers to ask for it or not, you must bring a copy of the durable power of attorney (signed and notarized) to the originator's office in order to apply for a reverse mortgage using your durable power of attorney privileges. In some states, you must also bring a doctor's note that states that your parents are, in fact, incompetent. Check with the originator before your first visit to make sure you have all the forms and documents you need — you're busy enough without making extra trips to the originator's office. Once there, the originator gives a copy to the title company for its records. If the durable power of attorney hasn't been officially recorded at the county recorder's office (the same place where the reverse mortgage is recorded), the originator does that, too.

You can save a step and do that yourself by walking into your county recorder's office, plunking down a notarized durable power of attorney, and saying, "I'd like this recorded please." They'll stamp it and file a copy, which protects you in the event that your durable power of attorney documents are somehow lost or destroyed.

Using a Living Trust as an Alternative

A durable power of attorney isn't right for everyone. Some people just aren't cut out to manage other people's lives; some can barely manage their own. It's a huge undertaking in many cases and it takes a lot of dedication. Now, everyone loves their parents, even if it's way, way deep down. But if you're feeling like durable power of attorney is a bit to committal for you, you have other options (we can talk about your commitment issues later).

You may have heard about wealthy spoiled kids who have a trust fund waiting for them when they turn 18. Granted, it happens more often in the movies than in real life, but trusts can be a useful tool in managing another person's finances. For our purposes, we're going to focus on the living trust (also called *intervivos*). A living trust is the only kind that can be helpful to you in getting a reverse mortgage for your parents, because it's the only one that guarantees the trust was created during your parents' lifetime, hence the name, "living trust."

Generally speaking, a living trust allows one person (the trustee) to handle the property title for another person (the beneficiary). What's confusing about the language of living trusts is that unlike your parents' will, which names beneficiaries who are usually the heirs like you or your other family members, in this instance you are the trustee and your parent is the beneficiary. It's a financial doppelganger.

What's not confusing is the basic benefit of a living trust: Your parent can be both the trustee and the beneficiary (which means they have control over everything on their own) until they become incapacitated and then you or another named trustee can step in and take over. There's no worry about you having too much control while your parent is still fully mentally functional. In this way it's similar to a springing power of attorney, but it has one big advantage: Living trusts are a respected part of the financial world. While people are often suspicious of a springing power of attorney, a living trust almost never cause problems. They are widely accepted as legal and reputable.

A living trust may be set in stone (irrevocable) or able to be changed or even canceled (revocable). The format you and your parents choose depends on your individual situation, but it's good to keep in mind that things change. You may decide after a few years that a durable power of attorney is the best path after all, or your parent may decide that your sister is really the one who should be in charge of the house. Talk to a professional about the benefits and potential pitfalls of both options.

Getting a living trust set up is fairly simple, but it's not the kind of thing you can do yourself, just as it's not a good idea to set up a durable power of attorney on your own. There's too much legal mumbo jumbo and too many considerations, like what effects it will have on your parent's other financial areas. The property in a living trust can sometimes (but not always) have an effect on your parents' taxes and government aide, like Medicare. You don't want to go to all the trouble of setting up a living trust and getting a reverse mortgage just to find out that it has negative implications for your parents' taxes. The same elder law attorney you scouted out for the durable power of attorney can be used to help create a living trust (see "Finding an Elder Law Attorney," earlier in this chapter). This is actually one of those times when your regular attorney can help you out, as long as he or she has some background in living trusts and other aspects of estate planning.

Part of the reason a living trust is so easy to do is because you pay someone else to do it, and you pay them a lot. There are legal fees, processing fees, transfer fees, attorney-needs-a-vacation fees — you get the idea. If you haven't already, skip back to earlier in this chapter to the "Finding a good elder law attorney" section and start looking for a good attorney who won't charge you an arm and a leg. Again, your parent's financial planning isn't the time to skimp on costs, but you may have some options as far as reduced-cost elder law attorneys.

One of the downfalls of a living trust is that even when your parent is incapacitated and you're managing the trust, it only gives you power over the property. In most cases, that's as far as you can go with it. You can get a reverse mortgage on the property, sell it, bulldoze it, paint it purple, whatever you want. But you have no control over the rest of the assets unless they are expressly laid out and transferred to you in the living trust. So if you are the trustee but forgot to mention that you will eventually need control over the rest of the estate (bank accounts, other property, family heirlooms, and so on) you're out of luck. That's why it's so important to have a capable attorney helping you tie up any loose ends.

Part V:
The Part of Tens

The 5th Wave   By Rich Tennant

"I'm well aware that we ask a lot from our
reverse mortgage applicants, Mr. Harvey.
However, sarcasm is rarely required."

In this part . . .

The Part of Tens is a standard device in every *Dummies* book, and ours is no exception. You may even want to read this part first, to get some instant-gratification answers! Use this part to answer some common questions most seniors have, find our favorite resources for seniors and their families, and check out the biggest mistakes that borrowers all too commonly make.

Chapter 15

Top Ten What Ifs When Considering a Reverse Mortgage

In This Chapter

▶ Dispelling some myths about reverse mortgages

▶ Answering your most common questions

*W*hether you make this the first chapter you read or one of the last, you likely have questions that aren't unique to your circumstances. Reverse mortgages beg a lot of questions, and most people need only hear the basic rules to begin a barrage of "what ifs." Many what ifs are answered throughout the book, and you can find the answers as you read. Others are included here, with information that can also be found in the preceding chapters.

No question is too silly, too basic, or too embarrassing to ask your counselor and originator. Trust us, they've heard it all. If you need to know something, the best and simplest way to find out is to ask. Speak up and let your confusions, reservations, and concerns be heard. Every question you ask brings you closer to a full understanding of your own economic situation.

What If I Want to Move?

This is probably the most often asked question among people considering a reverse mortgage. Consider this: You've signed off on your reverse mortgage and are living happily and comfortably in your home — then one day you start to realize that this is the time in your life when you can finally move to Curaçao and open that banana stand you always dreamed of. Or maybe it's becoming clear that you need a home with fewer stairs and more accessible appliances. Perhaps it's simply time to move on to an assisted-living home where you can take it easy while someone else does the cooking and cleaning for a change. Whatever your reason, you have the right to choose to move out of your home. There are no rules shackling you to your house and you are free to go as you please.

There's just one not-so-small catch. If you decide to move out permanently (or are gone for over a year), even if you don't sell the house, your loan becomes due to the lender. That's payment in full, which is a pretty big check to write. You have several options for paying back a reverse mortgage, the most common of which is selling your home. You're moving out anyway, so it's a natural choice that many people make. If you don't wish to sell or your other family members want to keep the house, you have to come up with alternative ways of paying back the loan. Check out Chapter 4 for lots of information about planning for repayment, and what to do when the time comes. Your adult children may like to have a look at Chapter 13 as well, which explains what their options are if you should pass away before the loan is repaid.

What If Only One Homeowner Is Eligible?

Sometimes a couple (or any combination of people living together) hear about reverse mortgages and want to jump right in. It's understandable that you would want to get your hands on that money as quickly as possible. Technically speaking, if at least one person in the household is eligible for a reverse mortgage, that person can go ahead with the loan no matter who else shares the same roof. After all, why should you live without when you can have an instant income flowing from your lender? Actually there's a very good reason not to: It leaves your roomie vulnerable.

In order to qualify for a reverse mortgage, you must be at least 62 and a homeowner with some equity. A couple aged 57 and 65 who own their own home only half qualify — that younger resident has to be removed from the title so the elder could get the loan, which is not a smart move. If the older person decides to press on and get a reverse mortgage anyway, he or she is be the only one who holds the loan, even though the younger can continue to live in the house (reverse mortgages don't pass judgment on living situations). So what's the problem? If that older person dies or moves out of the house and can't be contacted, the younger almost always is responsible for paying off the loan as an heir. That's a big debt to pay — the younger homeowner would probably have to sell the house to pay off the loan, which isn't always a welcome change.

What's more, there's a benefit to waiting for both members of the household to be eligible: The longer you wait, the older you get (wait, the good part is coming); the older you get, the more money lenders lend to you. A difference of five years can mean several thousand dollars! If you're in a situation where only one homeowner qualifies and you absolutely can't wait, try to find another solution to your money troubles. You can find some options in Chapter 8.

This is a good place to mention that if you are both eligible, but one has durable power of attorney over the other (this happens often when one spouse is mentally incapacitated and the other cares for him or her), you can both be on the loan, as long as the one with durable power of attorney signs the documents as "attorney in fact" or some variation. Chapter 14 talks about durable power of attorney, and although it focuses on adult children as durable power of attorney, you may benefit from reading up on it, too.

What If I Need More Money?

You have a reverse mortgage, you're balancing your checkbook, and you've realized that you need more cash if you're going to make it. You have a couple of major options:

✔ You can do a refinance if the lender's loan limits increase during your loan. For example, in 2004 the Home Equity Conversion Mortgage (HECM) limits were $160,176 to $290,319 depending on the county. But in 2005 they increased to $172,632 to $312,896. That's about a $12,000 difference, which can make a big difference in your available funds. To take advantage of a refinance, talk to your originator and ask to be notified when lending limits increase.

✔ If you're receiving monthly payments and you're facing a large expense that you can't pay with your savings, you can change your payment to a larger monthly payment, line of credit, lump sum, or a combination of monthly checks and another chunk of cash. For example, if you're receiving $600 per month and suddenly need $7,500 worth of repairs done to your car, you can take out that entire amount in a lump sum, which simply gets added to your loan balance and is deducted from the total amount available. This can be done by contacting the loan servicer and requesting that your loan be "modified." The servicer makes the calculations on your loan to determine the amount you are receiving monthly, which is then reduced in order to provide you the lump sum you need. This modification costs a grand total of $20, which will appear on the next statement you receive from your loan servicer.

However, if you originally received a lump sum or a line of credit and you spent it all, well, you're out of luck. That's why it's crucial to understand your monthly budget and plan accordingly. Chapter 2 gives you more information about budgeting and estimating expenses.

What If I Still Owe Money on My Previous Loan?

Because reverse mortgages are based on the equity you've acquired in your home, the more equity you have the higher the loan you can get. It's an abstract concept, but the money you're borrowing is actually already yours: It's a portion of the money you would get if you were to sell your house.

You don't necessarily have to own your home outright in order to qualify for a reverse mortgage, but you do have to be reasonably close. The reason is: Whatever you owe on your home needs to be paid off by your reverse mortgage. Whatever's left is yours to play with. If you owe $5,000 on your home and the lenders have agreed to let you borrow $100,000, that prior debt brings you down to $95,000. Generally, if you owe more than 25 percent on your home, you won't get the full benefits of the reverse mortgage and may want to consider another route if you can.

What If I Sell My House for More than the Loan Amount?

If you have a $75,000 loan and you sell your house for $389,000, you end up with $314,000 left over! Who gets it? Why, you do of course. It's your house, your money, your cash bonanza. If the loan has become due upon your death, your family (or whoever you've named in your will) is entitled to the left over equity.

A lot of fear surrounds reverse mortgages that no matter what you borrow or how much your home is worth, the lender is going to swoop in like a cartoon evildoer and take your home away when the loan is due. Many people fear that if they sell their home for a great price, they may lose it all by handing it over to the lenders. It's simply not true.

What If I Sell the House for Less than the Loan Amount?

You win. Well, you don't win, but it's a draw.

Lenders know that life is precarious and that nothing is certain, especially in real estate. That's why you pay a mortgage insurance premium (MIP) with an HECM loan, you get a lower loan limit with Fannie Mae, and you pay higher interest with the Financial Freedom loan — it's all protection for just such an occasion. If you owe $300,000 in loan and fees, but you can only sell your house for $210,000, all you need to do is sell your house for the best price you can, and your lender has to accept it as your loan repayment. Never mind that in this case, you're about $100,000 shy of the actual total. The golden rule of reverse mortgages is: You can never owe more than your home sells for.

This is actually the reason some people are afraid of reverse mortgages — the idea that you only have to pay back what your home sells for has been convoluted into a misconception that whatever your house sells for is what you pay back, large or small. But, as we discuss in the preceding section, "What If I Sell My House for More than the Loan Amount?", if your house actually sells for more than your loan amount, you get to pocket the equity. Now you know the facts and can set your friends straight about repayment. For more on this topic, go back to Chapter 7.

What If I Want to Get out of the Loan?

You have a few choices if you simply don't like the structure of the loan and no adjustments can make you happier. Because a reverse mortgage usually comes to an end by the borrower moving out, dying, or not maintaining the house, you only have a few options. Faking your own death is too extreme (and illegal) so we'll skip that idea; moving out may not be an option if you love your home but aren't so fond of the loan; And we certainly want you to keep paying your homeowner's insurance and not live in a house that becomes more dilapidated each year, so not maintaining your home is also out of the question. So what else can you do?

If you've changed your mind within the first three business days after signing the documents, you simply call up your originator and say, "I've changed my mind." This is called a rescission, and it shouldn't be taken lightly — everyone gets cold feet after a big financial decision. Chapter 11 has some checklists for exercising your right of rescission; read over it carefully before you change your mind for good.

You can also end the loan by paying it off. In most cases, it doesn't take you too long to figure out that this isn't the loan for you. You can liken it to those people who go to a restaurant, eat all but two bites of their meal and then call the waiter over to say "I didn't like it at all." Because most people who change their minds have had their loan for a relatively short period of time, it shouldn't be too hard to pay it back. On the other hand, if you got a lump sum, spent it all in your first four months, and then decided you aren't crazy about reverse mortgages, you may have a harder time paying it all back.

What If I Marry Someone Who also Has a Reverse Mortgage?

Don't laugh. Romance among seniors is more common than most people think. What with today's divorce rates, people staying single longer, and everything from cell phones to nonstick pans causing cancer, it's no wonder there are a lot of sexy single seniors. If two seniors with reverse mortgages want to marry (or live together) they have two main choices:

- ✔ One spouse can give up his or her reverse mortgage by paying it off (if one of you is selling your home to move in with the other this makes perfect sense). The only hazard here is that the other's reverse mortgage becomes due when he or she dies, regardless of who's still occupying the house.

- ✔ You can each pay off your loan (an especially good idea if you're buying a new home together and both selling your homes, making it possible to put a lot of money down on the new home) and enter into a new reverse mortgage together.

What you can't do is add one onto the other's loan. Since each reverse mortgage is tailor-made to a specific person, it isn't possible to throw another resident into the mix and keep the loan as-is.

What If a Couple Has a Reverse Mortgage and Gets Divorced?

The short answer is: You each move into a groovy pad and use the money from the sale of the home to pay off the loan in an amiable fashion.

The long answer is a little more complicated. If one person wants to stay in the home and the other (understandably) needs to move out, the loan stays in effect because the rule is that the reverse mortgage is due when the *last* borrower dies or moves out. Where it gets tricky is actually not our jurisdiction, but it's something to think about. The money from the reverse mortgage may or may not be eligible for alimony, and it can get pretty ugly between "he already used up $10,000 on golf clubs" and "she spent just as much on new furniture." The bottom line is this: If your marriage is on the rocks, don't enter into a loan together. You're just asking for trouble. If you need something to bring you together, try an orchid. Or therapy.

What If the Surviving Resident Is a Domestic Partner, Not a Spouse?

As long as the domestic partner is listed as a borrower (which by default means he or she must be listed on the title), the loan goes on unscathed. Nowhere in the reverse mortgage rules does it say that people with a reverse mortgage have to be married. Just make sure that two very important things are in place:

- ✔ The loan is signed by both residents, naming both as borrowers, and both are listed on the home's title.

- ✔ Both partners' wills clearly state that the home is to be left to the other. This shouldn't even be a factor since the reverse mortgage continues if the above condition is met, but it's better to be safe than pressured out of the home by your partner's pushy niece.

Chapter 16

Ten Resources for Securing a Reverse Mortgage

*W*e all need a little extra support here and there. Embarking on a big financial decision can be a little unsettling, or even scary, and we want you to have as many people at your beck and call as possible. Whether you're a senior who's looking for a reverse mortgage for yourself, or a pre-senior who's researching the idea for your parents (or even for your future), there are count-less organizations and individuals out there who can set your reverse mortgage wheels in motion.

We think we've given you a pretty darn good resource for reverse mortgages here, but there are additional organizations out there that also have great information. Sometimes you need to speak to a live person, other times it just feels good to see what you've read somewhere else as well. Whatever you need to guide you to make the right decision about your reverse mortgage, these resources (in alphabetical order) can help you make your dreams a reality.

AARP's Home Made Money

Available as a download online (you print it out yourself) or in a hard copy (a book sent to your home), this free 51-page booklet offers a general overview of reverse mortgages. The book is heavy on the HECM loan (see Chapter 5), but it also includes a section on the Fannie Mae Home Keeper (see Chapter 6), although it doesn't say much on private loans like the one offered from Financial Freedom (see Chapter 7). The good thing about "Home Made Money" is that it is completely unbiased, as is the AARP's way. That means you never have to worry that they're trying to sell you something or talk you into a loan that may not be right for you.

One particularly helpful aspect is the appendix, which explains rising debt and falling equity. This concept is often difficult to visualize, especially if you've spent 80 percent of your life earning equity in the home you own. Charts and simple language make this addition an especially nice tool for assisting a parent who seems a little confused. You can order the booklet by calling AARP at 800-424-3410 or visit the Web site at `www.aarp.org/revmort`.

AARP's Web Site

Take this book over to your computer right now and go to `www.aarp.org`. You can find reverse mortgage information at this site, of course, but you can also discover link after link of smart tips, discounted professionals like lawyers and financial planners, articles full of ideas for a healthy senior lifestyle, additional resources, and so much more. You don't have to be an AARP member to use the site, but you do have to be a member to take advantage of some of the benefits. You'd be amazed at what kind of services you can get as an AARP card-carrying member.

While you're on the site, be sure to read the plentiful articles on reverse mortgages. You can read about current reverse mortgage trends (who's getting them, where they're most popular, and so on), as well as any changes that may have occurred in loan limits or interest rates since you purchased this book. You can also link to the AARP Network counselor site and print out an application for counseling.

Administration on Aging

The Administration on Aging is a government-organized agency that offers one of the most comprehensive collections of information and education for seniors out there. You can find resources for every topic under the sun, from living arrangements to medical issues to mental health. The site also provides special sections for adult children and other caregivers, too, so encourage your family to take a spin on its Web site, `www.aoa.dhhs.gov`. If you're not Web savvy and you can't wait for your grandniece to show you how it's done, call them at 800-677-1116 to request information packets or get advice on where to turn. When you call, be sure to tell them what state you live in so they can direct you to organizations in your area.

BenefitsCheckup.org

Don't walk away from your computer quite yet. Before you even visit your reverse mortgage counselor, go to www.benefitscheckup. org, sponsored by the National Council on the Aging. This confidential Web site works like any other questionnaire: They ask a series of straightforward questions and you click on "yes" or "no" (or sometimes choose from a pull-down menu). Many questions have a little "help" button next to them, which further explain what they're looking for. It takes about ten minutes to complete, which is well worth it if it can find programs in your area that may let you stay in your home without having to pay thousands of dollars in loan fees and interest. Even if you're well off and don't mind the loan expenses, give it a whirl. It's fun to fill out forms!

When you get the results, print them out and take them with you to the reverse mortgage counselor. Your counselor can discuss your options with you more efficiently if you already have an idea of what they are. If you are an adult child or other non-senior, you can fill out the questionnaire for your favorite elder, but the ideal solution is to do it together and fill out the questionnaire as honestly and completely as you can. The resulting potential savings are well worth the time.

Counselor

The reverse mortgage counselor is your first contact in the reverse mortgage process. You can read all about counselors in Chapter 8, but in the meantime remember that the reverse mortgage counselor's job is to guide you through sorting out all of your options and to let you make your own decision. The counselors won't tell you what to do, but they will tell you what kind of impact each choice can have on your finances, your home, and your family in an unbiased way. Take their information to heart — these people know their stuff.

Use the time with your counselor to ask, tell, ask, tell:

- ✔ Ask what options are available to you.
- ✔ Tell them what your financial goals are.
- ✔ Ask for a comparison of options that fit your circumstances.
- ✔ Tell them what you're leaning toward and see if they agree.

No question is a stupid question. The counselors want to make sure you understand what you're getting yourself into if you decide to go with a reverse mortgage. Counselor sessions are confidential, relatively painless (usually only an hour or so long), and free. There are counselors who charge a fee ($75 is an average amount) but you can usually find another who may agree to meet with you "on the house" . . . sorry, we couldn't resist.

Fannie Mae

As one of the nation's largest home loan lenders, Fannie Mae knows mortgages, and they continue to be a leader in all types of home loans. Fannie Mae's version of the reverse mortgage, the Home Keeper or Home Keeper for Purchase (see Chapter 6), are two options that may just solve your money woes or give you that little bit of extra cash that allows you some breathing room.

Fannie Mae has developed several pamphlets that can get comfortable with taking out a new loan, and even a booklet called "Money from Home" that covers the basics of reverse mortgages. In addition, its Web site has lots of information you can use to get a reverse mortgage, such as preferred lenders (originators) and its own network of counselors. Fannie Mae's site also offers fact sheets, which spell out the basics of their loans, as well as the HUD Home Equity Conversion Mortgage (see Chapter 5). It's a good quick reference to use as a page marker in this book. Go to www. fanniemae.com and click on "find a mortgage" (on the left toward the bottom of the page) and then "reverse mortgages." Or call Fannie Mae at 800-732-6643 and ask for all of its literature on reverse mortgages.

Financial Freedom

Offering the newest of all the reverse mortgage options, Financial Freedom's Jumbo Cash Account plays with the big boys (see Chapter 7). Financial Freedom recognized a need for loans that covered homes worth more than the national average (which is what HUD and Fannie Mae base its loans on) and created a reverse mortgage that benefits homeowners with home values around a million dollars or more. Its Web site is chock full of interesting links — but our favorite Financial Freedom benefit is the reverse mortgage newsletters it offers free of charge. Sign up for it on the site (www.reverse.com) or call 800-500-5150.

Housing and Urban Development (HUD)

If you could take everything any homeowner ever needed to know and put it all in one place, you'd find yourself at the Housing and Urban Development (HUD) Web site. HUD has tons of information for seniors and a special section for reverse mortgages. The site, www.hud.gov/buying/rvrsmort.cfm, has links to specific reverse mortgage topics, like finding a HUD-approved counselor (always a safe bet) and HUD-approved lenders/originators (like-wise). You can also report crooked reverse mortgage dealings by contacting its hotline at 800-358-6216.

National Reverse Mortgage Lenders Association (NRMLA)

The NRMLA is just what it sounds like: a club for reverse mortgage lenders, also known as originators. The NRMLA has some basic free information called "Just the FAQs," among others. You can call to order all of its reading material at 866-264-4466, or just download it online at www.reversemortgage.org. You can also search for an NRMLA member in your state. Also, click on "Borrower Profiles" to read about other seniors who received reverse mortgages and all the zany things they did with their money. Okay, some are zany and some are pretty sensible, but they could give you some great ideas about how to use your money if you're on the fence.

The NRMLA site has a great reverse mortgage calculator, too. On the NRMLA home page, click on the calculator and get an estimate of what you can borrow based on your age, home value, neighborhood, outstanding debts, and what (if any) credit line you want. Just click on "Calculate" to see a breakdown of what you could get with three different loan options (two HECM and Home Keeper). What's really neat is that the calculator remembers you on your computer, so the next time you visit the site, you won't have to re-enter all of your information. But that's not all. When you click on "Loan Summary" you can see exactly how it figured out your estimated loan amount. This is an incredibly useful tool to help you decide which loan you may want to pursue, and something you may want to print out and take with you when you see your counselor.

Originator

At last we come to someone who doesn't offer you free services: the originator. You pay this person a lot to manage this transaction. The fees depend on the loan and the value of your home (see Chapters 5, 6, and 7), but you can assume you have to pay, at the very least, $2,000. What do you get for your money? You get one of the best reverse mortgage resources out there. A good reverse mortgage originator can answer every question you have with authority, patience, and a smile.

Use your originator to the fullest. Bring a notepad full of questions, and get ready to take some notes. As long as you're bringing things, have your adult children, financial advisor, and/or other friend tag along, too. Your originator should encourage you to have your family around.

Chapter 17

Ten Common Mistakes Borrowers Make

. . . .

In This Chapter

▶ Finding out what you shouldn't do when getting a reverse mortgage

▶ Getting tips on avoiding common mistakes

▶ Making smart choices

. . . .

*T*here's a wonderful thing about other people's mistakes: You get all of the lesson and none of the misfortune. Being a smart reverse mortgage borrower is important, since you're making a rather large fiscal commitment that can impact your entire life, and possibly that of your family. Reverse mortgages are designed to be a safe choice for seniors, but there are some things that can make them a better experience. Be proactive in your choices, and be sure to listen to the advice and wisdom of your counselor and originator. Below you can find ten of the most common mistakes that borrowers make when getting a reverse mortgage. Once you read them you should have no excuse not to avoid them.

Borrowing to Pay Off Small Debts

Sometimes you need a little extra cash to get what you need. It could be a real need, like medical bills, or a want, like a new car or overextended credit cards. Whether you owe money for wants or needs, this is not — repeat, not — the time to get a reverse mortgage. Let's say you have a $7,000 debt to your credit card company after a no-holds-barred holiday in the Riviera. If you take just the interest, closing costs, originator fees, and all those little incidentals and add them all up for a moderate-size loan, you could be looking at tens of thousands of dollars, and that's before you've even paid off the principal (the actual loan amount). Now you've spent two or three times as much money (or more) on the price of your loan than you would have if you'd just paid off the original debt. Does that sound like a smart financial decision? No way.

For smaller debts like these, you have some options. Start by talking to your bank about a small loan and see what they have to offer. They may have a low-interest loan with no additional fees. You can also try asking your family members for a loan; if you can get a little here and a little there, you may be able to meet your needs. The only time a reverse mortgage is appropriate for a smaller loan is if it's absolutely, positively, completely your last resort, and you're desperate, and you're willing to pay big fees for a small loan. Talk to your counselor about your options. You may find that there are government programs that can assist you if your debt is something like overdue property taxes or other programs. It's worth your hour-long appointment to find ways to avoid paying big bucks if you don't have to.

Draining the Loan

Reverse mortgages aren't an exact science. Your loan amount is based largely on an educated guess that no one has an ounce of control over: how long you'll stay in your home. Sure, lenders can look at the statistics and figure out what age you may be when the loan ends, but none of it is concrete. If you're 83 years old and getting a reverse mortgage, they may assume you'll have the loan for seven years and set your loan amount accordingly. If they agree to lend you $120,000 on a line of credit, that's just over $17,000 per year ($120,000 divided by 7 years) — a nice healthy income.

However, two things can happen that will put a big damper on that little nest egg:

- You may drain your money too fast, using it all up in the first few years.
- You may live in your home longer than you expected and run out of cash.

To avoid running out of money (whether sooner or later), budget carefully and don't carry large sums of money with you — we all know how much easier it is to spend money in your wallet than money in the bank. Unless you have a tenured monthly payment (fixed monthly payments as long as you live in the home), you need to keep an eye on your spending and make sure you're not going to be left without the money you need. If you need help, ask a loved one to give you a hand in managing your money.

Failing to Establish a Living Trust

An *intervivos,* or living, trust isn't a necessity for getting a reverse mortgage, but it can save a lot of headaches down the road if you and your children have one in place. Living trusts can be constructed so that seniors have complete control over their own affairs, including their reverse mortgage, until the day they can't manage real estate and financial responsibilities on their own. In Chapter 14 we talk about a living trust as an alternative to adult children getting durable power of attorney. However, anyone can benefit from having a living trust, and reverse mortgage borrowers may find that they feel more secure in getting a loan knowing that someone who loves them is there to take over if they should become mentally incapacitated.

The process of getting a living trust is fairly simple since you hire an elder law attorney to do it for you (see Chapter 14 for more on an elder law attorney) — anything is easy when you pay someone else to do it! You can set the terms in whatever way you're comfortable. A living trust means you're involved in the proceedings, so you have a say in who gets the honor of managing your real estate if you've gone 'round the bend. By failing to establish a living trust, you're leaving yourself (and your family) open to a whole host of potentially big problems.

Getting the Loan Too Early

Three things that get better with age are wine, reverse mortgages, and you!

The day you're eligible for a reverse mortgage is the day they light 62 candles on your cake. At 62, most people aren't ready to be called seniors; these days, 62 is the new 40. You're ready to start living life and loving it, whether you're retired, working, traveling, painting, riding your motorcycle, or whatever your passion is. Sounds like a great time to cash in on your home equity and get a reverse mortgage right? You'd think so, but unless you can't wait another day for that income, you may be better off waiting a few years.

Generally, your potential reverse mortgage loan principal goes up in value as you do. Although interest rates may rise in the next few years (which affects the value of the loan) the older you are, the more you can normally expect to get from a reverse mortgage. Generally speaking, you should gain about $10,000 in loan value for every five years that you wait to sign those documents. To decide whether you can afford to wait, ask yourself these four questions:

- ✔ Do I have enough money in savings to continue living comfortable for at least five years?

- ✔ Can I work for at least five more years to earn and save some money in the meantime?

- ✔ Am I anticipating a large expense that I'll need extra funds to cover (such as a surgery, new car, remodel, and so on)?

- ✔ Can I live safely in this home for at least five more years?

If you still think you need a reverse mortgage right away, go and talk to a reverse mortgage counselor about your options. Once you see how low your loan amount will be, you may be singing a different tune.

Getting the Loan Too Late

Waiting a few years to increase to total loan principal is one thing. Waiting so long you don't have time to enjoy it is quite another. The idea behind reverse mortgages is to allow you to live out your senior years in comfort, not to make you deprive yourself of comfort until you're 93, just to enjoy a bigger loan for a couple of years. You have to be able to imagine the advantages of a slightly smaller loan with more time to live it up.

Consider this: You're 70 years old, still relatively mobile and adventurous. You want to see the Great Wall of China before it's too late, so you and your son hop on a plane and your dream comes true, courtesy of your reverse mortgage funds. That's a memory you can always cherish. Now pretend you're 93, have never fulfilled your biggest wishes, and discover that although you have plenty of cash to throw around, your doctor doesn't want you to go more than five miles from your front door. Unless you're only finding out about reverse mortgages at 93, there's no reason to wait that long before you sign off on your loan. Use your best judgment, and get the loan when you believe you can appreciate the extra money the most.

Making Poor Investments

Many people believe that the smartest thing to do with the whole of their reverse mortgage funds is to invest it. This could be in stocks and bonds, in an off-Broadway production starring you, in your friend's small business selling everything for the bratwurst enthusiast, or any of thousands of other capital ventures. After all, historically most investments return at a rate of 8 percent! That could be a whole lotta moolah. But (this is the part where investing stops looking like such a grand idea) time is not on your side. Stocks may return at 8 percent, but that's over 50 years of highs and very, very lows. If you get caught at a low point, you'll be left with no money and no equity to bank on. Risky ideas are not the best option for your money if it's your only source of income and/or savings.

The trouble is, it's not always easy to tell what's a risky investment and what's a solid cash cultivator. Before you sink your money into anything, get some feedback. Go to your family, your financial planner, and talk to your reverse mortgage counselor about your ideas. Bounce the investment plan off people you trust and see what they think.

Another not-so-risky but not-so-smart-either idea is setting your money aside in a CD (certificate of deposit) at your bank. If you have an HECM loan with a line of credit (see Chapter 5), chances are good that you're earning more on the unused money in your loan, which you can access freely, than you are in a CD that locks up your money for a certain period of time. Again, contact a financial planner (or at least a family accountant) and let them show you how your investment ideas compare.

Neglecting the Home

You may recall that there are three ways for a loan to become due in full: You move out, die, or fail to maintain your property. If you neglect your home and let it go to "seed," the lender can end the loan and demand repayment. Of course, it's rare that the lender will come by and inspect your home, but there are a couple of red flags that go up if you're exhibiting certain behavior:

- ✔ **You stop paying your property taxes.** You're required to continue all of your regular city or state property taxes while receiving your reverse mortgage funds. An easy way to make sure this happens (forgetfulness is a common trait among reverse mortgage borrowers) is to let the lenders take care of this for you. You have the option to have your property taxes taken straight out of your loan and paid by the lender; use this feature if you think paying property taxes may slip your mind.

- ✔ **You stop paying your homeowner's insurance.** It's crucial that you keep up with your regular insurance payments. Not only does this protect you if anything should happen to your home or your possessions, but it also protects the lender's investment (so you can see why they'd be sticklers about this). Along with your property tax, you can elect to let the lender take over your homeowner's insurance payments. It's a good way to make sure you never fall behind.

✔ **You never follow up on your repair rider.** When your home is appraised, the appraiser may find that some areas of your house need to be addressed before they can recommend you as a good candidate for a reverse mortgage. It may be something relatively small like a malfunctioning water heater, or a big project like replacing the roof over your kitchen. That appraisal report goes off to the lender, who notes in a *repair rider* that in order to receive your loan, you need to fix this problem. If you choose to use some of your reverse mortgage money for that purpose, you have up to one year to have it completed by a licensed contractor. Your lender even sets aside an estimated amount for you to dip into. If you don't get the problem fixed to the appraiser's satisfaction, you may be looking at a loan that's due right away. Remember, always complete those repair riders before you spend your money on anything else.

Short-Lived Loans

You never owe anything on your loan (including fees and interest) until the loan has ended due to your actions. Everything you're about to read is illustrative for conceptual purposes.

The beauty of a reverse mortgage is that the longer you have it, the better of a value it is. Take this example: You get a $167,000 loan paid out monthly (over an estimated eight years), and pay $7,000 in fees and interest. If you keep the loan for only one year, you're paying an awful lot for the privilege of having a loan — about 33 percent of your total income (around $20,000) so far. If you move right away (or die) you'll have spent quite a lot of money for a comparatively minor loan. Would you do business with someone who wanted you to give them 33 percent in fees and interest? It just wouldn't make good money sense.

Now imagine you keep the loan for three years. You'll have spent about $11,000 in fees and interest, but you'll have received so much more from your monthly payments. At this point, you're only spending about 17 percent of your cash on the loan costs. That's quite a difference! Fast forward to year six of the loan: You'll have spent a total of about $15,500 on fees and interest, but now that number is only 12 percent of the total you've received. By the eighth year, your total loan costs are only about 10 percent of your total earnings — and that paints a much better financial picture! If you outlive the estimated life of the loan, you'll pay even less per year because you're getting money much faster than the lender can charge you. If you only need a short-term loan, consider a bank loan or other means of cash flow instead. Selling your home may be a good option if you plan to move soon anyway.

Taking Out More than You Need

This mistake applies mostly to people with HECM lines of credit (a very common choice discussed in more detail in Chapter 5). Just to refresh, the Home Equity Conversion Mortgage offers a line of credit as a payment option, which works like a savings account based on the equity in your home: Whatever you don't use earns an additional percentage of usable funds at pretty great rates. You have access to the money just like you would from a bank, and you can withdraw it in any amount you like.

The mistake comes when you take excess money out of the line of credit (more than you need) and let it sit somewhere else, such as a regular bank account, under your mattress, in your wallet, or in any other investment. Unless you know of some sure-fire risk-free investment source (if you do, please share your secret with us), none of these can work as hard for you as the accrued money you earn on a line of credit. Taking too much money out is like throwing away a few hundred dollars per month in interest.

Using a "Forward" Originator

Would you call a podiatrist for a toothache? Would you hire a street sweeper to clean your carpets? Just because two people have the same basic training doesn't mean either can take each other's place as experts. The same is true for forward (traditional) originators and reverse mortgage specialists. While forward originators are certainly capable of doing regular loans for people, many have barely heard of reverse mortgages, and most don't know the first thing about all the little nuances of the different reverse mortgage products.

If you have an originator who has helped you out in the past, they may be able to refer you to a reverse mortgage originator. You need an originator with experience, and the only way to ensure a quality loan is by using a reverse mortgage originator. Find yours by searching the AARP, National Reverse Mortgage Lenders Association, or HUD lists (see Chapter 9 for more on these resources).

Appendix

Glossary

· ·

*T*he following glossary of reverse mortgage terms can have you speaking like the pros. We've included some words that are not found in this book (we thought they were too technical or infrequently used) but which may come up during your own loan proceedings. Don't be afraid to take this with you when you go to your counselor or originator so you can keep up with any unfamiliar terms. At the end of this section, write in any words and their definitions that come up during the loan process and aren't covered here (which may be terms that are used only in very specific situations, or don't relate directly to reverse mortgages). That way you can have all of your important terms in one convenient place.

203-b limit: From Section 203-b of the National Housing Act, this code refers to the dollar limit that is used to determine how much you can get from an HECM loan in your county. This is based on the value of your home versus the average home price in your area in relation to the rest of the country. The lowest limits are for mostly rural counties and, in 2005, topped out at $172,632. Higher home value areas (usually urban areas and larger counties) are set at $312,896. These limits change every year or so to reflect current housing prices.

Acceleration clause: Usually there are only two ways to end your reverse mortgage — by moving out or dying. An acceleration clause says that a loan may be declared due and payable if you fail to maintain your home safely, pay your property taxes, or are remiss on your homeowner's insurance. It accelerates your loan pay date. All major reverse mortgages include this clause to protect the lender and you.

Adjustable rate mortgage (ARM): An adjustable rate is just as it sounds; the interest rate on your loan changes (adjusts) unlike a traditional 30-year fixed-rate loan that you may have had in the past. ARMs can adjust every month, every year, or every six months, depending on your loan. ARMs are based on federal interest rates, plus an additional amount added by the lender.

Appraisal: The estimate of the value of your home in a fair market. The appraised value is, in theory, what you could sell your home for if you were to put it up for sale today. The estimate is done by an appraiser, who comes to your home, inspects it, and compares it with three comparable properties.

Appreciation: The dollar amount increase in your home's value. Appreciation can work to your advantage in a reverse mortgage — if your home appreciates beyond the total loan amount due, you or your heirs will receive the difference if/when you sell your home.

Area Agency on Aging: A great resource for seniors and their families, this nonprofit organization operates locally and nationally. Find it online at www.aoa.dhhs.gov or call 800-677-1116.

Attorney in fact: Also called an agent, this is the person who holds durable power of attorney over another. In a reverse mortgage, this is usually an adult child who helps their parent secure a loan.

Cap: The limit that your ARM can go up or down during your loan. It varies for each loan. For instance, on a Home Keeper, your interest rate will never be more than 12 percent above your original rate.

Closing: The end of the application process, in which you sign the final papers, the originator records the loan with your county, and the loan officially begins.

Closing costs: The total of all fees and other charges, traditionally paid in full at closing. Since this can be quite expensive, this dollar amount can also be financed into your loan balance.

Co-borrower: Any other person who signs the same loan with you. The loan is due when the last remaining co-borrower moves out or dies or when the house is no longer maintained.

Comparables: Term used by appraisers to describe similar houses in your neighborhood that they use to help determine the value of your home. Also called comps.

Counselor: A requirement for any reverse mortgage, counselors lay out your options for you, give you a basis of education, and assess your candidacy for a reverse mortgage.

Deed of trust: The deed of trust is the one that is recorded with the county to secure your loan. This is the only one that affects a reverse mortgage and the only one you need to think about.

Deferred payment loans (DPLs): A DPL is a type of reverse mortgage, usually state sponsored, that gives you a loan specifically to repair or improve your home. You are limited to this use of the money, and the loan is generally much smaller than one of the three major reverse mortgage products.

Department of Housing and Urban Development (HUD): Government division that oversees the nation's housing concerns. Offers the HECM loan.

Depreciation: This is a loss of your home's value, which can actually work to your advantage in a reverse mortgage. If you borrow $100,000 and by the time you sell your home, your home is only worth $90,000, you are only liable to repay that $90,000. The leftover $10,000 is absorbed by the lender.

Durable power of attorney: Written permission for someone else to act on your behalf, usually an adult child. Someone with power of attorney can legally take out a reverse mortgage for the senior who has been entrusted to them.

Equity: The value of your home if you were to sell it, minus any debts you owe on it. For example, if you own a home worth $250,000 but still owe $75,000 on it, your home equity would be $175,000. Your reverse mortgage loan value is based partially on your equity.

Fannie Mae: A government-sponsored company that operates privately to buy and sell mortgages. They are the primary source of reverse mortgage funds and offer their own loan, the Home Keeper or Home Keeper for Purchase.

Federal Housing Administration (FHA): You can think of the FHA as the watchdogs of reverse mortgages. They are a branch of the Department of Housing and Urban Development (HUD), which offers the Home Equity Conversion Mortgage (HECM).

Financial Freedom: One of the largest private lenders, Financial Freedom offers the Jumbo Cash Account for higher-value homes.

Financing: Rolling the costs of getting your loan (originator fees, closing costs, and so on) into the total loan balance in order to pay these extra costs along with your loan repayment. Many people opt to finance their fees, which can be several thousand dollars.

Fixed rate mortgage: Most likely what you have currently, a fixed-rate loan is usually a 30-year term with an interest rate that stays the same for the entire life of the loan. These are falling by the wayside in recent years, in favor of ARMs. Long-term fixed rate loans are not an option in reverse mortgages.

Grant deed: A document that gives ownership to a property. This transfers property from one person or party to another.

Home Equity Conversion Mortgage (HECM): By far the most popular reverse mortgage, the HECM is offered by HUD and is insured through the Federal Housing Administration (FHA).

Home Keeper: Fannie Mae's reverse mortgage product, which offers higher loan limits than HECM and no mortgage insurance payment, but often lower loan principals.

Home Keeper for Purchase: A spin-off of the Home Keeper, this loan is designed to use the reverse mortgage to help buy a new home.

Index: The base interest rate, which varies depending on your loan type. This number, plus a margin, equals your reverse mortgage interest rate.

Jumbo Cash Account: Financial Freedom's reverse mortgage, the Jumbo Cash Account is intended for seniors with home values above the current Fannie Mae limits, but is best suited for those owning homes worth $700,000 or more. The loan is a credit line only — monthly payments are not an option.

Leftover equity: In a reverse mortgage, leftover equity refers to the money left over from the sale of the home after your lender has been repaid.

Lender: The company that actually funds the loan. Lenders discussed in this book include Fannie Mae and Financial Freedom, although others do exist.

Line of credit: Also called a credit line, this loan payment option allows you choose how much money you want to withdraw from your loan "account" and how often. There is a minimum draw amount of $500, which is meant to prevent someone requesting $29.75 to pay a utility bill.

Living trust: Allows someone (usually an adult child) to handle a property matters for you.

Loan balance: This dollar amount equals the amount you owe on your loan, including interest and any fees that were financed with your loan.

London Inter Bank Offered Rate (LIBOR) index: The rate at which banks lend money to each other in London, England, used by Financial Freedom to calculate your reverse mortgage interest rate.

Lump sum: One of three main payment options — you receive a check for the total loan amount at closing and manage it as you wish, but will receive no additional money from your reverse mortgage.

Margin: The extra percentage points an originator or lender can add to the base interest rate (set by the government). Margins are capped differently for each loan, but are generally between 1.5 and 5 percent.

Mortgage insurance: Associated with HECM loans, protects you and the lender in case your loan balance grows higher than your home value (in which case the lender would lose money on your loan). The payment for this insurance is called a mortgage insurance premium (MIP) and is based on a percentage of your interest rate.

Non-recourse loan: This describes all major reverse mortgages and states that you can never owe more than your home is worth when your loan is repaid.

One-month secondary market CD index: The interest rate Fannie Mae bases your rate on, as determined by the Board of Governors of the Federal Reserve System.

Originator: The person who actually makes your loan a reality. Originators provide documents, help you choose the right loan, send all of your paperwork through to the lender, and answer any and all questions you may have along the way.

Planned unit development (PUD): One of the housing types eligible for most reverse mortgages, a PUD consists of a subdivision or other project that shares common property (like a community pool or clubhouse).

Principal: The amount of your loan before interest, fees, or any other additions.

Property tax deferral (PTD): Another type of state reverse mortgage, PTDs help you pay your property taxes. This loan is a good choice if your sole reason for getting a reverse mortgages is to take care of these payments. They are very inexpensive to get, and occasionally do not need to be repaid at all.

Proprietary reverse mortgage: Any reverse mortgage that is owned by a private company. Of the three major reverse mortgage products, that includes Fannie Mae's Home Keeper and Financial Freedom's Jumbo Cash Account, although there are others.

Quit claim deed: This removes someone's name from title or ownership of a property. For instance, if a child's name had been added on title to their parents' home, the child needs to sign a quit claim deed to remove his or her name so the parents could obtain the reverse mortgage.

Repair addendum: If the appraiser recommends repairs, this document spells out the specific repairs needed, the conditions of the work done, and the timeframe.

Reverse mortgage: Any home loan that provides you with an equity advance (either monthly, as a lump sum, or in a line of credit) that is not payable until you move out or die (or at a specific time if you've chosen an uninsured loan, which is not covered in this book).

Right of rescission: The three-day time period after your loan closes in which you can still change your mind and revoke the loan.

Servicing: The maintenance on your loan after it closes (done by the servicer), which usually includes sending checks, updating information, changing your preferred payment options, providing you with regular statements to show how your reverse mortgage loan amount is growing, and day-to-day paperwork.

Supplemental Security Income (SSI): An income program for those over 65, which operates in addition to social security. SSI benefits may be affected by your reverse mortgage income.

Tenure payments: Monthly equal payments throughout the life of the loan, which continue until you move out or die.

Term payments: Monthly equal payments that are paid for a specified amount of time.

Title: A legal document that proves ownership of a property. When you apply for a reverse mortgage, your originator orders a title search to make sure no one else holds any claims to your property.

Total Annual Loan Cost (TALC) rate: The estimated cost of the loan to you, per year. This is a hypothetical projection, since you won't pay anything until the entire loan balance is due.

T-rate index: The U.S. Treasury Securities rate, which is used as the index for the HECM loan.

Uninsured reverse mortgage: Unlike those discussed here, this is a reverse mortgage that becomes due and payable on a specific date. These are sometimes a dangerous choice, so talk to your counselor and originator before pursuing an uninsured loan.

Index

planned unit development (PUD)
  definition, 255
  eligibility, 47, 90
planning for the future, 102
power of attorney
  comparing forms of, 213
  coverage of, 213
  definition, 212
  durable, 212–214
  elder law attorney and, 218–221
  limitation clause, 214
  money management, 222–224
  necessity, determining, 215–218
  responsibilities, 214–215
  reverse mortgage counselor,
    meeting with, 217–218
  signature format, 214
  springing, 212, 213, 215
  successor, 215
predatory lenders, 104, 150–151
prepayment penalty, 108
principal, 92, 255
principal loan amount, 54, 71
private lender loans, 104
processors, 144–145
proof of residency, 144
property tax, 33–34, 135–136, 142,
    189, 247
Property Tax Deferral (PTD) loan,
    135–136, 255
proprietary loan, 104
proprietary reverse mortgage, 255
public assistance, 35
PUD (planned unit development)
  definition, 255
  eligibility, 47, 90

• Q •

qualifying
  age and, 40–41, 230–231
  condominium, 47
  couples, 41–42
  equity, 43
  home condition and, 46
  Jumbo Cash Account, 109–110
  manufactured homes, 47–48
  misconceptions about, 12

multi-family home, 48–49
nonqualifying houses and units, 45
paying off current mortgage, 43–44
second homes, 49–50
single-family homes, 46
staying in your home, 44–45
title to home, 42
townhouse, 47
quit claim deed, 191, 255–256

• R •

rate cap
  definition, 252
  Home Keeper loans, 94
rate margin, 71
Real Estate Settlement Procedures
    Act (RESPA), 151
recording fee, 74, 96, 112
refinancing, 194, 206–207, 231
Remember, 6
renovations, 156–157
renting, 43, 202, 210
repair addendums, 165–166, 256
repairs, home
  appraisal and, 160–161
  costs, 172
  Fannie Mae rules, 90–91, 160
  repair addendums, 165–166
  as safety issue, 192–193
repaying the loan
  accrued interest, 55
  closing costs, 55
  contacting lender, 53–54
  death and, 59–61
  before it is due, 202–204
  moving out, 58–59
  origination fees, 55
  out of pocket, 205
  paying as you go, 57–58
  principal loan amount, 54
  by refinancing, 206–207
  selling the house, 199–204
  servicing fees, 55
  Total Annual Loan Cost (TALC), 56
  when it's due, 52–53
  when to repay, 57–61
rescission. *See* right of rescission

BUSINESS, CAREERS & PERSONAL FINANCE

0-7645-5307-0   0-7645-5331-3 *†

Also available:

- Accounting For Dummies †
0-7645-5314-3
- Business Plans Kit For Dummies †
0-7645-5365-8
- Cover Letters For Dummies
0-7645-5224-4
- Frugal Living For Dummies
0-7645-5403-4
- Leadership For Dummies
0-7645-5176-0
- Managing For Dummies
0-7645-1771-6

- Marketing For Dummies
0-7645-5600-2
- Personal Finance For Dummies *
0-7645-2590-5
- Project Management
For Dummies
0-7645-5283-X
- Resumes For Dummies †
0-7645-5471-9
- Selling For Dummies
0-7645-5363-1
- Small Business Kit For Dummies *†
0-7645-5093-4

HOME & BUSINESS COMPUTER BASICS

0-7645-4074-2   0-7645-3758-X

Also available:

- ACT! 6 For Dummies
0-7645-2645-6
- iLife '04 All-in-One Desk Reference
For Dummies
0-7645-7347-0
- iPAQ For Dummies
0-7645-6769-1
- Mac OS X Panther Timesaving
Techniques For Dummies
0-7645-5812-9
- Macs For Dummies
0-7645-5656-8
- Microsoft Money 2004 For Dummies
0-7645-4195-1

- Office 2003 All-in-One Desk
Reference For Dummies
0-7645-3883-7
- Outlook 2003 For Dummies
0-7645-3759-8
- PCs For Dummies
0-7645-4074-2
- TiVo For Dummies
0-7645-6923-6
- Upgrading and Fixing PCs
For Dummies
0-7645-1665-5
- Windows XP Timesaving
Techniques For Dummies
0-7645-3748-2

FOOD, HOME, GARDEN, HOBBIES, MUSIC & PETS

0-7645-5295-3   0-7645-5232-5

Also available:

- Bass Guitar For Dummies
0-7645-2487-9
- Diabetes Cookbook For Dummies
0-7645-5230-9
- Gardening For Dummies *
0-7645-5130-2
- Guitar For Dummies
0-7645-5106-X
- Holiday Decorating For Dummies
0-7645-2570-0
- Home Improvement All-in-One
For Dummies
0-7645-5680-0

- Knitting For Dummies
0-7645-5395-X
- Piano For Dummies
0-7645-5105-1
- Puppies For Dummies
0-7645-5255-4
- Scrapbooking For Dummies
0-7645-7208-3
- Senior Dogs For Dummies
0-7645-5818-8
- Singing For Dummies
0-7645-2475-5
- 30-Minute Meals For Dummies
0-7645-2589-1

INTERNET & DIGITAL MEDIA

0-7645-1664-7   0-7645-6924-4

Also available:

- 2005 Online Shopping Directory
For Dummies
0-7645-7495-7
- CD & DVD Recording For Dummies
0-7645-5956-7
- eBay For Dummies
0-7645-5654-1
- Fighting Spam For Dummies
0-7645-5965-6
- Genealogy Online For Dummies
0-7645-5964-8
- Google For Dummies
0-7645-4420-9

- Home Recording For Musicians
For Dummies
0-7645-1634-5
- The Internet For Dummies
0-7645-4173-0
- iPod & iTunes For Dummies
0-7645-7772-7
- Preventing Identity Theft
For Dummies
0-7645-7336-5
- Pro Tools All-in-One Desk
Reference For Dummies
0-7645-5714-9
- Roxio Easy Media Creator
For Dummies
0-7645-7131-1

SPORTS, FITNESS, PARENTING, RELIGION & SPIRITUALITY

0-7645-5146-9

0-7645-5418-2

Also available:

Adoption For Dummies
0-7645-5488-3

Basketball For Dummies
0-7645-5248-1

The Bible For Dummies
0-7645-5296-1

Buddhism For Dummies
0-7645-5359-3

Catholicism For Dummies
0-7645-5391-7

Hockey For Dummies
0-7645-5228-7

Judaism For Dummies
0-7645-5299-6

Martial Arts For Dummies
0-7645-5358-5

Pilates For Dummies
0-7645-5397-6

Religion For Dummies
0-7645-5264-3

Teaching Kids to Read
For Dummies
0-7645-4043-2

Weight Training For Dummies
0-7645-5168-X

Yoga For Dummies
0-7645-5117-5

TRAVEL

0-7645-5438-7

0-7645-5453-0

Also available:

Alaska For Dummies
0-7645-1761-9

Arizona For Dummies
0-7645-6938-4

Cancún and the Yucatán
For Dummies
0-7645-2437-2

Cruise Vacations For Dummies
0-7645-6941-4

Europe For Dummies
0-7645-5456-5

Ireland For Dummies
0-7645-5455-7

Las Vegas For Dummies
0-7645-5448-4

London For Dummies
0-7645-4277-X

New York City For Dummies
0-7645-6945-7

Paris For Dummies
0-7645-5494-8

RV Vacations For Dummies
0-7645-5443-3

Walt Disney World & Orlando
For Dummies
0-7645-6943-0

GRAPHICS, DESIGN & WEB DEVELOPMENT

0-7645-4345-8

0-7645-5589-8

Also available:

Adobe Acrobat 6 PDF
For Dummies
0-7645-3760-1

Building a Web Site For Dummies
0-7645-7144-3

Dreamweaver MX 2004
For Dummies
0-7645-4342-3

FrontPage 2003 For Dummies
0-7645-3882-9

HTML 4 For Dummies
0-7645-1995-6

Illustrator cs For Dummies
0-7645-4084-X

Macromedia Flash MX 2004
For Dummies
0-7645-4358-X

Photoshop 7 All-in-One Desk
Reference For Dummies
0-7645-1667-1

Photoshop cs Timesaving
Techniques For Dummies
0-7645-6782-9

PHP 5 For Dummies
0-7645-4166-8

PowerPoint 2003 For Dummies
0-7645-3908-6

QuarkXPress 6 For Dummies
0-7645-2593-X

NETWORKING, SECURITY, PROGRAMMING & DATABASES

0-7645-6852-3

0-7645-5784-X

Also available:

A+ Certification For Dummies
0-7645-4187-0

Access 2003 All-in-One Desk
Reference For Dummies
0-7645-3988-4

Beginning Programming
For Dummies
0-7645-4997-9

C For Dummies
0-7645-7068-4

Firewalls For Dummies
0-7645-4048-3

Home Networking For Dummies
0-7645-42796

Network Security For Dummies
0-7645-1679-5

Networking For Dummies
0-7645-1677-9

TCP/IP For Dummies
0-7645-1760-0

VBA For Dummies
0-7645-3989-2

Wireless All In-One Desk Reference
For Dummies
0-7645-7496-5

Wireless Home Networking
For Dummies
0-7645-3910-8